The Curriculum Handbook

Edited by
Terry Brown and Keith Morrison

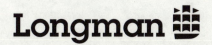

Longman Group UK Limited, 6th Floor, Westgate House, The High, Harlow,
Essex CM20 IYR, United Kingdom
Telephone: Harlow, (0279) 442601
Fax: (0279) 444501, Group 3 & 2

British Library Cataloguing in Publication Data
Curriculum handbook.
   1. Great Britain. Schools. Curriculum
   I. Brown, Terry II. Morrison, Keith
375.00941
ISBN 0–582–03086–2

ISBN 0-582-03086-2

Produced by Longman Group (FE) Ltd
Printed in Hong Kong

Contents

The editors

Terry Brown taught in direct grant, grammar and comprehensive schools before joining Durham University to develop their inservice programme. He has researched into the organisation of the curriculum in secondary schools and been involved in many courses concerned with the curriculum. He has been chairperson and, later, secretary of the Association for the Study of the Curriculum and for five years edited their journal *Curriculum*. He is now deputy editor of *The Curriculum Journal*. His recent publications include 'Bandwagon, ambulance or omnibus? A modular higher degree structure for teachers' and 'Middle management and the secondary curriculum: power, responsibility and accountability'. He is currently working freelance and has just completed a set of English course books for secondary schools.

Keith Morrison taught for many years in primary and secondary schools before moving into teacher education. He has been involved in several curriculum development and evaluation projects in both primary and secondary education, and is currently working on the development of a social philosophy of the primary curriculum. He is the author of two previous books and many publications on the politics of the curriculum, assessment and evaluation. His recent publications include 'Curriculum planning and the primary school', 'Bringing progressivism into a critical theory of education', 'Training teachers for primary schools: the question of subject study' and 'A cascade model of curriculum innovation'. He is currently Lecturer in Education at the University of Durham, where he is involved in initial teacher training and higher degree courses on curriculum analysis, development and evaluation. He has just completed a longitudinal multi-method evaluation of science teaching.

Notes on contributors

Neville Bennett is Professor of Primary Education at the University of Exeter. He was the country's first Professor of Primary Education.

Peter Burke is Chief Executive of the group secretariat of the Southern Examining Group.

John Dunford is Headteacher of the Johnston Comprehensive School in Durham City and a member of the Senate of the University of Durham.

George Gyte is the Chief Inspector of Northamptonshire LEA. Before that he was a secondary headteacher in Cleveland LEA and for a year Director of the Centre for the Study of Comprehensive Schools in York.

Jackson Hall was until very recently Director of Education for Sunderland and President of the Society of Education Officers.

Joan Sallis is Chairperson of CASE and was a member of the Taylor Committee.

Introduction

This handbook is intended to document curriculum initiatives and developments which are currently being undertaken in the United Kingdom or which have been started in the last five years. It is both a record and a directory, for researchers are provided with data to locate exactly where the initiatives are taking place. This introduction seeks to open up the context of the curriculum projects recorded here and to draw on the commentaries on recent developments provided by the authors of the first section.

The book is in seven sections; the first section presents a set of six papers which set the scene for the remaining six sections – details of specific projects and contributions to the curriculum made by a variety of organisations, institutions and agencies.

The overwhelming message about curriculum initiatives is that they stem from responses to recent legislation; it is as if curriculum developments and curriculum development organisations, institutions and agencies are now operating in a responsive rather than a proactive mode. The ramifications of this are clearly drawn in Hall's important paper in Section One. The nature of these responses varies along a continuum. At one end is critique – for example of the lack of a research or theoretical base to the national curriculum and its silence on learning theory – a point well made in Bennett's paper. At the other end is acceptance, acquiescence and relatively unquestioning implementation of DES and legislative prescription. Some parties are clearly seizing the opportunity afforded by the Reform Act to promote positive change and innovation. There are several key themes which are detectable throughout the book which this introduction exposes.

The politicisation of curriculum decision making

The 'politics of the curriculum' is a slippery term; on the one hand it can refer to the use which politicians make of the curriculum debate; on the other hand it can refer to questions of power and control of the curriculum. Both uses find voice in the book. For example, Bennett shows how the progressive movement, though confined largely to rhetoric rather than to practice, was seized upon as an easy target by zealous politicians. Further, one can see how many curriculum initiatives are imbued with the language of an industrial mentality much prized by the political Right, for example the rise of projects on Enterprise Education, Education and Industry, Business Education, Technical and Vocational Education, very many of them attracting large research funds and even coming complete with their own acronyms! Even the language has moved from child-centred phrases to such expressions as the 'delivery of the curriculum'. Gyte's paper adds to this the view that there will be an increasing role to be given to the development of a 'technologically literate workforce' in the 1990s. Moreover, if the accountability movement has had any impact, this can be most clearly seen in the rise of interest in evaluation studies. This is most notable in TVEI curricula where vast sums of money have been allocated for evaluating the impact of TVEI well into the 1990s, although there is a wealth of other material indicating monitoring and reviewing exercises in progress in a wide variety of curriculum fields. It is perhaps significant that very many organisations and institutions list 'reports' and 'evaluations' as being one of the principal written outcomes of a project. One is reminded of the adage that if you wish to accord importance to an area of the curriculum then you evaluate it!

The second use of the term 'the politics of the curriculum' concerns control of the curriculum. This is a *leitmotif* of the whole book, both overtly and implicitly. When one looks at the nature of funding of research and curriculum initiatives the most striking feature of it is that it is largely policy-driven research where the policies emanate from government legislation. Not that this is a novelty – the DES has traditionally deliberately confined its commissioning of research to policy directed research. What we are witness to now is the spread of this view of research. This manifests itself in many ways. Very noticeable is the dearth of any funded 'pure' research or research beyond the bounds of the national curriculum; if research is being done it is overwhelmingly in connection with the national curriculum implementation and its associated assessment requirements, and often being carried out in the larger Schools of Education in the country. This move to extending applied research is affecting institutions of higher education, curriculum development bodies and organisations, LEA and funding bodies. It is as though we are confined to working within given parameters – both theoretical and practical. There is little evidence of new paradigms being formed. If theoretical debate and research is being done at all it is small scale and largely underfunded or even unfunded. This is regrettable, as the theoretical field of curriculum debate *is* being taken forward by isolated bodies and individuals; for example there is increasing consideration being given to Critical Theory and a 'critical' stance to curricula and there is a growing role for 'cultural analysis' and social philosophy in curriculum debate; this does not find voice in the initiatives recorded in this book. There is, then, a clear lag of practice behind theory. One can discern then in the sections of the book an absence in educational circles of an open debate about the aims and long term purposes of education; in such an absence the vacuum is filled by the current political doctrines, purposes and ideologies of education and its social functions. Couple this with an imposed consensus on the content of the curriculum and one has a very potent centralised education decision-making structure.

Institutions of Higher Education are caught in this market, consumerist mentality, where funding is only attracted to policy driven research. There is a clear message in Section Seven of the book that if universities, polytechnics and colleges of higher education are to survive in research ratings – or even to survive in a climate of economic stringency – then it is up to them to provide consumers with what consumers think they need (or what they have been told to need!). Institutional viability depends on income generation, a market economy grips the education service. Institutions of higher education are having to extend their servicing functions – to DES, LEA and other commissioning organisations – and on several occasions are developing joint bids for funding. The politicisation of the curriculum extends beyond institutions of higher education to exam bodies. Burke's paper augurs the end of the power of exam boards and groups if they are not prepared to collaborate with government proposals. Whilst institutions concerned with curriculum development in Section Four of the book do not necessarily have the anxiety to attract research, being often professional associations, the impact of the national curriculum is nevertheless profound in that the clear majority of their concerns are driven by the national curriculum. Thus they too are collaborating with government proposals.

The effects of this latter interpretation of 'the politics of the curriculum' – the control of the content of the curriculum – can be seen in a variety of ways. Very clear is the threat posed to the breadth of the curriculum, a feature which both Sallis and Bennett argue should be resisted, Sallis arguing that there is more to education than that contained in a prescribed national curriculum, and Bennett showing how the government's own educational advisers – HMI – indicate that the best learning takes place in a wide curriculum. 'Relevance' and 'differentiation' should be interpreted widely, and there is a risk that there will be a move towards dull uniformity and standardisation wrought by the national curriculum, its assessment, and the reduction in the number of examination syllabi at key stage four. Notwithstanding this, there is evidence of the loss or reduction of Classics, Social Science, Drama, Home Economics, Media Studies, and the rise of Science, Technology, CDT, Information Technology and TVEI. Gyte's paper suggests that assessment is still a central area of debate, and with the government's emphasis on assessment in the national curriculum there is a wealth of research on assessment, Records of Achievement, Curriculum Evaluation (particularly of TVEI), profiling and record keeping. Whilst the diagnostic benefits afforded by increased assessment are documented in Bennett's paper, noticeable in the book is the silence on the way that increased assessment fuels the accountability debate, which debate in its turn is attractive to the political Right. If we recognise also the rise in research on management, INSET, governing bodies, and teacher appraisal, then one could interpret the scenario as the full working out of an 'industrial' view of the education service and its 'line management' models of organisation. Gyte's paper suggests that the effects of legislation on the requirement for schools to carry out an audit and then develop their curricular systems necessitate a massive staff development exercise – a feature echoed forcibly in Hall's paper. Further, Burke's paper shows how the effects of a 'rationalisation' plan for education and examinations are to narrow the number of syllabi to maybe only a handful for each subject throughout the country, and that the government is anxious to achieve this limitation.

A more sanguine view of the politicisation of the curriculum is taken in some papers. Dunford and Sallis both argue for the need to grasp the opportunity afforded by recent legislation to open up education to lay participation. Sallis argues that real parental participation must be cultivated if the strictures of the national curriculum are to be kept at bay; narrowness of scope will bring about narrowness of vision in curriculum planning. Dunford argues for partnership to be developed between the lay and professional sectors in education, particularly in governing bodies, the background to which is well traced in Hall's paper. Burke argues for partnership to be developed between exam boards and SEAC, though he regrets the loss of partnership between schools and examination boards which had been the long standing hallmark of the school-specific CSE examination syllabi. Gyte's paper advocates a new partnership between LEA and institutions of higher education, and indeed between schools and examination boards. The later sections of the book cite very many examples of relatively small-scale initiatives which are being undertaken by partnerships between LEA and HE institutions. In Sections Six and Seven of the book is charted the growth of often short-term secondments in order to do specific tasks – often in a collaboration between LEA and institutions of higher education. One has to question 'where is the pool or pooling of developed expertise'? Teachers come out for a few months to a year or two and then return to their classrooms. An overall view is needed to avoid patchy developments – a view set out in Gyte's paper. Such partnerships should be fostered at an early stage in the decision-making process. The amount of research on parental involvement, governing bodies and local consortia initiatives reported in the later sections of the books offers evidence to support the importance of their views. If one of the effects of the politicisation of the curriculum decision making process is to foster partnerships – to bring people and groups together – then this is perhaps to be welcomed.

If one accepts the notion of 'entitlement' – the case for which is raised in Hall's paper – and that the national curriculum could actually bring about a broader educational diet for some previously curriculum-starved children then there is evidence in the later sections that such breadth is being taken seriously in research locations. For example there is the flowering of cross-curricular issues – Environmental Education, Equal Opportunities, Economic Understanding, Citizenship Education, Health Education, and – very noticeably – Personal and Social Education. Research is being undertaken on interdisciplinary teaching and learning, on problem-solving strategies in both primary and secondary phases. Research is being carried out on Records of Achievement and new forms of record keeping where assessment is seen as integral to teaching and a spur to pupil motivation. This has to be set against the question of how these initiatives will survive in the actual curriculum of schools, bearing in mind that they are exhortations competing with the assessed, statutory requirements. Further, Hall's paper injects a salutary note on curriculum developments, cautioning us to beware the straitjacket effects of the national curriculum. One must comment further on the buoyant, positive tone adopted by the vast majority of research and curriculum development agencies. Very many organisations in Section Four deliberately state their support for local initiatives; there is a sense of enthusiasm in their documentation. In several instances organisations inundated us with far more material than we could comfortably use, and institutions contacted us to request more space to mention curriculum development projects. It seems then that there is no shortage of curriculum development projects taking place in all quarters of the country, and, apart from between LEAs, there is little duplication of projects. Gyte's paper suggests the need for a rationalisation of organisation at national level to avoid piecemeal development and provision.

The impact of recent legislation on all sectors of the education service has been to speed up the rate of curriculum change to an enormous degree. Schools and related institutions are, in their turn, having to speed up their programme developments to keep pace with new requirements. In many cases recent changes are requiring organisations and institutions to reconsider and restructure their roles. We have already indicated the service role incumbent on many institutions of higher education. One can detect in the literature of several organisations in Section Four their view of their function to disseminate and monitor developments. With regard to institutions concerned with the whole school curriculum (Section Five), the position is complex. Some claim to be doing nothing other than watch and pass comment if appropriate, others claim to cover *everything*, and thus indicate perhaps their naivety and possible lack of understanding in depth. A significant point to the entries in Section Five is that a large number of organisations which never expressed an interest until recently are now ploughing into the curriculum and producing very glossy materials for use in schools. For other institutions the changes are more fundamental. For example Burke's paper outlines how examination boards and groups are going to have to prepare for the demise of GCSE and possibly move towards extending their expertise in moderation and administration of national testing to take in the early key stages of the national curriculum. Further, Dunford's paper acknowledges the structural alterations to the roles of senior school staff and governing bodies that have been brought about since the Reform Act, whilst Sallis is concerned that genuine parental participation might be the casualty of rapid change, reduced to an empty ritual. One can draw an analogy with the industrial sector here – if industry does not accommodate itself to the climate of the present then it fails; so in education. Massive structural changes to longstanding organisations are necessary if they are to survive. As in industry, so in education the changes are not always painless.

    The handbook draws on the themes outlined above in all the sections. The papers in Section One set the scene for their specified area. What is noticeable is the resonance of the substance of one paper with the next; repeatedly the same themes are met. Following the papers in Section One there are six sections which report and order curriculum initiatives and developments which are being undertaken by the institutions and organisations listed. Entries are set in alphabetical order within each section. The data collected here is in response to questionnaires sent out to every government agency concerned with education, every relevant examination board or group, every relevant organisation concerned with school and curriculum organisation, every organisation concerned with a specific curriculum area, every LEA, and every institution of higher education. The questionnaires requested data which covered the 5–18 age range, i.e the ages of statutory schooling, and any curriculum initiatives which had been started in the last five years. In the event of a non-response to the questionnaire the section entry lists the organisation, its address and means of contact. What is encouraging is the high response rate. This means that this handbook has captured not only the *spread* of curriculum initiatives that are being undertaken in the country, but that it records the vast *bulk* of them. There is high validity then to the data. The questionnaire survey was exhaustive and thanks must be recorded here to the very full information which was received from the respondents. Each of the Sections Two to Seven is preceded by a brief introductory paragraph and the index is compiled at the end to enable readers to access curriculum development projects under subject headings. Readers who wish to find out what a particular institution or organisation is undertaking can of course go direct to that organisation in the appropriate section. Wherever possible an identified contact person has been named so that readers wishing to follow up a reference have an immediate point of contact. In some cases some entries will therefore have more than one telephone number or address. Further, a single project which covers more than

Introduction

one curriculum area may have more than one entry in the index. What is provided for the reader, then, is an up to date, easily accessible directory of curriculum initiatives which are taking place throughout the country.

Terry Brown   May 1990
Keith Morrison

Notes on the presentation of Sections 2 to Section 7

The data presented in Sections 2 through 7 originate in the main from questionnaire responses. The list below gives the phrases and symbols used to introduce the responses with a fuller explanation.

☎   telephone number
Ⓣ   telex number
Ⓕ   facsimile number (fax)
Ⓟ   contact person

Publications   professional communication channels, giving title and frequency of publications

Current initiatives   current curriculum initiatives gives title and then in parenthesis: the year project commenced; the year project is to be completed; and the age range of children addressed

Objectives   objectives of the organisation in relation to its contribution to the development and assessment of children and curricula

Remit   general description of agency or organisation

Awards given   titles of awards given by organisation

Contribution   organisations were asked whether they made a formal contribution to curriculum development by: consultation; raising theoretical curricular questions; provision of resource material; organising meetings and courses for voluntary attendance; producing discussion papers; producing assessment materials; others

1, 2, 3, etc   introduce the subject matter of individual projects; a money sum in parenthesis indicates the level of funding achieved; this is followed, where known, by the name of the funding organisation

■   introduces the purpose of that project
Ⓣ   introduces the project team
▼   introduces the documents available on the project

   telex number
   facsimile number (fax)
   contact person

Section 1

Setting the Scene for Current Curriculum Initiatives

1 The Primary Curriculum

Neville Bennett

In 1987 the then Secretary of State for Education, Kenneth Baker, described the English educational system as 'a bit of a muddle, one of those institutionalised muddles that the English have made peculiarly their own'. He compared it unfavourably with systems elsewhere in Europe. 'They have tended to centralise and standardise. We have gone for diffusion and variety. In particular, the functions of the State have largely been devolved to elected bodies; and the school curriculum has largely been left to individual schools and teachers' (DES, 1987). This had to change, he argued, by preserving the best of the present arrangements and doing away with the worst, through the establishment of 'a national curriculum which works through national criteria for each subject area of the curriculum'.

So what is the nature and source of this 'muddle'? and is centralisation and standardisation the answer to it? What is the 'best' of present arrangements that is to be preserved, and the 'worst' that is to be done away with? In order to answer these questions, as they refer specifically to the primary curriculum, an analysis is presented of contemporary primary practice, and its antecedents, before considering what changes the national curriculum will introduce or create.

Primary school practice

Presenting a coherent picture of curriculum practice, and its development, is no easy task. Surveys have been irregular, with limited and unrepresentative samples. Their foci have been determined by the prevailing concerns and theories of the time. Thus in the 1970s studies tended to concentrate on coarse-grain analyses of classroom and curriculum management, rather than on curriculum content, with the aim of ascertaining the extent to which progressive practices were being implemented. These concerns were gradually replaced in the 1980s by studies grounded in different theories of learning, leading to more detailed accounts of curriculum content and balance (Bennett, 1987).

Throughout the 1970s the rhetoric, if not the practice, of primary education was dominated by the Plowden Report (1967). The report was strongly prescriptive of 'progressive' education arguing that 'the curriculum is to be thought of in terms of activity and experience rather than knowledge to be acquired and facts to be stored'. The essence of this approach can be seen most clearly in its formulation of aims: '... the school sets out deliberately to devise the right environment for children, to allow them to be themselves, and to develop in a way and at a pace appropriate to them... It lays special stress on individual discovery, on first hand experience, and on opportunities for creative work. It insists that knowledge does not fall neatly into separate compartments and that work and play are not opposite but complementary'.

The debate which followed was characterised by what Richards (1988) called 'a kind of two party oppositional "politics" – between adherents of what has variously been termed as the "developmental", "progressive" or "liberal romantic" perspective on the one hand, and the "elementary", "utilitarian" or "conservative" perspective on the other'. The debate rapidly became polarised and deeply divisive, and was heightened, according to Delamont (1987), by the nature of the terms used, which had no clear meaning. 'The lack of any clear definition of what the terms mean is exactly the source of their emotional, political, value-laden and polarised force. They are totems, mythical entities, rhetorical devices and political labels'.

Despite the ferocity of the debate, classroom practice appeared little affected. Surveys throughout the 1970s and early 1980s clearly indicated the myth of what many believed to be a progressive revolution (Bennett, 1976; Bassey, 1977; Galton et al., 1980; HMI, 1978; Barker-Lunn, 1984).

Delamont (1987) summarised the accumulated findings as follows: 'despite the "progressive" *appearance* of junior school classrooms with tables, small groups and chatter, the interaction patterns are highly traditional. Most of the time the teacher is directing the class and giving out facts, monitoring silent seat work, marking books, hearing children read or doing "housekeeping". Only a tiny amount of a pupil's time is spent in direct contact with a teacher, and very little of what the teacher does is cognitively demanding'. Alexander's (1984) sceptical verdict on a decade of supposed experimentation was of teaching that is 'occasionally exciting, usually competent in the so-called basics at least, but not infrequently mediocre or inadequate'.

By the early 1980s investigators were beginning to report studies which focussed more clearly on curriculum balance. Bennett, Andreae, Hegarty and

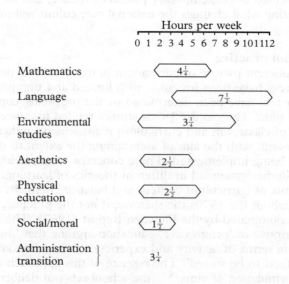

Figure 1.1   Time spent on different curriculum areas

Wade (1980) for example observed, in blocks of a whole week, the time allocated to curriculum areas, and pupil involvement on curriculum tasks in a national sample of infant and junior open plan schools. They reported very large variations in the curriculum balanced achieved. Figure 1.1 shows the average amount and range of time devoted to curriculum areas in junior schools.

Thus, for example, the average amount of time spent on mathematics nationally was four and a quarter hours per week, but varied from two hours in some classrooms to over seven hours in others. Similarly the average amount of time spent on language activities (reading, writing, spelling, etc.) was seven and a half hours per week but varied from a low of four hours to a high of twelve. Although the balance was somewhat different in infant schools, e.g. more time devoted to language, particularly reading activities, the variation was as great, and is supported by other studies (Bassey, 1977; Galton, Simon and Croll, 1980). What these findings indicated is that children received quite different curriculum diets dependent on the school they happened to go to.

Variation in curriculum was paralleled by variation in the extent of pupil involvement or engagement. On average pupils were involved in their work for about two-thirds of the time but this varied markedly from class to class, and from pupil to pupil in the same class. Class averages varied from a low of 50 per cent to a high of 90 per cent.

More recent studies have indicated to what purposes this time is put. Studies at infant level (Bennett, Desforges, Cockburn, and Wilkinson, 1984; Desforges and Cockburn, 1987; Tizard, Blatchford, Burke, Farquhar and Plewis, 1988; Bennett and Kell, 1989) and junior level (Bennett, Roth and Dunne, 1987) all attest to the tremendous disparities in curriculum from class to class. Bennett et al. (1984) for example documented all the work in maths and language throughout the spring and summer terms. In maths they concluded that the content of the curriculum as experienced by the children varied extensively both within-class and between classes and that provision did not seem to relate to any characteristics of the children; 'rather it seemed to emanate from teachers decisions on content and page'. Diversity was also evident in the structure of experience (in terms of the relationships between families of procedures in the same content areas) provided for maths work. In language they concluded 'There were large differences between classes in terms of what was attempted and what was obtained. These differences do not seem attributable to differences of catchment area or intake. Rather, they appear to arise from decisions made by individual class teachers or from the design of school schemes'. These analyses of the nature and content of curriculum in maths and language accord with other studies. Tizard et al. (1988), for example, observing teachers and pupils in inner-city areas, found very similar differences.

Some teachers had introduced written subtraction in year one of the infant school whereas other teachers had not yet introduced it in year three.

Curriculum delivery

Variations in curriculum content are matched by variations in delivery. This can be demonstrated with reference to the following model, which presents, in simplified form, a teaching cycle. Planning and preparation is followed by the presentation or representation of tasks/activities by the teacher. The children work on these activities within a classroom management system sufficient for a

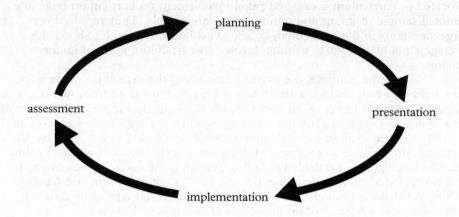

Figure 1.2   Schematic of ideal task planning

satisfactory level of involvement, and when completed their work is assessed by the teacher.

These assessments are, ideally, fed back to the children and fed forward into the teacher's next round of task planning. (See Figure 1.2)

Recent research would indicate that the aspects of the teaching cycle that teachers have most difficulty with are planning and presenting tasks which are appropriately related to children's capabilities, often referred to as 'matching'; and the assessment and diagnosis of children's understandings. HMI have expressed concern at poor levels of matching ever since the Primary Survey of 1978, particularly in areas like science and topic work. Their comments in the 1983 9–13 Middle School survey and the 1985 8–12 Middle School survey are typical. In the former they argued that 'both the more able and less able were not given enough suitable activities in a majority of schools', and in the latter report they state 'Overall, the content, level of demand and pace of work were most often directed toward the children of average ability in the class. In many classes there was insufficient differentiation to cater for the full range of children's capabilities'. This same message is also writ large in HMI surveys of probationary teachers (1988), and in their most recent reports on Science (1989) and History and Geography (1989). In the Science report HMI implicitly link matching and assessment. 'Few schools assess effectively children's progress in science. This often results in weaknesses in matching the work to the ability of the children and in planning for progression in science within and across year groups'. Lack of systematic assessment was also criticised in the History and Geography document.

The professional judgements of HMI accord with recent research in primary teaching with regard to matching, assessment, and their interaction (Bennett et al., 1984; Bennett et al., 1987; Bennett and Kell, 1989). Improving diagnosis appears to be the key to improving matching. Tasks cannot appropriately be matched without a clear view of children's understandings, but gaining that understanding is a sophisticated teaching skill. A popular metaphor for diagnosis is 'a window into the child's mind', and to see through that window needs a sophisticated combination of observation and questioning. It undeniably needs more time than what currently passes for assessment in most classrooms. Research indicates that diagnosis is not typical in contemporary practice, and this has obvious implications for teacher planning and pupil progression; as Ausubel (1968) argued twenty years ago 'the most important single factor influencing learning is what the learner already knows. Ascertain this and teach him accordingly.'

Sufficient has been presented above to show that lack of central or even local control of curriculum, together with a tradition of teacher autonomy, has resulted in primary practice being extremely diverse. Teachers have determined the allocation of curriculum time, the content to fill that time, and the mode of delivery. In other words all teachers have taught a different curriculum, dependent on their own particular aims and expectations. Conversely, all children have received a different educational diet and, as in other areas of human functioning, diet relates to growth.

Nevertheless it is not easy to demonstrate clearly differential learning, or school standards, at a national level because until now there has been no agreement on curriculum and no national testing programmes. The only data available are derived from the school inspections of Her Majesty's Inspectorate (HMI). These are based on professional judgements, doubts about which have been expressed concerning their reliability and validity. Despite this they carry much political weight, and have been instrumental in both lighting and fuelling a continuing debate about who should control the curriculum. Thus in 1983 DES began to talk in terms of an 'entitlement curriculum', defined as a broad framework representing a synthesis of the vocational, the technical and the academic: 'It seemed essential that *all* pupils should be guaranteed a curriculum of distinctive breadth and depth to which they should be *entitled*, irrespective of the type of school they attended or their level of ability or their social circumstances and that failure to provide such a curriculum is unacceptable' (DES, 1983). The Government followed this with the publication of a document entitled Better Schools in 1985 in which they presented a summary of HMI reports. The report concluded: '... the present spectrum of quality and the variations between schools are wider than is acceptable in a national system ... The findings of HMI point to several areas of substantial weakness in an unacceptably large proportion of our schools.' A weakness in three quarters of schools was curricular planning and implementation – 'above all, there are rarely effective mechanisms for ensuring that declared curricular policies are reflected in the day-to-day work of most teachers and pupils'. It criticised schools for an over-concentration on basic skills in literacy and numeracy unrelated to context, and for providing too little opportunity for work in the scientific, practical and aesthetic areas of the curriculum. The work was judged to be too teacher directed in half of all classes, leading to a lack of oral, and practical work. Teacher expectations were seen as too undemanding, leading to poor levels of match whereby able pupils are insufficiently stretched, and waste time in practising skills already mastered, and to the individual weaknesses of less able children not being diagnosed or dealt with appropriately. Pupils have not been led to appreciate the need to exercise rigour and perseverance, or to see the link between effort and mastery. Finally, assessment systems designed to ensure progress and continuity of learning for all pupils in all areas of the curriculum were not common.

The schools had been judged and been found wanting. In order to tackle the weaknesses apparent, and to improve standards, four areas of policy were adumbrated:

1. to secure greater clarity about the objectives and content of the curriculum
2. to reform assessment procedures so that they promote more effectively the objectives of the curriculum, the achievements of pupils, and the recording of those achievements
3. to improve the professional effectiveness of teachers and the management of the teaching force
4. to reform school government and to harness more fully the contribution that can be made to good school education by parents, employers and others outside the education service.

It is of interest, particularly in the light of what was shortly to follow, that the Government took the opportunity in 'Better Schools' to reiterate the statutory position regarding control of the curriculum – '… it would not in the view of the Government be right for the Secretaries of State's policy for the range and pattern of the 5–16 Curriculum to amount to the determination of national syllabuses for that period'. Instead it wished to proceed on the basis of broadly agreed principles about range and pattern, the establishment of which would 'not mean that the curricular policies of the Secretaries of State, the LEA and the school should relate to each other in a nationally uniform way… The Government does not propose to introduce legislation affecting the powers of the Secretaries of State in relation to the curriculum'.

Yet only two years later the Secretaries of State published a consultative document setting out the main elements of a national curriculum and the proposed legislation to secure its full implementation.

The National Curriculum

The Education Act defining the National Curriculum became law in July 1988. It aims to meet the criticisms of the schools set out in the above section. The Act lays down the main structure of the curriculum for all schools and the procedures for implementation. For all children aged 5–16 the curriculum will comprise three 'core' subjects (English, mathematics and science) and seven 'foundation' subjects (history, geography, art, music, technology, physical education and a modern foreign language). Religious education will be taken by all pupils as a 'basic' subject.

The National Curriculum is conceived in four 'key stages'. Key stages 1 (5 to 7 years) and 2 (7 to 11 years) cover the primary curriculum. Attainment in the National Curriculum is to be assessed at the end of each key stage using a combination of teacher assessments and national standard attainment tasks. These will be formative and criterion referenced and will describe pupil performance on ten levels covering progress from 5 to 16 years of age.

In order for children to meet these levels subject groups have devised 'programmes of study' and associated attainment targets which are legally binding on schools. Nevertheless teachers are free to determine their own teaching approach and curriculum materials. The National Curriculum Council, a body set up by the 1988 Act to advise on the detail of the curriculum has, in its guidance document A Framework for the Primary Curriculum, argued that the new curriculum offers a basis for clearer planning and will ensure that all children receive a broad, balanced and coherent programme of learning.

It is suggested that the aims of the National Curriculum will more likely be met where pupils are:

1. properly equipped with the basic tools of learning
2. given lots of first hand experience and practical tasks
3. led to ask questions, to reflect on experience and seek answers both individually and collectively
4. nurtured by teachers with high expectations
5. encouraged to become self disciplined and self evaluating.

This list, emphasising processes, participation and pupil autonomy, will encourage those who fear that the new curriculum will be content dominated. There also appear to be other advantages when contrasted with contemporary practice. It will guarantee that subjects which have in the past been given short shrift, such as science, will now be taught. Teachers will have to carefully address the issue of curriculum balance within the context of cross-curricular themes. And critical aspects of the learning process such as cooperative endeavour and oracy, currently neglected, will play a much more central role. Finally, of course, the continuous assessment of children's work becomes mandatory, thereby assisting children's learning and teachers' planning. At best then children will get a more similar, but more satisfying, educational diet.

Doubts nevertheless remain. It is clear for example that the structure of the National Curriculum has no research nor theoretical base. Indeed, as Aldrich (1988) points out after comparing the proposals with the curriculum in existence in 1904 '... the most striking feature of the proposed national curriculum is that it is at least 83 years old', and as such 'appears as a reassertion of the basic grammar school curriculum devised at the beginning of the twentieth century'. It is a curriculum which is not associated in the public mind with outstanding success in most of the nation's secondary schools.

Doubts must also be expressed about the hierarchical model of assessment. Implicit within this is a hierarchical model of learning which is not clearly linked to learning or developmental theory. That subject panels have experienced difficulty with this is evident to anyone who traces the supposed development in areas of attainment through key stages 1 to 4.

Most serious however is the ability of teachers to deliver effectively the new curriculum. Of particular concern must be teachers lack of subject matter knowledge in areas like science and technology. A recent national survey of primary teachers found that science, technology and music were the subjects that teachers perceived themselves to be least competent in. Nearly one quarter of all teachers claimed that they would need substantial inservice support in order to be confident to teach these subjects to the appropriate levels (Wragg, Bennett and Carré, 1989).

These teacher perceptions mirror those of HMI. HMI were particularly scathing of the teaching of science in their 1987 survey; one in five teachers taught no science at all, and what was taught was ineffective and inappropriate. Seven years later they still complained of unbalanced content, lack of genuine experimentation and too much note taking and dictation. They concluded that only half of the curriculum schemes were satisfactory and that standards of work were only satisfactory in one half of the schools (HMI, 1985). And in their latest reports, HMI (1989a, 1989b) cite teachers' lack of subject matter knowledge in science as the major obstacle to progress.

Lack of sufficient subject matter knowledge is a major concern in the process of teaching as well as in the content of the curriculum. Without such knowledge teachers are not well placed either to adequately diagnose children's work and provide effective feedback, or to plan and present tasks to children which are appropriately differentiated and matched.

Some of these issues are addressed in the first HMI report on the implementation of the national curriculum (1989b). On the one hand they report a general welcome by teachers for its introduction, who perceive the programmes of study as clear and helpful for planning and preparation. It has instigated a great increase in school wide discussion on curricular matters, and injected a degree of rigour and urgency into curricular planning which was not previously present.

On the other hand they reported that many schools will have to increase the range and quality of their work to meet the requirements of the key stages. Currently work is poorly matched and over dominated by tasks embodying mundane demands. Oral work is neglected. Most worrying however, both to the teachers and HMI, was assessment and record keeping. This is compounded by uncertainty about what is required in continuous assessment, and by deficiencies in existing arrangements which means that many schools are starting from a weak base in practice, and the lack of time available for undertaking work on assessment and recording. This same issue was prominent in the national survey carried out by Wragg, Bennett and Carré – when asked which classroom processes posed them most difficulties seventy percent of the teachers cited diagnosis of children's learning, sixty percent identified the continuous assessment of children's work and one half said record keeping.

Conclusion

At the time of writing the primary curriculum is in a state of transition. To be phased out is a system characterised by decentralised control, teacher autonomy and curriculum variety, to be replaced by a curriculum which is both centralised and standardised. This change, it is claimed, will strengthen curriculum planning and implementation, ensure breadth, balance and coherence, improve delivery and thereby improve standards.

Whether these predictions are well founded only time will tell. The prognosis for the short term is less than ideal. Considerably more time, money and attention has been paid to the delineation of the content of the curriculum, and the associated attainment targets, than to identifying and resourcing an effective implementation strategy directed toward the enhancement of teachers' knowledge, pedagogical skills and personal concerns. This policy, or lack of it, is difficult to understand since the weaknesses in primary teachers' subject matter knowledge and assessment procedures are well known, and are critical to the success of implementation. Yet the former has virtually been ignored, and the latter has received only two days inservice input, most often divorced from a consideration of classroom realities.

It is also well known that most of the world's best ideas founder on the rocks of implementation, and that externally imposed change invariably creates anxiety, increases workload and can leave the participants feeling temporarily de-skilled. Despite this the national curriculum is being introduced in piecemeal fashion, with guidance and details of assessment often following, rather than preceding, implementation. And all within a context of restricted time, training and finance.

The prognosis for the longer term is, in my view, much more optimistic. The resilience and professionalism of primary teachers is recognised and my prediction is that the turbulence of the short term will be followed by a period in which teachers will use their consolidated subject matter knowledge and professional skills to reflect on and reconceptualise their practice to provide learning environments which are more collaborative, more applied and more rigorous. The next generation of pupils can look forward to classrooms being more exciting, demanding places.

References

Aldrich R (1988) 'The National Curriculum: an historical perspective'. In Lawton D and Chitty C (Eds). *The National Curriculum*. Institute of Education, University of London.

Alexander R (1984) *Primary Teaching*. London, Holt, Rinehart and Winston.

Ausubel D (1968) *Educational Psychology: A Cognitive View*. New York, Holt, Rinehart and Winston.

Barker-Lunn J (1984) 'Junior school teachers: their methods and practices' *Education Research* 26, 178–188.

Bassey M (1977) *Nine Hundred Primary School Teachers*. Nottingham, Trent Polytechnic.

Bennett N (1976) *Teaching Styles and Pupil Progress*. London, Open Books.

Bennett N (1987) 'Changing perspectives on teaching-learning processes in the post-Plowden era' *Oxford Review of Education* 13, 67–79.

Bennett N, Andreae J, Hegarty P, and Wade P (1980) *Open Plan Schools*. Windsor, NFER.

Bennett N, Desforges C, Cockburn A, and Wilkinson B (1984) *The Quality of Pupil Learning Experiences*. London, Lawrence Erlbaum Ass.

Bennett N, Roth E and Dunne R (1987) 'Task processes in mixed and single age classes' *Education 3–13* 15. 43–50.

Bennett N and Kell J (1989) *A Good Start?: Four Year Olds in Infant Schools*. Oxford, Blackwell.

Delamont S (1987) 'The primary teacher 1945–1990: myths and realities'. In Delamont S (Ed). *The Primary School Teacher*, pp 3–20. Lewes, Falmer.

DES (1983) *Curriculum 11–16: towards a statement of entitlement: curricular reappraisal in Action* (Red Book Three). London, HMSO.

DES (1985) *Better Schools*. London, HMSO.

DES (1987) 'Kenneth Baker looks at future of education system'. Press release 11/87.

Desforges C and Cockburn A (1987) *Understanding the Mathematics Teacher*. Lewes, Falmer.

Galton M, Simon B and Croll P (1980) *Inside the Primary School*. London, Routledge and Kegan Paul.

HMI (1978) *Primary Education in England: a Survey*. London, HMSO.

HMI (1983) *9–13 Middle Schools*. London, HMSO.

HMI (1985) *Education 8–12 in Combined and Middle Schools*. London, HMSO.

HMI (1988) *The New Teacher in School*. London, HMSO.

HMI (1989) *The Teaching and Learning of Science*. London, HMSO.

HMI (1989a) *The Teaching and Learning of History and Geography*. London, HMSO.

HMI (1989b) *The Implementation of the National Curriculum in Primary Schools*. London, HMSO.

Plowden Report (1967) *Children and their Primary Schools*. London, HMSO.

Richards C (1988) 'Primary Education in England: an analysis of some recent issues and developments'. In Clarkson M (Ed), *Emerging Issues in Primary Education*, pp 3–23. Lewes, Falmer Press.

Tizard B, Blatchford P, Burke J, Farquhar C and Plewis I (1988) *Young Children at School in the Inner City*. London, Lawrence Erlbaum Associates.

Wragg E C, Bennett N and Carré C (1989) 'Primary teachers and the national curriculum' *Research Papers in Education*.

2 The Secondary Curriculum

George Gyte

The 1st September 1989 marked the beginning of the biggest and longest curriculum development project ever undertaken in England and Wales: the introduction and implementation of the national curriculum (Walker,1989). Indeed, as a curriculum experiment, it will not be until the year 2001 that the first youngster will have experienced in full, the impact of this major innovation on their eleven years of maintained education.

Since the mid-seventies the search had been underway to construct a common curriculum in comprehensive schools which ensured 'each student was treated as an individual, with an equal right to the school's human and material resources and access to the same curriculum' (Walker, 1989). Much educational heartsearching took place over whether this was best addressed through defining principles for the curriculum, areas of experience, entitlement concepts, on a subject basis, or through a combination of any of these approaches.

James Callaghan's 1976 assertion that there was 'a strong case for the so called core curriculum of basis subjects' (Callaghan, 1976) was taken a substantial step further by the then Sir Keith Joseph, Secretary of State for Education and Science, in Sheffield in 1984 when he referred to the need for 'broadly agreed curriculum objectives and levels of attainment at various stages by pupils of different abilities'. The 1987 manifestos of all the main political parties made references to a national curriculum and hard on the heels of the election result came the specific proposals for the National Curriculum. The Education Reform Bill received Royal Assent in July 1988 with its Chapter One curricular provisions largely intact. Thus fifteen years of intensive debate was clarified into a subject based national curriculum consisting of ten foundation subjects, three of which (mathematics, science and English) are regarded as core subjects. The remaining foundation subjects are history, geography, technology, music, art, physical education and a modern foreign language. In Wales, Welsh is a core subject in schools where it is the medium of instruction and a foundation subject in all others. With the exception of a modern foreign language (obligatory only in NC years 7 to 11) all foundation subjects are compulsory throughout the years from 5 to 16 (NC years 1–11). In addition all schools are also required to include religious education in the curriculum.

The years of compulsory schooling have now been divided into four key stages: two in primary and two in secondary education. The secondary years are spread across the ages 12, 13 and 14 for Key Stage 3 (NC years 7–9) and ages 15 and 16 for Key Stage 4 (NC year 10–11). The importance of the key stage is that assessment of the national curriculum attainment targets and programmes of study takes place at or near the end of each key stage.

Thus the national curriculum years 7–11 have reached, by statute, this measure of clarity over intention; the years 12 and 13 (and hence the 16–19 area) remain outstanding. Schools and colleges, government, LEAs, employers and other end users try to come to terms with a framework for education and training which involves a core curriculum and student entitlement. Kenneth Baker, as Secretary of State, threw down the challenge; picking it up and shaping it into a coherent framework which builds on the national curriculum and recognises the transition requirements for a diverse student population still seems a daunting proposition. I shall return to this issue later in the chapter.

Given the legislative requirements, schools have responded with considerable vision, skill, managerial dexterity and imaginative pragmatism in their efforts to implement the programmes of study and attainment targets associated with the core subjects and technology. Work on these first four national curriculum subject areas has without doubt raised the profile of planning, managing and implementation strategies required in order to effect the necessary changes to the secondary curriculum. Furthermore schools have had to ensure that the approaches adopted now to secure successful institutional development planning are ones which can anticipate and accommodate future statutory and other requirements.

What planning approaches have been adopted in many secondary schools as they have prepared for and began the implementation process? Firstly a curriculum audit has had to be undertaken in order to find out the current position and define the changes required: the staffing and training needs, the resourcing implications and the buildings adaption/alterations necessary in order to fulfil the programmes of study. Whilst it may be said that schools have undertaken in the past a curriculum review which would have covered much of the same ground, I don't think the curriculum targets had such clarity as they have now. Nor has there been the necessity to ensure that the planned curriculum meets statutory requirements, that gaps or overlaps between subject areas are clearly identified, that a year group's curriculum objectives are analysed so as to identify that within and that beyond the National Curriculum, that curriculum subjects concerned with the same objectives or National Curriculum targets work cooperatively to avoid unnecessary duplication in schemes of work. Indeed, never before has the secondary curriculum been such a planned experience encompassing the lessons learned from the Technical Vocational and Educational Extension, the Lower Attaining Pupils Project, the Records of Achievement Project, the Local Education Authorities Training Grant Scheme, school focused training plans and now the National Curriculum core and foundation subjects, cross-curricular dimensions, themes and skills.

It is small wonder that the enormity of this task against a backcloth of other major initiatives such as those involving Local Management of Schools, Teacher Appraisal Schemes and pilot projects over Assessment of the National Curriculum, has caused the red light of teacher and institutional overload to burn brightly in 1989–90. It came as no surprise then to find the new Secretary of State for Education and Science, John McGregor, looking for ways of reducing the burden on heads and teachers whilst maintaining the Government's commitment to 1992 as the date for the introduction of all national curriculum subjects.

Some key problem areas

Kenneth Baker obviously works on the principle that if you intend to make a different educational omelette you have to break all the required eggs at the same time: hence the plethora of initiatives fighting for the same agenda space and timelines. One can understand the political zeal to achieve all change within the span of a single Government's mandate; one can't accept the lack of prioritisation accompanying such a large scale management of change operation in the education service. So far as the secondary curriculum is concerned it has left a number of pressing problems which need resolution.

I have already stated the management issue of competing priorities vying for attention. Headteachers nevertheless have the task of defining the staging of change in their schools and would no doubt appreciate a period of verbal and written abstinence from all except the National Curriculum Council and their Local Education Authority (though they may desire a re-assertion of 'brevity is next to Godliness' in missives from both these two!) as they grapple with the curriculum agenda so far and suffer from priorities overload.

The second major problem focuses on curriculum progression. Good schools have been working hard at issues surrounding continuity, liaison and progression between phases for a number of years. The national curriculum has highlighted the requirement to be clear-minded about curricular liaison and progression structures both *between* and *within* schools. A detailed understanding of curricular organisation, teaching styles, learning approaches and schemes of work leading into and out from key stages is an important prerequisite to enabling each child and student to realise their potential as well as each school achieve a qualitative improvement in its educational task. Breaking down the traditional barriers between primary and secondary schools is one thing, recognising there are important barriers and constraints to the progression challenge *within* schools is just as important.

This leads into our third area of concern, that of assessing, recording and reporting on achievement. The highwire act of the Black report (TGAT) was to balance the tension between professional sensitivity to the child and student as a developing individual, and the desire of the parent or public to know in a simple way how much they have learned and understood of the National Curriculum. This the report did, despite criticisms for being complex and involved. However, the need for teachers to record and monitor pupils' curricular progress against attainment targets and programmes of study involving both teacher assessment and standard Assessment tasks requires a demanding schedule. Such a schedule will necessitate training and development work for teachers in the tasks themselves, year heads and senior managers in the planning, coordination and logistics of the information database requirements as well as recording and reporting systems and procedures for parents, governors, LEA and other audiences. Thus there was some considerable dismay over the recently announced delay about Records of Achievement. Not only are they universally admired and urged by the CBI and leading industrialists, they are championed by teachers because they also place an emphasis on skills, experiences and learning acquired in areas outside both the national and the wider school curriculum as well as emphasising the centrality of the learner's own contribution to the recording of achievement. Keeping the momentum going concerning Records of Achievement without Government recognition of the necessary resource implications will be difficult given other competing demands. Yet the Record of Achievement provides the vehicle for making a reality of the secondary curriculum become more than the sum of the ten foundation subjects and religious education. Indeed it is the only means by which achievement and, as importantly, recognition in the National Curriculum Council's dimensions, skills, and themes can be satisfactorily acknowledged.

Of course, the third problem area in the secondary curriculum is the most contentious and is that concerning the 14–16 curriculum, the impact of Key Stage 4 on GCSE and whether there would be continuing room and scope for the vocational examining bodies. In this area, more so than anywhere else in the secondary curriculum, the tensions are caught over curriculum differentiation and vocationalisation and what has been termed the overcrowded curriculum. The Secretary of State's speech on 25 January 1990 to the Society of Education Officers annual meeting established his purpose:' my objective is not to lay down a detailed prescription but to establish a broad framework for Key Stage 4 which gives schools wide flexibility and scope for planning a suitable curriculum for all their pupils ... It is no part of the Government's purpose to over-regulate Key Stage 4 so that room for innovation is lost and worthwhile options are effectively driven out' (McGregor, 1990).

Thus it was clarified that for the core subjects of mathematics, English and science, all students will take a full course leading to GCSE, but for other national curriculum foundation subjects and for religious education a variety of options will be available in addition to GCSE. Thus, modularity and combinations of subjects into courses leading to GCSE will be allowable providing they confirm with the attainment targets and programmes of study. In addition further options will be available where schools wish to prepare their students for vocational qualifications and to include material from outside the national curriculum.

Mr McGregor also stated that he expects all students to continue with the core subjects, technology and a foreign language to 16 and that most pupils will do all 10 foundation subjects. However, he also made clear the most controversial decision yet, that exceptionally there should be scope for the ablest students,who might have reached GCSE at level 8 in the remaining foundation subjects, to drop those subjects before the end of Key Stage 4 to enable them to undertake other options outside the 10. In this seminal speech then Mr McGregor has at a stroke, reduced the centrality of both the national curriculum and the GCSE as the common currency for all students to 16. Instead he has enabled the least and most able to opt out, and so far as the latter group is concerned built a sizeable cuckoo in the planning nest for comprehensive schools.

Future developments
What is now clear, is that far from the national curriculum calling a halt to the debate about the nature and purpose of the secondary curriculum together with the attendant dialogue with examining bodies, employers and other end users about how it is to be structured, assessed and accredited, in fact the arguments surrounding 14–16 and its fit and progression relationship with 16–19 have gathered momentum. Indeed, given the green light by the Secretary of State in his January 1990 speech to the Society of Education Officers, there will be a range of encouraging developments related to modular structures, and unit accreditation approaches crossing GCSE, vocational examinations and the national curriculum programmes of study and attainment targets.

Furthermore those initiatives will be strengthened in the post 16 world.

In recent years the TVEI has inspired discussions concerning inter-related accreditation possibilities between A level and vocational examinations in order to offer more flexible pathways for students, and thereby increase the number of students staying on in education and training. The early years of the 1990s will focus sharply on our national failure to match our industrial competitors in this latter respect, and the requirement to push hard to remain a high technology economy with a skilled, flexible and technologically literate workforce.

In a similar way, the pre-16 curriculum will see important developments occur on cross-curricular issues. The National Curriculum Council's brave attempt at clarification of terminology in this area has been most helpful: dimensions (eg personal and social education, multi-cultural education and equal opportunities), skills (information skills, communication skills), and themes (eg economic and industrial awareness, careers education and guidance, health education, environment education, citizenship). The search is on to find the most appropriate ways of mapping, managing and coordinating the curricular implementation of these issues within schools. Furthermore the recent accent on citizenship emphasised by the work of the Speaker's Commission on Citizenship and the Prince's Trust, highlights the need for greater coherence of understanding and provision in schools. It is quite likely the 1990s will see a continuing debate as well as research about what is meant by citizenship in terms of the social, civil and political entitlements and responsibilities of individuals and the part they play in the wider community. The way in which schools and colleges help young people develop as citizens is now assuming a major curricular as well as extra-curricular dimension.

Research trends

The mounting agenda facing secondary schools and colleges and the lack of a good evidence-based approach to understanding the complex choices and workloads highlights a glaring problem in our service. There is no national commitment to a coherent research and development strategy which underpins national policy and thus recent legislation. Until this is recognised and addressed satisfactorily we will continue to have the present piecemeal and patchy research provision we have emanating from inadequate budgets with no long term commitments. Thus we have the NCC addressing curriculum definition and implementation, SEAC focusing on the why, how and what of assessment and LMS/LMC re-writing the script concerning the nature and resourcing of the curricular experiences of children and students. Yet there is no coherent national framework which funds and harnesses a reasonable level of research and development provision in our institutes of higher education to test out the validity and impact of this 'attempt to lever up the quality' of the system.

Already it is clear we shall need some high quality research exploring the nature of comparisons within and between schools as a consequence of standard assessment tasks and other agreed performance indicators and measures. In addition the nature of the emerging partnership over assessment between schools, LEA and examination boards at Key Stages 3 and 4 will be an area for formative research and evaluation in order to ensure that teacher assessment meets appropriate criteria for reliability and validity within inter-school LEA moderation arrangements, as well as to answer the question as to whether it is improving the quality or not.

Whilst assessment and school achievement comparisons can be seen as important areas for research trends, they signal also an important pointer for the future. After the experience of ERA and its aftermath, policy analysis will assume a greater significance in the future, and so it should. It is the absence of just such a dimension which has led to the recent spectacle of educational 'stop–go' policies bewildering the service managers and disillusioning the professionals. If the next few years see a closer and more structured relationship over educational research, development and policy analysis, between schools, LEAs and institutes of higher education then a very sensible step forward will have taken place.

References

Callaghan J (1976)   Ruskin College speech
McGregor J (1990)   'National Curriculum for 14–16 year olds'. SEO Conference 25 January 1990
Walker G (1989)   *Comprehensive Themes* C.S.C.S.

3 The Effects of Recent Legislation on the Curriculum

Jackson Hall

The 'great debate' begun by the then Prime Minister, James Callaghan, in a speech at Ruskin College in October 1976, ended in March 1985 with the publication of 'Better Schools' (HMSO, 1985) in which the Government set out its views on the curriculum, reviewed its policies for school education and announced its conclusions. The Ruskin speech had set the agenda and the basic issues were:

(a) the improvement of standards of learning;
(b) the alignment of the schools to the needs of society;
(c) the content and control of the school curriculum;
(d) the quality of the teachers and their accountability;
(e) the roles and responsibilities of the DES, LEAs and governing bodies

   Sir Keith Joseph, Secretary of State from 1981 to 1986, made no secret of his conviction that a rapid improvement in standards could be achieved by applying free market economy principles to the school system. He led a strong body of opinion in the Conservative party that believed that this might be achieved by an education voucher scheme; giving parents power as consumers would make schools more responsive to parental choice and stimulate the competition between schools which would generate higher standards. He finally decided, however, that the practical difficulties of a voucher scheme were insuperable. 'Better schools' therefore outlined a strategy designed within the framework of the 1944 settlement although it confirmed the significant shifts of emphasis in the roles and responsibilities of the DES, the LEAs and governing bodies which were already evident in the development of educational policy after 1976.
   Although 'Better Schools' concedes that there is 'much to admire in our schools', it adds that 'the high standards achieved in some schools throw into relief the shortcomings, some of them serious, of the others. Nor are the objectives which even the best schools set themselves always well matched with the demands of the modern world (para.2). It states that 'the standards now generally attained by our pupils are neither as good as they can be, nor as they need to be if young people are to be equipped for the world of the twenty-first century (para.9). Nevertheless, 'Better Schools' concluded 'that the action now necessary to raise standards in school education can in the main be taken within

the existing legal framework' (para.212) and that the 'one area of the law of school education where change is needed in the interests of raising standards' was a further reform of the governing bodies of county, controlled and maintained special schools (para.214).

The Government had already tackled the reform of governing bodies in the 1980 Education Act. Under this act, each school (with very limited exceptions) had to have its own governing body with at least two parent governors and one or two teacher governors; membership was optional for the headteacher. These changes were intended to strengthen the professional capacity of the governing body and to enable parents to exert more influence on school policies. Secondly, the act required the publication of much more information about the school including, for the secondary school, the publication of examination results – a step towards public accountability. Other provisions of the act strengthened the rights of parents in choosing a school for their children. The act reflected the government's belief that consumer pressure (through the governing body and the exercise of parental preference) would stimulate higher standards of performance.

The 1986 Education (No.2) Act implemented the commitment announced in 'Better Schools'. It removed the LEA's discretion to appoint a majority of the governors and added co-opted governors representative of community interests – in order to 'harness more fully the contribution that can be made to good school education by parents, employers and others outside the education service'. The act is also significant, however, because its provisions effect the secular curriculum. It:

(a) requires the LEA to publish and keep up to date its policy for the secular curriculum and places a similar duty on the governing body which must take the LEA policy statement into account, and also any views expressed by the community; it must also consult the chief police officer in its area, who consequently has an opportunity to influence the curriculum, presumably in relation to crime prevention and the duties of citizenship;
(b) requires the governors to consider separately, keep a separate record, and keep up to date their view as to whether sex education should be included in the school curriculum; if it is not, they must specify their reasons; if it is, they must set out in writing the content and organization of the teaching; where given, sex education must be taught 'in such a manner as to encourage pupils to have due regard to moral considerations and the value of family life'[1];
(c) requires LEAs, governors and heads to forbid partisan political activities in the school and to take all reasonable steps to ensure that a balanced view is presented of political issues when they arise.

This legislative excursion into the secret garden did not increase the Secretary of State's powers over the curriculum. Given the Government's views

---

[1] Under the 1988 Education Reform Act, the LEA and the Governors' statements must be compatible with the requirement of its provisions. The Governors may 'modify' the LEA statement but they cannot ignore it. The governors are also bound by Section 28 of the 1988 Local Government Act under which local authorities are forbidden to: (i) intentionally promote homosexuality or publish material with the intention of promoting homosexuality; and (ii) promote the teaching in any maintained school of homosexuality as an acceptable family relationship.

about the urgent need for curriculum reform, however, there were two weaknesses in its strategy. The first was the absence of an authoritative change-agent to ensure that broad agreement on the curriculum objectives and content expressed in HMI publications and DES policy statements would be implemented in all schools. The second was the absence of a reliable, general mechanism to generate school improvement and evaluate performance. Government policy up to 1987, although moulded by principle, was opportunistic and incremental, at odds with its conviction that higher educational standards could only be achieved by more radical means. Nevertheless, 'Better Schools' stated that 'The Government does not propose to introduce legislation affecting the powers of the Secretaries of State in relation to the curriculum' (para.37).

By 1987, however, the Government had decided on the strategy embodied in the 1988 Education Reform Act which specifies a national curriculum backed by assessment and gives the Secretary of State unprecedented powers over the curriculum. It also introduced mechanisms – the publication of pupils' attainments, 'open' enrolment, the local management of schools (LMS), and opting out – which create a market dimension in the school system in the belief that 'competition, choice and freedom' will stimulate schools to achieve higher standards of performance. The Consultation Document (DES, 1987) justified this decisive breach with past policy on the grounds that progress had been 'too variable, uncertain and often slow' to meet the need to 'raise standards consistently, and at least as quickly as they are rising in competitor countries' (para.6). The act does not, however, repudiate the working drawing of the curriculum – it had not reached blueprint status – presented in 'Better Schools'; unless this is understood, the act's curriculum provisions may be misinterpreted, as they were in many early reactions.

The national curriculum
The national curriculum consists of:

(a) the core subjects which are
  (i) mathematics, English and science; and
  (ii) for schools in Wales which are Welsh-speaking, Welsh;
(b) the other foundation subjects which are
  (i) history, geography, technology, music, art, and physical education;
  (ii) for the last five years of compulsory schooling a modern foreign language specified by the Secretary of State; and
  (iii) for schools in Wales which are not Welsh-speaking, Welsh.

For each of these subjects, the Secretary of State may by order specify:

(a) the knowledge, skills and understanding which pupils of different abilities and maturities are expected to have by the end of each key stage (ie. at about 7, 11, 14 and 16 years of age) – referred to as the attainment targets;
(b) the matters, skills and processes which are required to be taught to pupils of different abilities and maturities during each key stage – referred to as the programmes of study; and
(c) the arrangements for assessing pupils at or near the end of each key stage for the purpose of ascertaining what they have achieved in relation to the

attainment targets for that stage – referred to as the assessment arrangements.

The school curriculum, which must include the 'basic curriculum' (ie. the national curriculum and religious education), only satisfies the requirement of the 1988 Act 'if it is a balanced and broadly based curriculum which (a) promotes the spiritual, moral, cultural, mental and physical development of pupils at the school and of society; and (b) prepares such pupils for the opportunities, responsibilities and experiences of adult life.'

The subjects and the timetable

LEA and grant maintained schools must provide the 'basic curriculum' which consists of the national curriculum plus religious education. Since religious education is not included in the national curriculum, it is not subject to the Secretary of State's powers over the core and other foundation subjects. The new requirement is that the Agreed Syllabus must 'reflect the fact that the religious traditions in Great Britain are in the main Christian, whilst taking account of the teaching and practices of the other principal religions represented in Great Britain'.

It is the statutory duty of the LEA, the governing body and the head to ensure that the school curriculum satisfies the statutory requirements and the DES has pointed out (DES, 1989) that 'It is not enough for such a curriculum to be offered by the school: it must be fully taken up by each individual pupil' (para.2.2). There are, however, limited but closely regulated exceptions to the general requirement for pupils to study all the core and other foundation subjects up to 16:

(a) those who take GCSE subjects early and get good grades in the 'other foundation subjects' will be allowed to substitute an alternative subject;
(b) slow learners may be allowed to drop a foundation subject to concentrate on the others;
(c) alternative arrangement for practical work may be made for those with physical disabilities;
(d) statements for pupils with special educational needs may modify or disapply any or all of the requirements of the national curriculum although the statement must set out the revised provision to be made and meet the requirement for all pupils to follow a broad and balanced curriculum;
(e) temporary exceptions may be made for pupils waiting for a statement or a revised assessment under the 1981 Act, and for other pupils for whom the national curriculum may be temporarily unsuitable (eg. pupils affected by severe emotional upsets or who have had long periods of absence).

As initially proposed, the national curriculum would have occupied 80–90 per cent of the timetable. The time allocations have been replaced by the 'for a reasonable time' formula (although programmes of study are based on assumptions about the timetable), and the estimate has fallen to 70–80 per cent, to which must be added an allocation for religious education. Clearly, however, the problems of the over-crowded curriculum are not mitigated by legislation; schools will not under-allocate time for the national curriculum and its demands may leave too little time for other curriculum needs.

The objectives for the primary curriculum are to emphasise competence in language and mathematics, to promote more systematic teaching of history and geography and, in particular, to strengthen science and design and technology. 'Better Schools' advised primary schools to take more advantage of teachers with expertise in particular areas of the curriculum by giving them 'the time, the status and the encouragement to enable them to prepare and offer support to their colleagues and to exert the necessary influence on the whole curriculum of the school' (para.22), and by increasing specialist (as distinct from class) teaching for older pupils. The fact remains that primary schools are short of the range of expertise needed, especially to tackle science and the range of design and technology expected. This raises a general question. If teachers do not have the subject knowledge (and many do not) and consequently have to rely on exemplifications of work in programmes of study and on what the publishers produce, how effective will the teaching be? There must be doubts about the quality of teaching on this basis.

With regard to secondary schools, it has been predicted that some subjects (eg. a second foreign language, economics, sociology, and especially Latin and what little is left of Greek) will disappear, and that science (seen as the three separate sciences), home economics, business studies and careers education could also suffer. Some of these will survive, up to a point, within programmes of study. Drama is not neglected in the English programmes, and sociology or economics could feature in a modular course which satisfies the requirements for history and geography. The design and technology programme is intended to cover the range of work in art and design, business studies, CDT, home economics and IT; the question is not the adequacy of the programmes but whether there is time for them within the timetable.

Although subject-based teaching remained very strong in secondary schools, the 60s and 70s saw the development of integrated and, to a lesser extent, more general courses (eg. in personal, social and moral education), especially in the junior years although to some extent (especially for the less able) in the senior years too. The introduction of the GCSE reduced the variety of courses which proliferated under the CSE dispensation in the senior years, and the introduction of the national curriculum will take this process further and discourage integrated, cross-curricular and general courses in the junior years. Those remaining will mostly require radical revision to meet the new requirements. In short, the general thrust of the national curriculum is towards more subject-based teaching in the secondary school as well.

It will also re-shape and attenuate the option system in most secondary schools – in this respect it responds to HMI criticism that many option systems have deprived pupils of a balanced and coherent curriculum experience. On the evidence of 'Better Schools', the DES sees the basic curriculum as a full timetable for many pupils. The view expressed there is that the 15–20 per cent of the timetable left for options in Years 10 and 11 should 'provide an essential opportunity for enriching the curriculum with elements which appeal to a minority of pupils …(and) also make it possible to reinforce the compulsory or constrained part of the curriculum for less able pupils' (para.69). At best, the National Curriculum makes it difficult to timetable more than two additional subjects in Years 10 and 11 and, in any case, the school's ability to offer additional subjects may well be restricted by shortage of staff and other resources – which would preclude the solution of the problem by lengthening the school day as the city technical colleges have done. The demands of the national curriculum for scarce time and resources pose serious problems, to put it mildly, for the provision of a second foreign language and adequate time for science. Nor is there any doubt that the national curriculum exacerbates problems which have yet to be faced for GCE A level courses in science and mathematics.

Cross-curricular themes and issues, a developing rather than a mature feature of the curriculum in most schools, are not necessarily inherent in subject content and the subject-driven demands of the national curriculum threaten their provision. Although the subject working groups are requested to advise on their place in the programmes of study, cross-curricular themes have received less attention than they deserve in the reports published so far. They are not visible features of the national curriculum and, if there is no assessment requirement, time, attention and resources for them will depend on the school's priorities, and perhaps on the initiative of individual departments or teachers. The DES acknowledges that 'accommodating cross-curricular issues within the whole curriculum requires careful planning, particularly in Years 10 and 11' and promises that 'advice will be made available on alternative methods and strategies' with no more than a cautious assurance that 'work done so far indicates that attainment targets for foundation subjects can provide a basis for study and assessment of some cross-curricular issues' (DES, 1989, para.4.7).

The national curriculum: a straitjacket?
The Consultation Document (DES, 1987) claims that the national curriculum will ensure that all pupils, regardless of gender, ethnic origin, disability or geographical location, will have access to broadly the 'same good and relevant curriculum', minimise disruption in the education of pupils moving from one area of the country to another, and be a better preparation for the needs of adult life.

This is a strong case for a national curriculum for the years of compulsory schooling, and not least for restricting choice at the secondary stage. Firstly, the deficiencies of the primary and secondary school curriculum are too well and persistently documented to be ignored and the arguments against premature specialisation at the secondary stage have been well-rehearsed over the years. HMI strictures on many option systems were justified on sound educational principles, apart from the criticisms that dropping subjects too early can be a handicap later in life and that, on occasion, choices were influenced by gender stereotypes or racial bias. There is admittedly a case against a compulsory foreign language but the difficulties of making an exception of a major subject tend to be overlooked and it is arguably a challenge that should be taken up. Secondly, the national curriculum is a safeguard against irresponsibility, slackness and incompetence; in these respects, the national curriculum is deliberately restrictive, reflecting the Government's reactions to reports about the politicisation of the curriculum by maverick LEAs and teachers and, more generally, HMI reports about the wide disparities of school quality. Thirdly, in addition to the exemptions for individual pupils, there is provision for the Secretary of State to permit or direct a school to provide a curriculum differing from the national curriculum for the purposes of curriculum research and development. Exemptions will be rare, however, and may well be given mostly to grant maintained schools because they are accountable directly to the DES.

Whatever the advantages of the national curriculum, there is a danger that it will be a straitjacket which will inhibit curriculum development, discourage good practice, and jeopardise cross-curricular themes because programmes of study and attainment targets are subject-driven. The bar on pupils of compulsory school age following a course leading to an external qualification unless it has been sponsored by the Secretary of State or a body recognised by him constrains secondary school initiative. In the case of primary and middle schools particularly, the pressure of accountability may encourage subject teaching at the cost of good practice. Having to publish pupils' attainments may encourage 'teaching to the test' generally. In some schools, there will be pressure from the governing body and/or from parents to stick to the letter of the prescription, a disposition that will be shared by staff in some schools. There is also the pervasive influence of bureaucratic regulation and direction, which tends to be restrictive and will certainly increase; it is difficult to believe that the Annual Curriculum Return to the DES every June reporting the times allocated to subjects will itself influence primary schools towards subject-teaching but an accumulation of signals, pressures and procedures can become influential, even unintentionally.

Seen simply as an aggregation of timetable subjects (which was how many saw it initially), fears that the national curriculum would be a straitjacket binding schools to a subject-driven curriculum had substance. These fears have been allayed by assurances that the subject specification is only a descriptor. The recommendation in the report of the Task Group on Assessment and Testing (TGAT) that more than one subject should, where appropriate, contribute to a given attainment target is reassuring although the subject working group reports have so far been somewhat disappointing in this respect. The NCC, however, in 'A Framework for the Primary Curriculum', states that: 'The description of the national curriculum in terms of foundation subjects is not a description of how the school day should be organised or the curriculum delivered ...the strategies used for planning and delivery of the national curriculum should reflect good practice' (para.1.1) ...'The national curriculum is not a straitjacket' (para.1.2).

Initially, there were fears that programmes of study and attainment targets would be detailed and prescriptive[1]. Although the guidance to subject working groups states that 'Within the overall programme of study ... there must be space to accommodate the enterprise of teachers, offering them sufficient flexibility in the choice of content to adapt what they teach to the needs of the individual pupil', the Secretary of State's remit to the English working group asked for 'a detailed description of the content, skills and processes which all pupils should be taught ... '. In the event, however, the programmes approved so far are neither detailed nor narrowly prescriptive; they are consistent with good practice and leave ample scope for professional discretion. Similarly, the attainment targets also require professional interpretation.

In general, the legislation is being implemented in terms which encourage good practice and leave scope for professional initiative. It is of course essential for programmes of study, if they are to be effective, to command professional respect and commitment, and this is more likely if they

---

[1] These will be more detailed for the core than for the other foundation subjects; only guidances are expected for art, music and physical education.

are not too detailed and prescriptive. They also have to reflect and encourage 'best practice' – the mathematics working group, for example, sought in its guidance to reflect 'the spirit of the Cockcroft Report, and the developments since then relating to new technology'. Furthermore, before programmes of study are given statutory authority, the Secretary of State must consult and take into account the views of representative bodies, including professional associations. Nor should it be forgotten that the programmes of study are themselves on trial after they come into operation, and that professional opinion about them will take shape and find expression. This feedback will include HMI and NCC reports, as well as an unprecedented flow of information about their effectiveness. Although the Secretary of State has acquired formidable powers over the curriculum, authority in a very real sense is, in the longer term, inherent in the service and this is the ultimate safeguard. A national curriculum backed by assessment must say a good deal about content and the logic leads to an entitlement curriculum. In practical terms, the question is not whether the National Curriculum is a straitjacket but whether the prescription is educationally sound and leaves sufficient scope for professional interpretation and initiative. The evidence so far is that it does.

Nevertheless, the argument in principle, not about the National Curriculum but about the Secretary of State's powers over it, is not weakened by the use made of them so far. The worst straitjacket would be a curriculum shaped by the interests of partisan politics. The Chairman of the Historical Association's Education Committee has warned (*Times*, 25 August 1989) that national curriculum history will not be taught with 'confidence, enthusiasm and support … (if it) … is believed to be influenced in a partisan way or likely to be altered by a change of government … the Government, any government, should keep its distance'. To expect statutory powers never to be used seems wishful thinking, however, and the Catholic bishops were more realistic in pointing out that these powers mean that 'the Secretary of State and his advisers will have the last word on what shall be taught in Catholic schools even if this conflicts with the ideals and practice of Catholic education'. The Secretary of State's statutory powers over the curriculum have, in principle, serious implications for a pluralist, democratic society.

Implementing the curriculum

DES Circular 7/88 describes LMS as 'one of the key reforms of the Education Reform Act'. Discussions about LMS tend to focus on the school's new responsibilities for its budget but LMS covers the spectrum of school management – the management of the curriculum and learning, staffing and staff development, resources (not just financial) and, not least, the management of accountability. LMS therefore makes a school development plan imperative. The plan should outline the school's current provision; appraise the school's strengths and weaknesses; programme, in accordance with the government's timetable, any changes needed to meet the requirements of the national curriculum; timetable and plan a programme for curriculum and organisational development which specifies what is required in the way of staff support and staff development; and set out the arrangements for monitoring and evaluating progress.

The development plan will require the preparation or revision of syllabuses, and a review of the school's assessment and reporting practices and policies. In all of this work, the school must take into account the LEAs curriculum policy, and also the attainment targets, programmes of study and assessment arrangements as they are issued. The school will need to decide how the curriculum is to be organised bearing in mind the need to teach national curriculum subjects 'for a reasonable time', how the cross-curricular themes should be provided, and the organisation of teaching groups. The provision for children with special educational needs, including those with statements, will have to be determined in accordance with the prescribed procedure.

The purpose of LMS is that decisions made by the school about the use of resources should contribute to more effective teaching and learning. Preparation of the development plan therefore entails a review of the school's current use of its resources, and decisions about the changes that are needed and feasible to support its educational objectives. The staff is its chief resource and the planning should include an audit of their expertise against what is needed so that any changes in the complement and composition of the staff that may be necessary can be put in hand; the needs of the national curriculum could mean redundancy for some teachers unless they can undertake, if necessary after inservice training, other teaching duties. All staff will need training and this too requires careful planning; well-used, the five days designated for inservice training by the 1987 Teachers Pay and Conditions Act are a new and valuable resource.

School development plans will vary in quality but they should become a creative instrument for improving the curriculum. Planning which underpins curriculum development with systematic staff development, institutional support and resources has a fair chance of success; the curriculum initiatives of the 60s and 70s revealed that staff goodwill, enthusiasm and high hopes are not enough – although it would be foolish to think that progress is possible without them.

The immediate problems which implementation poses are the supply and distribution of teachers, their qualifications, their quality and their motivation. Government policy will have to be more successful than it has been in tackling these problems if all pupils are to 'have the same opportunities wherever they go to school' (DES, 1987, para.7). Since the government can be called to account for the staffing needs of the national curriculum, its commitment to teacher supply should be strengthened but demographic and market trends are likely to make recruitment more difficult in the foreseeable future. The problems are aggravated because the national curriculum requires many more teachers of mathematics, science, CDT and languages (more than half of the National Curriculum) – the very teachers who have been in short supply for fifty years. A more general challenge to the government, but certainly at least as serious for the prospects of the legislation, is the need to improve the profession's morale which has suffered severely from the years of criticism, contraction and disruption. In this respect, very much depends on the levels and structure of the salaries offered, and on the effectiveness of the national arrangements under which the teachers' and LEAs' negotiating rights are restored.

Apart from difficulties in the supply of teachers, however, there is the stark fact that most primary and some middle and secondary schools are too small to have the range of expertise that the national curriculum requires. 'Better Schools' acknowledged that 'The main constraints (in providing a broad and balanced curriculum) lie in the number of teachers and their collective qualifications and skills, and in the size of the school. The smaller the school, the more serious these constraints are likely to be' (para.64). Deficiencies may be met up to a point by, for example, sharing staff, joint appointments, perhaps in some cases by fund-raising for additional staff, but these are palliatives, not solutions. Small schools will have no option but to prioritise the demands of the national curriculum. In general, it will be more than ever important to make good appointments and to manage staff efficiently; the current wastage of professional expertise, perhaps especially in primary schools, is well-documented and pressure to make better use of it can only be beneficial.

The act's curriculum objectives depend beyond question on ambitious assumptions about the quality of school leadership and the school's capacity for curriculum development. The legislation gives every teacher an individual role as a curriculum developer and also a collegial role in planning and providing a curriculum geared to the knowledge, understanding and skills specified for each key stage. To harness this individual and collective contribution requires creative management by heads and their senior colleagues and it is far from certain that many schools have the professional and institutional maturity to meet this challenge – on the other hand, they never will have unless they are given this responsibility. It would be irresponsible, however, for the Secretary of State and the LEAs not to give the support that schools need to meet this challenge. How well they will support the schools has yet to be seen.

The National Curriculum combines both core and entitlement concepts of the curriculum in distinguishing between core and other foundation subjects. If this is taken to mean that core subjects have superior status, they may benefit from unduly favourable staffing and resource decisions. In any case, however, schools (especially in the primary sector) may understandably concentrate on the core subjects initially and commit resources to them that will be difficult to modify later to meet other curricular needs. The basic, more general point is that governors, teachers and parents value different subjects differently and will act accordingly; the legislation cannot guarantee that every subject will be given its due and it is therefore far from certain that every school curriculum will be as broad and balanced as it might be.

The influence of assessment on the curriculum
The Consultation Document (DES,1987) claimed that assessment would raise standards of attainment by; (a) 'setting clear objectives for what children over the full range of ability should be able to achieve' and thus 'help schools to challenge each child to develop his or her potential' (para.8(i)); and (b) 'checking on progress ... at various stages, so that pupils can be stretched further when they are doing well and given more help when they are not' (para.8(iv)).

The TGAT report argues (para.14) that graded assessment schemes show that pupils respond well to short-term attainable objectives, and that failure should not be seen as 'personal inadequacy' but as an opportunity for the teacher to diagnose and tackle the learning difficulty constructively – assessment is presented as a teaching aid to improve the effectiveness of the curriculum. This is true up to a point but diagnosis of the difficulties of teaching and learning is more difficult, the remedial teaching techniques less well-developed, and the educational yield therefore less certain than the report acknowledges.

Attainment targets and assessment arrangement for each key stage should result in more informative pupil records which in turn should promote progression and continuity by reducing the time wasted within and between schools. Schools will have to cooperate in curriculum planning; this is not as easy as it sounds and it will be particularly difficult for the middle school because it shares Key Stage 2 with its primary school(s) and Key Stage 3 with its secondary school(s). The harmonisation of programmes of study and attainment targets and GCSE syllabuses awaits a national settlement to which secondary schools will have to adjust. It has been argued that assessment at 16+ should replace the GCSE but the GCSE is bound to continue, probably until there is a more coherent and effective system of education and training for the vast majority of the 16–19 age group.

In practice, progression and continuity are not easily achieved because it is difficult to differentiate even between proximate levels of attainment. For example, the English working group report specifies for the level 4 reading target 'a widening range of prose and verse' and for level 5 'a still wider range of prose and verse' (Cox, p.42). There is a difference but what is it? This illustrates the problems that progression and continuity pose for teachers in their day-to-day work in the classroom. The use of attainment targets to achieve progression and continuity is a promising strategy but it has yet to be tested and developed before it delivers its promise of progression and continuity.

Assessment could result in significant changes in the organisation of the curriculum. The NCC points out (Circular no.3) that 'the organisation of classes by age may not in all circumstances be the most effective ... An added consideration is that some children require earlier access to the wider resources available in secondary schools. There are also implications for the arrangements made by secondary schools to receive pupils with differing levels of attainment in different subjects. The basic issue here is the organisation and structure of the curriculum; grouping abler younger pupils with older pupils, whether by streaming, setting or vertical timetabling, could institutionalise selection long before 11+ and have a knock-on effect for secondary schools through early transfer. Assessment coupled with a competitive school system could result in some children being 'expressed' through the primary into the secondary school – although the practice would penalise the primary school financially.

Diagnostic assessment will contribute to the effectiveness of the curriculum but assessment in order to classify pupils is a much more doubtful proposition, especially because labelling is so deeply embedded in the culture of many schools. The curriculum should motivate pupils but the motivation of less able pupils whose weak performance at 7 year old is confirmed at 11 and again at 14 seems bound to suffer. Classification will also cause anxiety and tension in many homes, or confirm indifference in others, and the TGAT argument (para.15) that it will not impair relationships between some parents and the school is unconvincing. It seems far more likely that classification will in some cases be damaging to the pupil/teacher/parent relationship which can contribute so much to the effectiveness of the curriculum. Furthermore, especially in schools where pupils' attainments are depressed by socio-economic factors, there might be a significant number of disaffected parents.

As an aid to the curriculum, classification seems at odds with the pupil Record of Achievement approach which focuses on what the pupil has done and can do, and promotes cooperation between pupil and teacher in the belief that this improves motivation, confidence and performance. Hopes that the Record of Achievement will offset the damage caused by classification seem less realistic than the fears that Records of Achievement will come to be seen as a second best.

Assessment should expose the school's curricular strengths and weaknesses and its development plan should be shaped to develop or remedy them as the case may be. The information should also enable the LEA to target its advice and assistance more effectively. Assessment for these purposes should stimulate curriculum improvement. But the use of assessment to permit comparisons of school performances every year is another matter. This information is intended to influence parental choice and, since the school budget depends largely on its role, successful schools will be rewarded and the less successful penalised. The purpose is to generate competition between schools in the belief that this will stimulate them to achieve higher standards but, even if this results in an overall improvement of standards, it may be at the expense of the curriculum in the schools adversely affected and a wider variation of standards between schools. Planning by attrition will not necessarily result in the closure of poor quality schools, pupils in these schools will suffer and this means that not all pupils will be offered the 'same good and relevant curriculum'. Furthermore, the competition is not fair because the performance levels are not to be corrected for socio-economic factors. The TGAT report recognises that the quality of the curriculum should be measured by the progress rather than the attainments of the pupils, and supports the publication of assessment results only 'in the context of reports about that school as a whole, so that it can be fair to that school's work and take account so far as is possible of socio-economic and other influences' (para.18) but this is far from convincing as a corrective measure and it could be counter-productive into the bargain.

Conclusion

It will be some years before the effects of the legislation on the curriculum can be fairly assessed. The level of resources for the curriculum will be one of the critical factors and the modesty of the Government's estimate of the costs of implementing the Act is surprising and disappointing. It is of course true that LMS promises better value for money and higher standards of performance, and that schools generally may reap some benefit if the 1988 Local Government Act requiring various services, hitherto mostly maintained by local authorities, to be put out to competitive tendering yields the promised savings as well as better value for money. On the other hand, the community charge will not encourage high spending by LEAs. The fortunes of the national economy will, as always, affect the future of the service for better or worse.

The notion that legislation is certain in its effects and successful in its objectives is an illusion. The greatest obstacles to higher standards of performance are the difficulties of learning and the problems of teaching. The legislation does not make these easier but it should strengthen the obligation to tackle them. Overall, the legislation is a challenge to the service to translate bureaucratic interpretations of political decisions into good and improving professional practice in the schools. How successfully this challenge is met depends mainly on the teachers, how well they are trained, and how effectively they are led in the schools. In the words of the Consultation Document, 'The full force of the teachers' professionalism will need to be put behind the national curriculum and assessment if both are to be beneficial to pupils and other "customers" of the education service' (DES, 1987, para.67). There is much to do to improve the morale and efficiency of the teaching force if the promises of the Education Reform Act are to be realised.

The legislation has little to say about the teachers. The 1987 Teachers Pay and Conditions Act instituted the valuable five days inservice training for all teachers during the school year, and there is the provision of the 1986 Education (No. 2) Act under which the Secretary of State has supported by specific grant more substantial inservice training programmes since 1987. Another section of this Act empowers the Secretary of State to introduce national arrangements for teacher appraisal. This should improve teacher performance and thus contribute to the effectiveness of the curriculum; this has yet to be proved but there was dissappointment in many quarters at the Secretary of State's decision (1989) to postpone its introduction. The reason given for the decision was to relieve the schools of an additional burden at a time when they are already under considerable pressure from the scale and pace of change. Nobody believes, however, that the pressure of change will slacken for some years to come and, if the claims made for teacher appraisal are justified, it should be seen as an integral part of the reform programme.

The legislation marks a shift from the imprecise ethic of education as a public service but it seems to fall between two stools. On the one hand, it promises a specific (and ambitious) entitlement in the form of the national curriculum; on the other hand, it introduces market mechanisms which may compromise this entitlement at least for some pupils.

References

Better Schools (Cmnd. 9469), (1985) London, HMSO.

Cox (1988) English for ages 5 to 11. London, DES.

DES & Welsh Office (1987) The National Curriculum 5–16; a consultation document. London, DES.

DES Circular No. 7/88 (1988), Education Reform Act: The Local Management of Schools. DES, London.

NCC (1989) Circular No. 3, National Curriculum Council, 15–17 New Street, York Y01 2RA.

National Curriculum Task Group on Assessment and Testing, a report (1988) London, DES.

Further reading

Brooksbank K and Anderson K (Eds), (1989) *Educational Administration* , 3rd edition. Longman, London.

Coffield F and Edwards T (Eds), (1989) Working within the Act. (obtainable from the School of Education, University of Durham).

Coopers & Lybrand. (1988) Local Management of Schools: a report to the Department of Education and Science. London, DES.

Emerson C and Goddard I (1989) *All about the National Curriculum.*Oxford, Heinemann Educational.

Lawton D (Ed) (1988) *The Education Reform Act: Choice and Control.* London, Hodder and Stoughton.

Maclure S (1988) *Education Re-formed.* London, Hodder and Stoughton.

Warnock M (1988) *A Common Policy for Education.* Oxford, Oxford University Press.

4. Gaining Public Understanding of the School Curriculum

Joan Sallis

The proposition that it is the educator who determines what children learn is a very recent growth. The idea of education as a private transaction concerning only those transiently involved in providing and receiving it is even more so. The dangerous gap between public perception and reality in the debate about the school curriculum probably first began to appear in the years following the 1944 Act and to become a serious threat to educational advance only in the 1960s. The efforts of the primary school to educate the whole child, which continued until someone caught them at it, and of the secondary school to educate all the whole children under one roof, largely left the public behind. It is ironic that this loss of public understanding and support should have coincided precisely with the growth of parent organisations, the demand for choice, information and involvement, and the development of parent representation in school government, but it was so.

The history of public oversight of schools goes back further than most people imagine – at least 600 years. Long before there were schools for all, when schooling was almost a spectator sport, it was generally accepted that it was nevertheless a public purpose, not a private transaction. This now seems to me very remarkable, but its logic was that a process which shaped values and opinions, which produced the people who would educate the children of others, heal the diseases of others, solemnise the marriages and write the wills of others, produce the literature, art and music to be enjoyed by others, had to be the object of public negotiation and oversight.

Thus great efforts were made, even when schools had been provided by charities or wealthy private benefactors, to find some institutional means of subjecting the school curriculum to the influence of lay trustees or governors who would represent the interests of the public. These efforts culminated in two great Victorian Commissions, the Clarendon Commission and the Taunton Commission, whose reports in the middle years of the nineteenth century crystallised much of the thinking of earlier times. Thus the Clarendon Commission pronounced in 1864 that : 'The introduction of a new branch of study, or the suppression of one already established, and the relative degree of weight to be assigned to different branches, are matters respecting which a better judgement is likely to be formed by such a body of governors as we have suggested ... than by a single person, however able and accomplished ... What should be taught, and what importance should be given to each subject are therefore questions for the Governing Body; how to teach is a question for the Head Master.'

The Taunton Commission only a few years later spoke severely of schools which 'give undue prominence to what no parents within their reach desire their children to learn'. The task as the Commission saw it was 'to adapt the schools to the work which is now required of them, by prescribing such a course of study as is demanded by the needs of the country'.

This sounds very modern. It is vital to bring it to the notice of educators, since they so often assume that the demand for lay involvement in curriculum policy is an aberration of our time, and an attack on a professional preserve which was hitherto sanctified by law and history. There is no such sanctity, and it is rather the notion of teacher control of the curriculum which is the aberration. That notion developed because of the failure of those who had the legal responsibility – LEAs and governors – to exercise it. Because of that failure, and the associated failure of educators to carry the public with them during a long period of rapid expansion and extensive experimentation, we have government intervention on the present scale. That intervention is directed not only to the establishment of a national curriculum, but also to the creation of more rigorous consumer control through the provisions on open enrolment, information, formula finance and opting out. This all adds up to an attempt to restore a lost consensus about what children should learn. Many believe, as I do, that it is a pity that it had to happen that way. But unless there is understanding of why it happened the mistakes of the last thirty years will be repeated with tragic consequences. For it is now more important than ever that the teacher should work not in isolation, but with the informed support of parents and governors. If we fail in this the national curriculum will be a constraint on creativity, not its agent. The natural and unanswered anxieties of parents will drive schools down unnecessarily narrow paths. Many of the excellent advances in both primary and secondary practice over the last few decades will be halted. The values associated with meeting all needs in schools may be so swamped by the pressures of formula-driven funding as to constitute in all essentials a voucher system. The continuing evolution of the national curriculum which should take place could be stunted. A great deal is at risk, but there are also enormous benefits to be won.

I wrote of the government's attempts to restore a lost consensus about what children should learn. I wrote too about the determination of the service to educate the whole child and all the whole children. It is in this process, as well as in the tremendous expansion and experimentation of the years following the Second World War, that the understanding of the public has got left behind. Before 1944 a majority received only elementary education, which amounted to a grounding in the three Rs, religion, perhaps some history and geography, if you were lucky rudimentary science, and perhaps some practice in filling inkwells which was good preparation for useful if repetitive jobs afterwards. There had been little perceptible change in the content for half a century. It was scarcely the subject of debate. Those who received secondary education were volunteers, broadly speaking had motivation, home support, and an understanding of what it was all leading to.

Then came the enormous change implied in secondary education for all and later comprehensive reorganisation, the broadening of the secondary school curriculum, the development of new subjects and the problems of motivation.

In the primary school the notion that learning did not take place in tidy compartments of subject and age took over, and many landmarks disappeared. Child-centred methods were widely misunderstood, and some experiments like the ITA got a bad press. At the same time there was widespread social change, what Harry Ree has called 'The Death of Dad' – crumbling of many forms of authority and social cohesion – and schools were having to take on board many more of children's problems than those directly and obviously related to their learning. There was a structure, but for many parents it remained unseen, and they worried about the loss of landmarks. Many teachers in this period became defensive, as though they feared that teaching the modern way, while hard enough to do well, might look to a casual observer like a less professional activity, similar to what went on in the kitchen of a rather nice home. There was a tendency to over-professionalise many aspects of child care, and many parents were told by teachers that methods had changed so much that they might confuse their children if they tried to help them. This led to the alienation of many less confident parents from schools and still further reduced their self-esteem, a process for which schools have paid dearly.

This is all familiar stuff and I apologise for repeating it. but it is essential to identify problems which the national curriculum and other changes may make acute. I turn now in more detail to what seem to me to be some of the dangerous turnings at the particular roundabout we have reached in the history of public involvement in children's learning.

The greatest danger perhaps is that the process of involving governors and parents will become an empty ritual. This is difficult to avoid when the process of change is so rapid and teachers themselves find it hard to keep up. A few things need to be emphasised. Firstly and most crucially, it is essential that teachers and particularly head teachers see the process as a positive one. There is much resentment of the crude consumerism of the 1988 Act, and this is likely to spill over onto the very differently motivated partnership which the 1986 Act (almost forgotten in some quarters) seeks to introduce into the educational debate. The 1986 Act is only about how schools make their decisions, NOT about undermining local government, de-professionalising teachers, forcing schools into cut-throat competition. If the opportunities it affords to share values and enlist allies among ordinary people in the fight to keep education as a need-based service are neglected, vacuums may be filled in a highly undesirable way.

It may also be overlooked that the 1986 Act provides for LEA and school curriculum policies to be drawn up, negotiating precisely for the individual school those parts of its activity which are not prescribed, and adapting its programmes to its own neighbourhood. It would be easy to assume that this vital process has been subsumed in the national curriculum, thus neglecting an essential and creative area of debate, and bringing about those very rigidities which schools fear. It needs to be said often that there is still scope for a local curriculum and local adaptation of national provisions. Often school curriculum proposals are brought to governors and parents in too finished and impenetrable a form. Teachers are so conscientious, so perfectionist, so proud, that they can scarcely contemplate going public on something half-baked. It is part of the need to be a step ahead as well. But outsiders feel diffident about commenting on something which seems so near finality that they often merely rubber-stamp it, thus losing the sense of ownership which will make them good ambassadors and good advocates. It would be better to involve them at earlier stages and leave a few loose ends for them to get hold of.

I wrote of the natural desire of the teacher to be a step ahead, and that works against another good habit which is sharing difficult documents straight from the DES or LEA. The documents come so thick and fast, particularly on the curriculum, that it is tempting, instead of spreading them out straight from the fat brown envelope, to say 'I'll take this home at the weekend and when I've digested it we'll talk'. Make it my own and *then* go through the pretence of communicating. That in fact is why so many heads see communication as an extra responsibility in top of all the other impositions, not an integral part of management. Indeed they often don't see participatory structures as part of management at all, don't take a pride in their quality as they do in other aspects of school leadership. That needs to change.

One dangerous turning to avoid is too eager a response to the competitive climate. Education has always progressed by the spread of good practice. It would be tragic if, instead of sharing their good ideas in curriculum and other areas for the benefit of children, schools were to hide their work like children doing a test. Sharing should be part of the common values system of staff, governors and parents. Similarly 'marketing' should not go to the head. The best advertisement for a school is that it involves its public in its policies, since nobody is going to get obsessive about choice when they have something much more valuable, namely influence. That's the biggest bargain offer of all.

The primary school particularly, but the secondary school too in the arts and in personal and social education, is exposed to the grave danger that it will be led to narrow the curriculum unnecessarily. Afraid to stray from the paths that lead to the tests, teachers could forget that flowers grow beyond the paths, and that many children have few windows opened for them except at school.

It is vital that governors share the school's vision of the broad curriculum and its purposes, so that they in turn can share that vision with parents. They must share too, their confidence that the school's methods will deliver the goods. Parents will be understandably anxious about this, and many, perhaps most, have *never* understood how what happens in the classroom leads to the acquisition of recognisable skills, never known why children draw round their neighbour's feet, weigh rice, sail corks, visit the churchyard or the supermarket. It will become more urgent now to communicate these things, and to communicate the many messages of HMI to the effect that basic skills are most effectively taught, not when heavily concentrated on, but through a broad curriculum.

A further danger is that the contemporary emphasis on 'relevance' will be crudely interpreted. A reminder that if we don't educate children to contribute to a prosperous society we can't afford good schools, museums, theatres, was timely. So was the reminder that there is challenge and dignity even for the most able in the more obviously wealth-producing activities as well as in the professions. Yet alarm bells ring when one hears relevance so tirelessly urged by powerful and influential people who have reached their positions of power and influence through the great privilege of an irrelevant education, and are choosing it for their own children. Relevance must be for all, and it must be deeply and broadly conceived and shared. It must include that response to the unreturning moment of wonder and curiosity, and it must include the need to enrich the adult hours not spent at work. Parents will be very suspicious of any narrowing of their own children's goals when different goals remain on offer for others. This message is very important to those members of the business community who get involved in schools. They must be encouraged to see the needs of the employer, not just for people with skills, but for employees with the capacity to make good relationships, to relax, to enjoy life, to adapt, to see their working lives in the context of a varied and exciting world.

What of the community of ordinary parents in a school, not governors, not PTA officers, in the world beyond the Education Reform Act? It is vital that the changes should not be just one more means of making them feel unnecessary to their children's success. They must be *included* from the beginning. Indeed with so much more emphasis on active learning, on coursework and continuous assessment, if parents as a whole do not become more involved we could be creating new forms of privilege, with an under-class of children whose parents are not confident supporters of their learning. Home help with learning schemes must flourish. Parents, already made welcome in most schools, must be made to feel necessary as well.

Parents' new legal rights to read various curriculum documents and governors' working papers must be made real. Schools must give much more attention to how information can be made routinely available and genuinely accessible. We should have a policy of promoting parents' rooms in all schools as soon as practicable, a symbol of parents' place as partners in the process.

Schools must give priority to overcoming the inhibitions of parents who find schools intimidating, and increasing their self-esteem. Those families who have never really felt that they could contribute anything to their children's education since the 'revolution' of the 60s and 70s could all too easily be made to feel even more hopeless in the face of the national curriculum with all its potential complexity. It must somehow be made to seem user-friendly before new feelings of exclusion develop.

What I am seeking is not easy. Professionals feel best able to share when they are most confident, and now, when they themselves are wrestling with change, the temptation to become more remote and defensive may be almost overwhelming. Yet this is a time when above all we need professional humility, the will to say 'I cannot do this job without you, their parents, without you, our governors, without you, the public'. For there has never been a time when the understanding and support of the public for the learning process has been more needed.

5 The Role of Examination Groups in the Curriculum

P.K. Burke

The Examining Boards have been greatly affected by the educational reform of the 1980s, and at the time of writing – early October 1989 immediately following the second annual conference of the Joint Council for the GCSE – there is an air of uncertainty about their future. On the one hand, firm assurance from the DES about the Government's commitment to GCSE as the main means of assessment within the national curriculum at Key Stage 4 would appear to offer them a secure prospect. On the other hand however, a closer inspection of the various policy statement emanating from Elizabeth House combined with the advice submitted by SEAC, reveals a number of remarkable inconsistencies which suggest that support for GCSE may be purely cosmetic and political and that it will in due course be assimilated within the national curriculum assessment arrangements. At that point it would no longer be identifiably different from the systems of assessment at Key Stages 1–3 and GCSE per se would have disappeared. What the fate of the Boards might be in that eventuality will be examined later in this chapter. Suffice to say at this point that it is the author's view that if they are to survive it will require them to undergo a metamorphosis, the nature and extent of which is likely to be difficult for many of them to contemplate.

The introduction of GCSE had a profound effect on the Boards. Not only did it require them to adopt new attitudes to their fundamental business of recognising and rewarding achievement, it also marked the beginning of the end to their traditional independence, because the establishment of the GCSE Groups entailed some loss of each member Board's sovereignty and autonomy. The consequences of GCSE have therefore been as much political as educational, and the Boards now find themselves subjected to further and similar pressures arising from the national curriculum assessment proposals. Unless they can respond in a positive and united manner in the near future, there is a very real danger that their future role as agencies of curriculum and assessment development may be severely diminished.

Prior to the introduction of GCSE the Boards were able to respond to, and sometimes promote, changing curriculum and classroom practice through their control over syllabus development. The very high level of active teacher involvement in their work ensured that they were made aware of changing assessment needs, thereby enabling syllabus changes in the main to keep pace with curriculum developments. And in a number of significant cases of course the Boards worked closely with external agencies to create curriculum change and not just respond to it. The School History Project 13–16, the various Nuffield Science schemes and the Geography 16–19 Project are fine examples of such joint curriculum development ventures. The major contribution of the Boards to all this was the development of appropriate syllabus provision, and the preparation and administration of the supporting examinations. GCSE however gave the Boards much less freedom of action and scope for innovation in the vital area of syllabus development. Although teacher involvement has remained at a high level - but even here there is some concern for the future which will be raised later – the introduction of the national criteria laid down much tighter parameters for syllabus constitution. In addition, the syllabuses were developed on a Group and not on a Board basis and were sometimes hindered and distorted by opposing views and philosophies of the various GCE and CSE partners. Finally and perhaps most significantly, the majority of the syllabuses when completed, were required to obtain approval from the Secondary Examination Council (SEC) before they could be offered to schools and colleges. The whole process therefore became more protracted and more rigorously controlled than before. Yet it would not be correct to assert that overall syllabus provision within GCSE has failed to meet the emerging curriculum needs of mid 1980s. Certainly the number of syllabuses has been dramatically cut as compared with the position under GCE 'O' level and CSE but within this reduced supply it has still been possible for example to provide for the bespoke and sometimes highly idiosyncratic requirement of TVEI courses. More generally the Groups have been anxious to meet the assessment challenge of the increasingly popular modular curriculum by providing flexible assessment and moderation arrangements which complement the perceived teaching and learning advantages which 'modules ' are said to offer.

All is about to change however, and in a style destined to be more extensive and restrictive than was the case with GCSE. There are a number of forces at play. First, the replacement of the SEC by the School Examination and Assessment Council (SEAC), a body with statutory powers to oversee all aspects of national curriculum assessment matters. Secondly, the procedures and criteria for the approval of qualifications, which will lead to a further extensive reduction in syllabuses and syllabus certification titles available to schools and colleges.Thirdly, GCSE syllabuses in all subjects must be modified to accord with the national curriculum programmes of study, profile components, attainment targets and reporting levels, which are much more specific and prescriptive than was the case with national criteria. Finally, there is the as yet undefined criterion of 'need' which SEAC will apply to all existing and future syllabus provision. Taken together, these factors will bring about the rationalisation of syllabus provision which the government is anxious to achieve, and the GCSE Groups will have little or no power to prevent it. Indeed their very future existence will depend heavily upon the degree to which they collaborate to bring it about.

The scenario which is likely to emerge from this process of rationalisation is one which will be totally unfamiliar to teachers in England and Wales, used to having a wide choice of syllabus and examination provision to support their curriculum. In the core and foundation areas of the national curriculum, the most they can expect to see will be no more than three or four

GCSE syllabuses in each subject/curriculum area; in other subject areas, perhaps only one or two syllabuses might be on offer. What is more, none of these syllabuses will 'belong' to any particular Board or Group, but will be described as 'SEAC approved' or 'nationally approved'. As long as the available syllabus provision is sufficient to accommodate the range of teaching and learning approaches through which teachers will wish to deliver the national curriculum, this picture may not be an entirely bleak one at least from the school point of view. But to the Boards and Groups it represents a virtual total surrender of their previous control over syllabus development and provision, and some might say undermines their role in future curriculum development. Whether or not this turns out to be the case will depend on the extent to which they can now set aside their traditional, competitive instincts and practices, and work together to take advantage of the new and different opportunities which are currently open to them. Speed will be of the essence however for there are other agencies – educational publishers, university departments of education and private consultancies, for example – eager and perhaps better prepared to seize the initiative.

So what course of action must they pursue to bring about the metamorphosis referred to earlier in the chapter ? Above all else, they must face up and respond to the political realities of the education scene of the 1990s, but more of that in a moment. Referring back to the availability of a few 'nationally approved' syllabuses, they must argue strongly for each Group to be allowed to set its own examinations on the syllabuses, at least for the core/foundation subjects. They must then adopt and promote the cause of regionalisation, under which a school or college would only be permitted to take the examination offered by its regional GCSE Group, although it would be able to choose to study any of the national syllabuses. This would mean sacrificing the principle of 'freedom of choice' – of syllabus and of Groups – which centres currently possess and which many of the Boards and Groups cherish, but in a situation of relatively few syllabuses operated in common, there is no longer any argument, apart from overt commercialism to sustain this free-market operation. There are on the other hand strong arguments in favour of a regionalised administration of a national examination system. It would provide continuing opportunities for teacher involvement in the work of the examining agencies and ensure that the examination reflected local needs and circumstances. It would create scope for experimentation in assessment and moderation strategies, and it would leave the door more ajar for future curriculum development. The alternative prospect of national syllabuses and a single national examination on those syllabuses taken by all students might endanger all of these advantages.

These would be the first steps towards a change that would lead to the abandonments of the existing national remit of the Boards and Groups and the adoption of a regional responsibility which would provide the basis of their new 'raison d'être'. It is worth mentioning in passing at this point that although this chapter has been written in the context of GCSE and national curriculum developments, the same pressures for rationalisation and change are already evident in the field of AS and A level examinations, and there is no good reason why they should not also come within the scope of the same regional administrative arrangements. Indeed, arguments for curriculum and assessment coherence from age five to eighteen demand that they should.

From their regional responsibilities, other opportunities might present themselves to the Groups. At the time of writing, it seems likely that SEAC will recommend to the government that the administration of the national curriculum assessments at Key Stages 1–3 should be assigned to the LEAs.

The administration of national tests on a large scale and the moderation of teacher assessment is not a matter in which the LEAs are greatly experienced, and there are already suggestions that they may collaborate to set up the necessary structures and systems and operate them on a consortium basis. Yet the Groups have the experience, the structures and systems, and they already have the links established with secondary school. It would only be a matter of extending these arrangements to cover the primary and middle school sectors. If the Groups were able to demonstrate the correct degree of sensitivity to the curriculum and assessment needs of the lower age-ranges, and were willing to enter into genuine partnerships with LEAs and schools in their regions, then they could have every expectation that they might undertake the administration of Key Stages 1–3 on their behalf. Failure to achieve this might leave their administration of Key Stage 4 exposed to further rationalisation in the future, especially if it appeared to be a more expensive operation than that offered by the LEAs. Administrative harmony across all four key stages would clearly have political attraction for some.

More important in the short term however may be the need to assist SEAC and the government to harmonise the *assessment* arrangements at Key Stage 4 with those at the earlier stages. This means addressing those inconsistencies which exist between GCSE and national curriculum assessments at age 16. What is intended to be a planned and coherent curriculum provision, offering continuity and progressions throughout the age of compulsory schooling, surely demands similar coherence in the supporting assessment arrangements. That should be available if Key Stages 1–3 are properly piloted, and implemented and a satisfactory relationship between teacher assessments and Standard Assessment Tasks (SATS) established. But GCSE will not provide a smooth transition from Key Stage 3 to 4, and but for the fact that it already exists, no one would dream of introducing it at this time. That is not to say that it has not been successful, nor that it is out of step with the ambition of the national curriculum. There is much evidence to show that it has brought a dramatic change to classroom practice, especially in some subjects, and it has provided greater motivation to students with a consequent improvement in performance. It has also taken the first few tentative steps towards so-called 'criterion-referenced assessment', and is therefore in keeping with planned national curriculum assessments based on attainment targets. But the requirement that national curriculum achievement levels 4–10 should equate with the standards of GCSE grades G–A force an unnecessary distortion on the new system. The retention of a separate GCSE certification will also be a source of future confusion to parents, students, teachers and employers, as well as to further and higher education. Under the proposals as currently set out, two students in the same class and in the same school will study History beyond Key Stage 3. One however may follow a GCSE History course whereas the other may not, and would be assessed under normal Key Stage 4 arrangements. Both students could however quite conceivably end up with the same level of achievement, say a level 8. The first one would have the result recorded on a GCSE certificate, the second in some other form, possibly in a Record of Achievement. The opportunities for misinterpretation and misunderstanding are enormous, and the risk would be that the whole recording and reporting process would be brought into disrepute. Far better therefore for the Groups to argue, at this early stage, for the abandonment of a set of initials – GCSE – and to urge instead the importance of building upon the experience and benefits which GCSE has brought about, so as to make them available to all students in the future. Such a tactic is also more likely to secure their own position in the future pattern of things.

So the vision that is emerging – a regional examination structure offering coherent assessment and administration across Key Stages 1–4, and preferably including AS and A level – can become reality if only the Groups are able to take the steps required of them in the near future. Further advantages arising from the resulting close links with schools and LEAs could then accrue. Schools will be required to design whole school policies for curriculum and assessment; inservice training of teachers in the primary, middle and secondary sectors in the broad area of assessments will be a continuing priority for some years to come; the organisation and evaluation of moderation of teacher assessments must be undertaken and alternative approaches tested as teachers acquire more confidence and greater professionalism in undertaking the assessment of pupil performance; the concept of 'differentiation' will need careful scrutiny, and review and refinement in students with special needs within the scope of the national curriculum; the implementation of Records of Achievement criteria will need to be co-ordinated and schools advised as to how they might plan all their curriculum and assessment activities around this particular initiative. These are the areas in which vital curriculum and assessment development will be required in the 1990s, and given the right circumstances and structures they will be legitimate areas of activity for the Groups. Consider the benefits which would arise for example, if from properly planned inservice training and moderation programmes, the Groups were able to offer 'accredited status' to teachers who satisfied the necessary standards in carrying out their national curriculum assessment work.

There is one further step which the Boards must take however before these opportunities can be claimed. They must merge their separate identities and become single, unified regional examining bodies. With a small number of nationally-approved syllabuses shared by the Groups, and ideally with regional examinations, there is no good reason at all for the continued existence of the separate GCE and CSE Boards. They belong to another era, and their retention can only frustrate the need for coherence of assessment and administration which will be so essential in the future. The longer they remain in being the less the likelihood that the opportunities identified in this chapter will come their way. But merged into unified regional bodies with full and proper representation of LEA and teacher interests on their committees, working with and on behalf of the schools and LEAs, they can become the focus of curriculum and assessment initiatives in the 1990s.

They will however need the full-hearted support of practising classroom teachers if they are to succeed in this new and different role. There is some evidence from the GCSE examinations in 1988 and 1989 that heads are increasingly reluctant to allow their staff the necessary time out of school to undertake examining work. It is not just a question of the lack of funding to cover the release of the teachers, but this is a major consideration. A properly negotiated arrangement, replacing the 1970 agreement governing the release of teachers for examining work, has recently been drawn up, and it is to be hoped that heads will respond sympathetically to the terms of the new agreement. Without the proper level of teacher involvement there is a very real risk of an examination system which is not accountable to those students and schools it is intended to serve.

The prospect for the Boards/Groups is therefore clear. They must accept and respond to the changing circumstances in which they are designed to operate. If they can do this, they can have a new and exciting role, very different from their traditional narrow work, at the centre of the curriculum and assessment changes which the national curriculum will generate. Failure to do so will bring the risk of condemning themselves to isolation from the mainstream, responsible for what may become an increasingly anachronistic assessment system at the age 16, and thus in changes of ultimate irrelevance before the end of the century.

6 Managing the Curriculum with Governing Bodies

John Dunford

Through the introduction of the national curriculum, the 1988 Education Reform Act has greatly increased the control of central government over the school curriculum. Yet paradoxically it has also increased many of the powers at the level of the individual school. In particular, governing bodies have become much more influential in the life of the school. This has created new opportunities and new tensions in school education and the management of the curriculum has become a more complex and delicate task. This chapter examines the curriculum responsibilities and composition of the new governing bodies. It looks at the ways in which these responsibilities are being carried out and the tensions which are being created in relationships at local level. It concludes that there are many dangers but that, with care and tact on all sides, the new situation can be turned to the advantage of schools.

School governors have become, *de facto* as well as *de jure*, more closely involved with all aspects of school life; hence school management must now be more holistic as governors, finance, staffing, curriculum, resources and buildings have become more interdependent in the success or failure of the institution. The management of relations between the school and its governors is no longer distinct from the management of the curriculum.

Managing the governing body is an increasingly important skill for Head Teachers and senior managers in schools and colleges. Before 1988 few schools held more than one meeting per term of the governing body. The main item on the agenda was the Head Teacher's report and the longest discussion was often the state of the buildings in general and the leaking roof in particular. The meeting rarely lasted longer than two hours and sometimes less than one.

Since 1988 this pattern of activity has altered considerably. The buildings have deteriorated further and a great deal of time is still spent discussing maintenance and repair, but more fundamental changes have taken place in governors' responsibilities and one of the greatest areas of change concerns the involvement of governing bodies in the curriculum of the school.

The new responsibilities
The 1986 Education Act, which re-modelled school governing bodies, changed their responsibilities in a number of ways. It became the duty of the LEA to produce a curriculum policy, which governors have to consider when drawing

up the curriculum aims for their own school (Section 17). If the governing body disagrees with the LEA policy, the governors are permitted to modify it. The act lays down that it is the duty of the head teacher to ensure that the curriculum of the school is compatible with the LEA and governing body policies and that the correct curriculum policy is followed (Section 18).

Only in the area of sex education does the LEA have no jurisdiction: a statement of policy on sex education is the responsibility solely of the governing body who must ensure that the sex education has 'due regard to moral considerations and the value of family life.' (Section 46)

The governors and head teacher are also charged under the 1986 Act with the responsibility for ensuring that any political education which takes place offers 'a balanced presentation of opposing views.' (Section 45)

The governing body is obliged to issue an Annual Report to parents (Section 30) and to hold an annual meeting for parents (Section 31). Governors and head teachers have had to work closely together on the preparation of the Report and the staging of the annual meeting, although these meetings have been sparsely attended in most schools.

Since the 1988 Education Reform Act, the governors also have a duty to consider the national curriculum, as well as LEA policy, when drawing up their own curriculum policy.

They must ensure that the school follows the national curriculum. Any complaints about a school's curriculum are now subject to the LEA complaints procedure, which LEAs had to devise after the 1988 Education Act. It is to be hoped that this cumbersome procedure is not used too often as it is likely to involve a considerable amount of work for governors and head teachers. A further burden imposed by the Act is the disapplication procedure, through which certain children may be absolved from stated parts of the national curriculum.

The new governors
Who are the governors now charged with fulfilling these tasks and how are they reacting to their new responsibilities? The 1986 Act provides for up to five representatives of the LEA and an equal number of parent governors, depending upon the size of the school. The LEA representatives – often, but not exclusively, councillors of the majority political party – are nominated by the Education Committee. As councillors, they represent a constituency, but as school governors they represent only themselves and the Education Committee which elected them. In practice they are often able to put forward an LEA viewpoint and they may also represent the interests of the people in their political constituency, although this area may be peripheral to the area normally served by the school where they serve on the governing body. Governors are limited to four school governorships; under LMS, even this number may cause conflicts of interest if the schools are in the same locality.

Parent governors are elected for four years and, unless they resign, they may serve out their full term of office even though their child has left the school. Having been elected by a ballot of all the parents, they have a clearly defined constituency whose interests they have been elected to serve. Nevertheless it is not easy for parent governors to change from the microcosmic view of a school, as seen through the lives of their own children, to the macro view which is required of a school governor. Nor is it easy for them to consult with other parents, especially in a large secondary school. Their familiarity with the education of their own children can, however, be used to advantage by governing bodies.

The one or two teacher governors are elected by the teaching staff. Like the parent governors, they represent a constituency but, as full governors of the school, they are a part of its management and have to take a wider view when participating in decision-making about all school matters. The Head Teacher may opt to be a full governor, or not, but has rights of access to meetings. An increasing majority of Head Teachers have opted to be full members of the governing body of their school.

The LEA representatives, parents governors, teacher governors and the Head meet to co-opt up to six people to the governing body, at least one of whom must be a member of the local business community. Although some well-organised LEA political groups have used this power of co-option to create a political majority on the governing body, it has also been used by groups of parents to increase their number. It was intended to be used to bring in people with experience in areas such as finance, personnel management, marketing and building, and many schools have used the power of co-option in this way. It has not been used to acquire curriculum experts, since schools have not felt inadequate or under-represented in this field. However, eight per cent of governors are teachers in other schools and so the number of serving teachers on governing bodies is often higher than the government intended in its legislation. This number is boosted by a further eight per cent who are lecturers and other professional educationalists and a proportion of ex-teachers among the retired people who have been co-opted in many schools (Survey 2: Schools, NFER, 1989). Another survey suggests that, in fifty per cent of governing bodies, the 1988 governor elections saw no change in the local politician who occupied the chair. Many new chairs, however, are parents and non-political co-opted members with previous experience on the governing body. The same survey found that over sixty per cent of governors are men and that the majority of governors are articulate and middle class. (*Times Educational Supplement*, 30.6.89).

The new structures
Few governors are curriculum experts and most are overwhelmed by the complexity of the curriculum, especially in secondary schools. Yet they are aware of the extent of their responsibilities and this had led to two relatively new features. First, there is the clearly expressed desire for more training in all areas of governorship and LEAs are charged with the organisation of this. Second, there is the wish to know more about what happens in 'their' school. This has led to an increased degree of openness by schools towards their governors. Sensibly, schools have not waited for governors to knock on the door, but have extended invitations to governors to become more involved in the life of the school. This has gone well beyond the traditional invitations to the school concert. Governors have in some schools become attached to particular areas of school organisation, such as buildings, finance, non-academic staff, special needs or pastoral care. In other schools governors have agreed to take a special interest in a particular curriculum area, such as language development, humanities or science. They visit their host area, look at resources and may be invited to attend departmental and faculty staff meetings. Teachers may at first be suspicious of what they regard as an intrusion into their professional sphere, but they soon recognise the benefit of having a governor

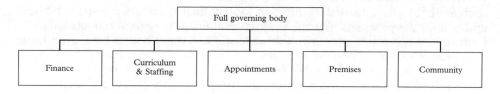

Figure 6.1 A typical committee structure for a large secondary school

who is able to put forward the views and needs of their department at appropriate meetings. Involvement in depth with some area of school life creates better informed governors and this is undeniably beneficial in a well-managed school.

Another by-product of the complexity of the task now facing governing bodies is the establishment of a network of sub-committees. A typical committee structure for a large secondary school is shown in Figure 6.1. The curriculum committee decides upon a curriculum plan for the following year, studies curriculum innovations in the school and looks at the implications of government and LEA circulars. Its term of reference would be along the following lines:

1. To receive reports from the Head and the Director of Studies on the curriculum of the school.
2. To invite other teachers to report directly to the sub-committee on innovations and performance in the curriculum areas for which they are responsible.
3. To review and evaluate the school's curriculum, including its aims and objectives.
4. To report to the governing body on the school's implementation of the National Curriculum and other curriculum matters which come within the jurisdiction of the governing body.
5. To make recommendations to the governing body and the finance sub-committee on curriculum matters.

Items which before 1988 passed through the full governing body without comment are now the subject of extended questioning and discussion at the sub-committee. The membership of this committee usually comprises the chair of governors, the head teacher, three or four other governors, several elected teachers (not necessarily the teacher governors) and the Director of Studies or deputy head (curriculum) ex-officio. This sub-committee does not usually have executive powers, such as may be vested in the finance or appointments sub-committees; nevertheless the existence of a Curriculum Committee is a recognition of the new powers of governors and an acknowledge of the extent which the curriculum is no longer the sole property of teachers in the school.

The new tensions
Traditionally the head teacher's responsibility for the curriculum of the school has meant that there has been little conflict in this area between teachers and

governing bodies. Most LEAs (although there have been notable exceptions, such as ILEA) have tended to interpret loosely their curriculum responsibilities and, within the parameters of the external examination system, schools have been free to determine their own curriculum. Governing bodies have been kept informed of major curriculum changes, but have largely been out of the picture. The 1988 Education Reform Act has changed the basis of all these relationships. LEAs will become more intrusive as they seek to fulfil their monitoring role; governors will be more active in curriculum decision-making as they try to come to terms with their new responsibilities; and schools will not only have to contend with LEAs and governors, but will have to follow government guidelines on the national curriculum and associated testing arrangements. The early 1990s, when the new relationships are being established, will be a time when head teachers in particular will be anxious about the possibility of conflict. The extensive curriculum changes which must be introduced during this period will give ample scope for the over-zealous governor to intervene in the detail of curriculum management. The public debate which has surrounded the introduction of the national curriculum has given many people the impression that the ownership of the school curriculum has (in the words of current government orthodoxy) passed from the producers – the teachers in schools – to the government and to the consumers – parents and local employers. This is not the place to argue whether this is right, or even whether this is what has actually happened; it is sufficient to note that some active school governors believe this to be so and will fulfil their role accordingly.

In discussing above the composition of governing bodies, we observed some signposts of possible tension. The question of admissions to popular schools is one such potential problem: how will parents and local councillors who live outside a school's normal intake area reconcile their responsibility to people in their locality with their wider responsibilities for the admission policy of the school? The curriculum will not be the only area, therefore, where tensions may exist, but it is likely to be the major area. So much change has to take place in the 1990s that it must be taken in steps; priorities will have to be worked out and it is very unlikely that governing bodies will be unanimous about priorities for change. Every year for the rest of this century schools will have to face great changes to the curriculum in the Core and Foundation subjects, which will create a massive workload for teachers. But governors and schools will also want to consider equal opportunities, multi-cultural education, links with local industry, sport, extra-curricular activities and many other issues. A governor whose child is in the school may find it difficult to agree that improvements in such important areas should be delayed while the teachers concentrate on the immediate problems of introducing the new work programmes of the National Curriculum. As governors gain in experience and confidence about what used to be the secret garden of the school curriculum, they will be more likely to intervene in areas such as reading schemes, geography policies and approaches to technology. This creates great potential for conflict between a Head Teacher and school governors. As the governors have overall control of curriculum policy and the Head has responsibility for the day-to-day execution of that policy, conflicts will arise in circumstances where the Head cannot persuade the governors to adopt what the professionals feel is in the school's best interests.

There are many comparable situations in other spheres, where policy control is vested in lay governors and the policy is carried out by professionals.

District health authorities, universities and polytechnics all have a large number of lay members on their governing bodies. These people are experienced in other walks of life, but try to keep well informed about the matters within their jurisdiction by serving on sub-committees, reading background papers and visiting parts of the institution. Guided by the senior professionals in the institution, they make their decisions and rarely come into conflict with the wider body of professionals. The new school governing bodies are similar in structure to these committees and their example suggests that widespread conflict over the curriculum between governors and teachers is unlikely to take place, but this is not to suggest that the dangers are entirely absent and school managers will have to work with care and tact in order to avoid conflict. In doing this, schools will be anxious not to create precedents which might upset the balance of authority between the professionals and lay governors.

One strategy for this situation would be to give away as little information as possible to lay governors, but this would be a mistake. The curriculum, as we noted in the opening section, cannot be seen in isolation from the other responsibilities of the governing body and, in areas such as finance and marketing/publicity, the head and governors will have to work together. Trying to co-operate closely in some spheres and keep the governors at arms' length in others will not succeed. A much more commonly adopted strategy will be to involve governors more in school life and so ensure that their decisions are informed by up-to-date knowledge. Lay governors tend to see school matters in a different perspective from professionals. This may result from the experience of their children who attend the school, their view of the needs of employers or a particular interest in a topic such as foreign languages. The best governing bodies will have a balance of all such viewpoints and will harness the tensions that will inevitably exist. Governors with particular interests or expertise will come to be seen as an asset to the institution and will be used accordingly.

Active governors

Adults other than teachers (AOTs) have been involved in the teaching situation in many schools, both primary and secondary. This has passed well beyond the occasional visit by a speaker who comes in for a lesson and then disappears. In some schools, AOTs have become real partners with teachers in moulding the children's learning process. They can help to plan and evaluate the course in which they are involved, as well as to teach it. Active governors are likely to take part in this sort of activity and to encourage others to do so. Their involvement in planning courses also leads naturally to membership of other school working parties which in the past have been composed entirely of teachers. The introduction of Records of Achievement and Appraisal are obvious examples of areas where external input would benefit internal decision-making. Governors do not usually initiate curriculum change in schools but, as the activities described above develop, they will grow more confident and will be in a better position to relate their other experiences to the school situation.

One area in which schools have never excelled is evaluation and governors with industrial experience will help schools to improve in this field. Certainly they will want to have objective evidence of the progress of innovations and will be looking to senior management to provide this. Schools will need to develop a range of statistics – sometimes called performance indicators – in order to monitor the quality of curriculum developments in a way that will be satisfactory to governors.

Local Management of Schools, introduced nationwide by the 1988 Education Act, will concentrate the minds of governors on all aspects of school life, not merely on finance. Especially in schools which are badly hit financially, the governors will be trying to protect the curriculum and this will require a more detailed knowledge of what is taught than governors have previously needed. If the financial situation is tight, governors will have to be knowledgeable and innovative in order to preserve a sufficiently broad framework on which a successful school curriculum can be built.

Towards a successful partnership

The National Curriculum will not provide a detailed recipe on how schools should organise its delivery. Governors and school management will have to work together to create the conditions in which children can learn successfully. This partnership is the essence of the future management of the curriculum. The Education Acts of 1986 and 1988 have reflected the widely-held opinion that schools must be more accountable for their activities to the local community and to parents; the legislation has created the conditions in which local people can make a greater input to a school through its governing body. In some localities this opportunity may not be taken by parents and others, but in most schools the future reality is a growing participation by parents and others. With open management by schools, this external input will strengthen governing bodies, improve decision-making and support the work of schools. The extent of the work involved for head teachers and governors in making this partnership successful should not be under-estimated.

Section 2

Curriculum Initiatives from Major National Agencies

Curriculum Handbook

This section contains details of major national agencies which are concerned with curriculum initiatives. This includes several branches of the DES based in London and at other centres in the UK. Clearly many of these agencies either sponsor, or receive funding for, research in a variety of curriculum fields. Because of the size of some of the agencies here some of the entries in this section are in outline form only with supplementary details provided so that readers can access more specific follow-up information for themselves. For example the DES-funded research is listed by headings only.

Several of these agencies list their projects through 'in-house' registers which are also used for dissemination to interested parties. These are indicated in this section.

1. Aid and Development Agencies Committee on the National Curriculum Council
15–17 New St, York Y01 2RA
☎ 0904 622533
ⓟ Secretary

2. Assessment of Performance Unit
Department of Education and Science, Elizabeth Hse, York Rd, London SE1 7PH
☎ 071 934 9000
ⓟ Director
Assessment of Performance Unit: Science
Centre for Studies in Science and Mathematics Education, School of Education, University of Leeds, Leeds LS2 9JT
☎ 0532 334622
ⓟ S. Daniels
Projects and curriculum initiatives
1 Profile and profession study (1987–92, 11–13 (15) age group)
Nature 400 pupils tested at 11 and again at 13 (and at 25 if funded), carried out by staff of 11 with DES/SEAC funding
▼ Reports

3. Association for Educational and Training Technology
Blithe Centre, BMA Hse, Tavistock Sq, London WC1H 9JP
ⓟ Secretary

4. Council for Educational Technology for the UK
3 Devonshire St, London W1N 2BA
ⓟ Information officer

5. Department of Education and Science – DES
Elizabeth Hse, York Rd, London SE1 7PH
☎ 071 934 9000   ⓣ 23171
ⓟ Chief inspector, curriculum
Publications Free, *Current Educational Research Projects Supported by the Department of Education and Science,* 1989; also DES press notices (and a published index to press notices), circulars, statistical bulletins, statistics of education, HMI reports (and a published index to HMI reports)

Current initiatives
The DES is currently commissioning research on 81 projects. These are organised under 10 areas:
Schools 1   Financial delegation (1 project); 16–19 education (1 project)
Schools 2   Special educational needs (16 projects); transition from school to work (6 projects); drugs education (1 project)
Schools 3   Curriculum (7 projects)
Schools 4   Examinations and records of achievement (3 projects); assessment of performance unit (8 projects)
Further and higher education 1   Higher education (3 projects)
Further and higher education 2   Further education (6 projects); youth service unit (3 projects)
Further and higher education 3   Adult education (4 projects); student affairs (2 projects)
Teachers pay and general   Teacher appraisal (3 projects)
Teachers supply and training   Teacher training (4 projects)
Architects and building   (13 projects)
Nature of contribution of organisation
The Department only commissions projects which are 'policy-related', i.e. a) will help to guide policy decisions that need to be taken; b) will help to improve the quality of the educational process in areas of policy concern; c) will facilitate the implementation of policy decisions; and d) will evaluate the effects of the implementation of policy decisions. It is prepared to consider proposals submitted by research institutions from outside the Department, provided they satisfy one of these criteria or can, if necessary, be modified to meet the current research needs of the department.

6. Department of Education and Science for Northern Ireland – DENT
Rathgael Hse, Balloo Rd, Bangor, County Down BT19 2PR
☎ 0247 270077   ⓕ 0247 456451
ⓟ K. Reid, EOII, coordination branches
Responsible for ensuring that all children in the 5–16 age range receive education that a) promotes the spiritual, moral, cultural, intellectual and physical development of pupils and thereby of society; and b) prepares such pupils for the opportunities, responsibilities and experiences of adult life. It discharges its responsibilities for the curriculum and assessment through a range of agencies. Of these the main contributors are:
i) the Northern Ireland Curriculum Council – a statutory body with the remit to advise on the common curriculum (i.e. the compulsory elements) for 5–16 year olds and on the whole curriculum for 5–18 year olds. The Council may with approval of the Department, commission research and development projects from schools, school authorities, institutions of higher education and other bodies;
ii) the Northern Ireland Schools Examination and Assessment Council – a statutory body

responsible for advising on and overseeing the assessment arrangements for the common curriculum and for providing public examinations including GCSE and GCE AS and A Levels;

iii) the Education and Library Boards. The advisory and support services of the five Education and Library Boards provide support for schools in the implementation of the common curriculum and assessment and in any aspect of the whole curriculum for which schools seek support. The Boards may, with the approval of the Department, undertake curriculum development projects with individual schools and groups of schools. The Education and Library Boards can be contacted on the following telephone numbers: Belfast 329211, Belfast 391188, Armagh 523811, Omagh 44431 and 44931, Ballymena 3333;

iv) the colleges of education, the universities and other bodies may undertake curriculum development projects with the approval of the schools and appropriate school authorities.

Current initiatives
1 Schools curriculum support scheme (1987–, 5–11 age group).
2 Primary guidelines (1985–9, 3–11 age group).
3 IT in design education (1988–90, 11–14 age group).
■ This project explores and investigates existing IT resources in the field of designing, identifying potential support to facilitate the understanding of basic procedures involved in the activity of designing and marketing
▼ Resource materials; classroom support materials; curriculum models; classroom ideas
4 Healthy eating project (1988–90, 11–16 age group).
■ This project concerns the development of a province-wide strategy for healthier eating in school canteens and to coordinate a policy between the five Education and Library Boards
▼ Teaching reference package
5 Secondary science curriculum review (SSCR) (1981–90, 11–16 age group).
■ To review the needs of pupils and identify the broad aims of a science education programme appropriate to the full ability range.
▼ Reports/evaluations; resource materials
6 Law in schools project (1989–92, 14–17 age group).
■ To research the needs of schools in Northern Ireland for teaching materials on law
▼ Books; audio cassettes; video
7 Writing and reading project (1987–92, 5–16 age group).
■ To provide reading material with a 'local' flavour
▼ Books
8 11–16 programme (1984–90).
■ Curriculum review and development through a partnership between the Department, Education and Library Boards and participating schools, focusing particularly on those young people who do not relate positively to secondary school and who

achieve little from it
▼ Reports (from the 11–16 programme information office), resource materials; policy documents
9 Records of achievement (1985–89, 11–16 age group).
▼ Reports/evaluations; policy documents
10 Young historian scheme (1989–91, 14–18 age group).
■ To encourage and facilitate the study of history; to promote education for mutual understanding and cultural heritage through history in clusters of post-primary schools with particular emphasis on GCSE and A Levels
11 Microelectronics in schools (1989–90, 7–11 age group).
■ To develop the use of electronic mail to promote education for mutual understanding, and in particular to support joint work in the environment, in clusters of primary schools.
▼ Interim report of the Development officer
12 European studies project (1986–92, 11–18 age group).
▼ To help pupils to understand relationships between Ireland and Great Britain within the context of Europe; to provide scope for pupils to carry out joint study topics in history and geography in which the exchanging, sharing and evaluation of informations has a central role; to encourage the development of information skills using a variety of media to communicate between schools
▼ Draft project handbook; teaching modules; publicity leaflets; conference reports

7. Department of Education and Science and the Welsh Office
Cathays Park, Cardiff CF1 3NO
☎ 0222 825111
Ⓟ Information officer

8. Further Education Unit – FEU
Grove Hse, 2–6 Orange St, London WC2H 7WE (10 regional centres planned)
☎ 071 321 0433 Ⓕ 071 321 0528
Ⓟ J. Love, Information officer
Publications *FEU Newsletter*, termly
Remit FEU exists to support the public sector further and higher education service in all matters relating to the curriculum. It is an advisory and intelligence body. It formulates guidance as a result of a wide programme of consultation with the field and of research and development on curriculum issues.
Current initiatives
1 Competence–based curriculum development (1988-90, FE age group).
▼ Report/evaluation
2 Towards a framework for curriculum entitlement (1989, FE age group).
▼ Policy documents
3 Towards an educational audit (1985-9, FE age group).
▼ Reports/evaluation; resource materials; 3 bulletins under series title 'Educating the Auditors'
4 Supporting YTS (1989, FE age group).
▼ Reports/evaluations; resource materials

5 Curriculum development for students with severe learning difficulties (1985-8, FE age group).
▼ Reports/evaluations; resource materials
6 Curricular impact of WRNAFE (1986-9, FE age group).
▼ Reports/evaluations
7 Continuing professional development for LEA advisers and officers (1988-9).
Ⓟ L. Neil

9. NCC Information Section
National Curriculum Council, 15-17 New St, York YO1 2RA
☎ 0904 622533
Ⓟ Ms C. Etherington, Information officer

10. National Foundation for Educational Research – NFER
The Mere, Upton Park, Slough, Berks. SL1 2DQ (and two regional centres)
☎ 0753 74123   Ⓕ 0753 691632
Ⓟ Mr S. Barber, Press officer
Publications *Educational Research*, 3 times per year: *Research Papers in Education*, 3 times per year; *Topic,* 3 times per year; *Journal of Moral Education*, 3 times per year; *NFER News*, 3 times per year. Free publication, *NFER Current Projects*, annually. The NFER also keeps a register of educational research in the UK for which a nominal service fee is charged.
Current initiatives
The NFER is currently working on over 30 projects which are organised under 6 areas: Department of assessment and measurement which, working closely with NFER-Nelson, publishes tests of mathematics, English, verbal reasoning and non-verbal reasoning. It is also developing assessment materials for the national curriculum, an occupational test series, and materials for microcomputer testing.
Department of professional studies   9 projects.
Department of evaluation and policy studies 7 projects
Department of curriculum studies mathematics, 3 projects; centre for research in language and communication, 4 projects
Department of information research and development   4 projects
Other projects   3 projects

Objectives The NFER is an independent body undertaking research and development projects on issues of current interest in all sectors of the public educational system. Its approach is scientific, apolitical and non-partisan. By means of research projects and extensive field surveys it provides objective evidence on important educational issues for the use of teachers, administrators, parents and the research community. The Foundation's research activities are backed up by an extensive network of supporting services in computing and statistics, in survey administration, in information, and in the development and use of tests. These services are available to other users within the limits of available resources.

11. Records of Achievement National Steering Committee
Department of Education and Science, Elizabeth Hse, 39 York Rd, London SE1 7PH
☎ 071 934 9000
Ⓟ Information officer

12. Schools Examination and Assessment Council – SEAC
Newcombe Hse, 45 Nottinghill Gate, London W11 3JB
☎ 071 229 1234;   Ⓕ 071 243 054
Ⓟ Allan Chick (Head of Information)
Publication SEAC Recorder (newsletter), termly
Remit The School Examinations and Assessment Council (SEAC) is an independent Government Agency and was established by the Secretary of State for Education and Science, under the terms of the Education Reform Act, in August 1988. Its functions are to keep all aspects of school examinations and assessment under review, to carry out programmes of research and development and other related activities and to advise the Secretaries of State for Education and Science and for Wales on matters connected with examinations and assessment.

13. TVEI Unit
5th Floor, 236 Greys Inn Rd, London WC1X 8HL
Ⓟ Director

Section 3

Curriculum Initiatives from Accreditation Agencies

Curriculum Handbook

This section contains details of agencies concerned with the accreditation of examinations and assessment which affect students aged between 5 and 18. In the main, this means the GCSE Examination Groups and their constituent Board members. We have, however, interpreted the remit a little more widely than that to include some agencies whose work indirectly affects the school curriculum.

Although the separate Boards are now linked together in Regional Groups, it is difficult to disentangle a regional group identity; the working unit still appears to be the individual Boards, acting cooperatively.

It seems inevitable that there will be major upheavals in this section over the next few years as assessment procedures — and agencies' — for the national curriculum emerge. Survival for agencies, as Peter Burke points out in Section 1, will depend on the agencies' ability to adapt to new circumstances and to develop new roles. At present, these agencies rightly pride themselves on their closeness to and cooperation with the teaching profession. It is to be hoped that this feature will be retained in changing circumstances.

1. Associated Board of the Royal Schools of Music – ABRSM

14 Bedford Square, London WCIB 3JG (and 300 regional centres)
☎ 071 636 5400   ⓣ   25489
Ⓕ 071 436 4520
Ⓟ Ronald Smith, Chief executive and Director of examinations
Professional communication channels *Libretto*, Newsletter; syllabuses.
Remit   The Associated Board was founded in 1889 to set standards for teachers and pupils and thereby to raise the level of musical performance and knowledge. It now examines over half a million candidates each year in more than 80 countries worldwide.
Awards given   Preparatory test (for instrumentalists after 6–9 months tuition); grades 1 to 8 in all singing, theory, and instrumental subjects
Objectives   The Associated Board has a consultation process through teachers' meetings and courses. It has a formal Consultative committee and an Examination Board. Syllabuses are regularly reviewed with the relevance of the examinations to present-day educational requirements firmly in mind.

2. Associated Examining Board – AEB

Stag Hill Hse, Guildford, Surrey GU2 5XJ (and 2 regional centres)
☎ 0483 506506   Ⓕ   0483 300152
Ⓟ J. Day, Secretary general
Publication   Annual report; annual syllabus book.
Remit   The AEB is a public examining body charged with the task of providing assessment of candidates from schools, colleges and other centres in the United Kingdom and overseas.

Awards given   Basic Tests; GCE A level; GCE AS level; GCSE (as a partner in the Southern Examining Group); various other tests for specific purposes.
Objectives   The Board works within a framework established by the Department of Education and Science and overseen by the Schools Examinations and Assessment Council (SEAC), the latter of which is responsible for formal approval of syllabuses proposed by the Board. Although the Board's main business lies in GCE (A and AS levels) and GCSE examinations, it also offers a suite of Basic Tests and a range of other assessments, partly school/college-based, partly for professional institutes such as the Association of Driving Instructors and the Institute of Employment Consultants. The Board welcomes discussions with interested parties over developments in the field of curriculum and assessment.

3. Business and Technical Education Council – BTEC

Central Hse, Upper Woburn Place, London WC1H OHH
☎ 071 388 3288   Ⓕ   071 387 6068
Ⓟ Ms Margaret Clay, Marketing services
Publications   Bulletin; Update
Remit   BTEC specialises in purpose-built education. Its qualifications are relevant to the world of work, and are nationally and internationally recognised as evidence of the quality, standards and integrity of the competencies achieved by the qualification holders. BTEC awards are progressively receiving conditional accreditation by the National Council for Vocational Qualifications (NCVQ).
Awards given   BTEC Certificates and Diplomas at First, National and Higher National Levels with Continuing Education units, Certificates and Diplomas specifically for adults; the BTEC Certificate of Achievement accredits achievement in one or more units.
Objectives   BTEC has the task of advancing the quality and availability of work-related education for those in, or preparing for, employment. Consequently they work with other agencies such as NCVQ, the Training Agency, Employer and Professional organisations, and vocational education and training providers. The framework of BTEC awards is flexible enough to meet most vocational requirements. The syllabuses and awards are kept up-to-date by a process of continual review.
BTEC works closely with the providers of education and training to ensure that national standards are maintained, via its quality assurance and control systems fo validation, moderation and monitoring procedures. A centre normally chooses from the wide range of BTEC material available, or devises its own to meet specific employer or employee needs. In the latter instance, these are then submitted to BTEC for approval. BTEC's expertise is available to those who wish to ensure the quality of their programmes.

4. City and Guilds of London Institute – C & G
46 Britannia St, London WC1X 9RG
☎ 071 278 2468   Ⓣ 026 6586
Ⓕ 071 278 9460
Ⓟ Publicity manager
Publications *Broadsheet*, 3 times a year; *Schools Bulletin*, twice a year.
Remit The advance of technical and scientific education as a service to the individual and to industry, commerce and the public services.
Awards given City and Guilds vocational and general educational certificates; (with BTEC) Foundation programmes of Pre-Vocational studies and Certificate of Pre-Vocational Education.
Objectives C and G schemes in English and Basic Competence in Information Technology have been approved by SEAC for use in secondary schools. Schemes in Maths and Science are under consideration.
Contact Division 31 at C and G for up-to-date details.
In partnership with BTEC, C and G has developed Foundation Programmes of Pre-Vocational Studies for 14 to 16 year olds. Designed to equip young people with skills and knowledge to deal with everyday situations in an adult world, they can be used alongside GCSE. The Certificate of Pre-Vocational Education (CPVE), also offered with BTEC, is for pupils who have reached statutory school leaving age. Courses may be up to two years but the minimum time for a CPVE programme is 500 hours.
For further information about the foregoing, please contact the Joint Unit for CPVE and Foundation Programmes at C and G.

5. College of Preceptors
Coppice Row, Theydon Bois, Essex CM16 7DN (and 10 regional centres)
☎ 037 881 2727   Ⓕ 037 881 4690
Ⓟ Professor Holmes, Dean
Publications *Education Today*; *College of Preceptors Newsletter*
Remit The College of Preceptors prepares examinations for practising teachers.
Awards given ACP; LCP; DipASE; FCP
Objectives The syllabuses of the College are revised regularly to ensure that teachers are au fait with the demands placed upon them by innovations in the national curricula. Recent innovations in the management of education, the legal bases of education, and craft, design and technology are reflected in syllabuses for teachers preparing for a degree level award, the Licentiateship of the College of Preceptors (LCP).
The Associateship (ACP) allows teachers to examine in approved reports new features of curricula in primary and secondary schools.

6. Joint Matriculation Boards – JMB
Manchester M15 6EU
☎ 061 273 2565   Ⓕ 061 273 7572
Ⓟ P Mr C. Vickerman, OBE, MA, MA(Econ), Secretary

Publications Annual report; full list of publications available from the Secretary; these include GCE Regulations and Syllabuses (annual) and General Requirements for entry into the constituent Universities (annual).
Remit The JMB is the largest GCE Board in terms of UK subject entries, developing new syllabuses and conducting examinations at Advanced and AS levels. The Board's policy is one of soundly based innovation. The JMB also offers: University entrance test in English for speakers of other languages; Staged assessments in literacy (SAIL); Tests of numeracy through problem solving. The JMB is the GCE partner in the Northern Examining Association for the GCSE (see separate entry). Finally, on behalf of its constituent universities (Manchester, Liverpool, Leeds, Sheffield and Birmingham) the Board administers the general requirement for entrance to their first degree courses.
Awards given General Certificate of Education; Certificates of Literacy and Numeracy; University Entrance Test in English for Speakers of Other Languages.
Objectives As a GCE Board, the JMB has always been concerned to ensure that the range of syllabuses it offers reflects and anticipates the changing needs of the curriculum and that methods of assessment adopted encourage good teaching practice as well as being reliable. The JMB has played a leading role in involving teachers in the assessment of their own students within post-16 examinations. Within the Northern Examining Association, in which the JMB is the GCE partner, the JMB contributes to the GCSE examination, the Northern Partnership for Records of Achievement and other initiatives at 16 plus.
Major innovations are frequently initiated through pilot studies with groups of schools and colleges interested in a new subject or a new approach to an existing subject. Schools and colleges, either individually or collectively, may put forward proposals for new developments for consideration by the appropriate Subject Commitee.
The Board's Annual Reports provide information about the work of the JMB, outline current syllabus and curriculum developments and give details of the results in each year's examinations. Copies may be obtained free of charge from the Secretary.

7. London Chamber of Commerce and Industry Examinations Board – LCCI
Marlowe Hse, Station Rd, Sidcup, Kent DA15 7BJ
☎ 081 302 0261   Ⓕ 081 302 4169
Ⓟ Mr Ernest Lee, Assistant director, examinations and assessment or Mr David Smith, Assistant director, external relations
Publications *COMLON*, a quarterly journal; booklets of regulations/syllabuses; Examiners' Reports
Remit The LCCI offers employment-led

examinations/assessment schemes in a wide
range of subjects: the qualifications are open
to students/trainees of any age. Examination
content and form is varied and has been
decided in consultation with many sectors of
the education service, educators/trainers,
industry/commerce, and government
agencies. It welcomes discussions with
interested parties about developments in
assessment and/or the curriculum and the
validation and accreditation of private or
customised training.
Awards given   LCCI
Objectives   Vocational qualifications offered
by the LCCI include: Foreign Languages at
Work Scheme (FLAW) — a teacher-assessed
course, moderated by LCCI, leading to
student profiles; Foreign Languages for
industry and commerce (FLIC) — on demand
throughout the year in any language; Spoken
English for Industry and Commerce (SEFIC),
for non-native speakers — on demand
throughout the year; secretarial language
examinations (SLC, ASLC, SLD) in 3
languages; group secretarial examinations
(SSC, PSC, PESD); first and second
certificates for legal secretaries; first and
second certificates in office technology; NCVQ
awards: business administration I, II, III, and
IV, National Retail Certificates, and other
competence-based awards to be announced;
'On Demand' examinations — practical word-
processing and elements of data processing,
typewriting and audio-typing; four annual
series of examinations in a wide range of
business/office studies subjects at 3 levels,
with the facility to combine clusters of subjects
to qualify for group awards.

8. London and East Anglian Group for GSCE – LEAG
Stewart Hse, 32 Russell Sq, London WC1B
5DN   (and 4000 regional centres)
☎   071 436 5351   Ⓣ   291813
Ⓕ   071 631 3369
The other constituent boards of LEAG are:
East Anglian Examinations Board, The
Lindens, Lexden Rd, Colchester, Essex CO3
3RL (Tel. 0206 549595); London Regional
Examining Board, Lyon Hse, 104 Wandsworth
High St, London SW18 4LF (Tel 081 870
2144).
Ⓟ   Chief Executive
Publications   LEAG Circulars, 3 times a
year; regulations and syllabuses (annually);
occasional publications.
Remit   The objective of LEAG is the
advancement of education by the preparation,
conduct and administration of GCSE
examinations and other tests, examinations
and means of assessing and recording
academic achievement and the issuing or
endorsement of certificates or other
statements of achievement.
Awards given   GCSE; Graded Assessments
Objectives   LEAG offers GCSE syllabuses
in nearly 100 subjects, including 'mainstream'
syllabuses for 16 year olds who have followed
a two-year course, one-year Series 17

syllabuses for students aged 17 or over and
external syllabuses for students who, for
example, are studying privately at home.
LEAG has developed a number of Graded
Assessment schemes for students aged
11–16, including mathematics (GAIM),
science (GASP), modern languages (in
French, Urdu; German and Spanish to follow)
(GAMLL), and craft, design and technology
(GACDT). These schemes offer a means of
achieving a GCSE qualification by continuous
assessment and the opportunity to fulfil the
demands of the national curriculum insofar as
this requires internal teacher assessment.
LEAG is a member of the Consortium for
Assessment and Testing in Schools (CATS)
responsible for the development of standard
assessment tasks at national curriculum Key
Stages 1 and 3. LEAG is collaborating in the
development and certification of Record of
Achievement schemes.

9. Midland Examining Group – MEG
Through its constituent examining boards:
East Midland Regional Examinations Board,
Robins Wood Hse, Robins Wood Rd, Aspley,
Nottingham NG8 3NR   (Tel. 0602 296021);
Oxford and Cambridge Schools Examination
Board, Elsfield Way, Oxford OX2 8EP   (Tel.
0865 54421)   and Brook House, 10
Trumpington St, Cambridge CB2 1QB   (Tel.
0223 64326);
Southern Universities Joint Board, Cotham
Rd, Cotham, Bristol BS6 6DD (Tel. 0272
736042)
The West Midlands Examinations Board,
Norfolk Hse, Smallbrook Queensway,
Birmingham B5 4NJ   (Tel. 021 631 2151);
Cambridge University Local Examinations
Syndicate, Syndicate Buildings, 1 Hills Rd,
Cambridge CB1 2EU   (Tel. 0223 61111)
Publications   MEG Examiner, newsletter;
regulations and syllabuses
Remit   GCSE syllabuses and assessment
Awards given   GCSE

10. National Council for Vocational Qualifications – NCVQ
222 Euston Rd, London NW1 2BZ
☎   071 387 9898   Ⓣ   071 387 0978
Ⓟ   Mr Alastair Robertson, director,
communications
Publications   National Record of Vocational
Achievement (NROVA) leaflets; NCVQ videos;
NCVQ Annual Report; NCVQ Information
Notes; NCVQ Newsletter; other NCVQ
publications (full list on request).
Remit   NCVQ has national responsibility for
vocational qualifications.
Awards given   National Vocational
Qualifications (NVQs) Levels 1–4.
Objectives   The NCVQ has 9 specific tasks:
to secure standards of occupational
competence and to ensure that vocational
qualifications are based on them; to design
and implement a new national framework for
vocational qualifications; to approve bodies
making accredited awards; to obtain
comprehensive coverage of all occupational

sectors; to secure arrangements for quality assurance; to set up effective liaison with bodies awarding vocational qualifications; to establish a national database for vocational qualifications; to undertake, or arrange to be undertaken, research and development to discharge these functions; and to promote vocational education, training and qualifications.

11. The National Nursery Examination Board – NNEB

8 Chequer St, St Albans, Hertfordshire AL1 3XZ
☎ 0727 47636
ⓟ Ms Sheila Bellamy, Administrative officer
Publications *NNEB Newsletter*
Remit To enable students to work with children from 0 to 7 years of age
Awards given NNEB and CPQS Certificates
Objectives The Board is an Examining and Validating body which awards Certificates to students who have successfully completed a specially designed course approved under the Board's regulations. The Board awards the Certificate in Nursery Nursing and the Certificate in Post Qualifying Studies. The curriculum is designed for students to follow a course of education and training which enables them to work with children from 0 to 7 years of age in a number of employment settings. There is no upper age limit for student entry to courses and mature students are welcomed. The courses can be studied on a part- or full-time basis.
The Board is currently seeking ways in which it can accredit prior learning and is at present developing the curriculum in response to the criteria put forward by the National Council for Vocational Qualifications.

12. Northern Examining Association – NEA

ⓟ through its constituent examining bodies.
For centres in the NEA area:
Mr D.J. Gillan, MEd, BSc, Associated Lancashire Schools Examining Board, 12 Harter St, Manchester M1 6HL   (Tel. 061 228 0084   Fax 061 228 0186);
Mr D. Kelly, BA, North Regional Examinations Board, Wheatfield Rd, Westerhope, Newcastle-upon-Tyne NE5 5JZ   (Tel. 091 286 0084   Fax 091 271 3314);
Ms. K Tattersall, BA, MEd, North West Regional Examinations Board, Orbit House, Albert St, Eccles, Manchester M30 OWL (Tel. 061 788 9521   Fax 061 788 7452);
Mr. B. Park, MA Yorkshire and Humberside Regional Examinations Board, 31–33 Springfield Avenue, Harrogate, Yorkshire HG1 2HW   (Tel. O423 566991 Fax 0423 523678) and Scarsdale Hse, 136 Derbyshire La, Sheffield S8 8SE   (Tel. 0742 557436 Fax 0742 553758)
For centres outside the NEA area: Mr. C. Vickerman, OBE, MA, MA(Econ), Joint Matriculation Board, Manchester MI5, 6EU (Tel. 061 273 2565   Fax 061 273 7572)
Publications Annual Report; GCSE

syllabuses (annual). Lists of publications available from the constituent Boards.
Remit The NEA is the largest of the Examining Groups for the General Certificate of Secondary Education and comprises a GCE Board (JMB) and four regional Boards (ALSEB, NREB, NWREB, and YHREB). The NEA provides a complete range of GCSE syllabuses and offers a variety of Mode 3 syllabuses. Cooperating with the 37 northern LEAs, the NEA is the GCSE partner in the Northern Partnership for Records of Achievement.
Awards given GCSE; through the Northern Partnership for Records of Achievement, the accreditation of northern schools and colleges for records of achievement.
Objectives The NEA has played a leading role in examining at 16+, including its sustained contribution to the development of Joint GCE O-level and GSE examinations which preceded the GCSE. Through the combined traditions of the JMB and the regional boards, the NEA has encouraged teachers' involvement in the assessment of their own pupils' work and the submission of syllabuses by individual centres and groups of centres to meet particular needs.
The NEA is able, because of its regional structure and consequent close relationship between Home Boards and their schools and colleges, to respond to developments in the NEA regions as well as having the capacity to meet national challenges in examining at 16 plus and other areas of curriculum development and assessment.
The NEA's Annual Report provides information about developments in assessment and gives the results of each year's examinations. Copies may be obtained free of charge from any of the NEA boards.

13. Northern Ireland Schools Examinations Council

Beechill Hse, 42 Beechill Rd, Belfast BT8 4RS
☎ 0232 704666
ⓟ Chief officer

14. Oxford and Cambridge Schools Examination Board

Ewert House, Banbury Rd, Oxford OX2 7BZ
☎ 0865 54291
ⓟ The Secretary

15. Royal Society of Arts Examinations Board – RSA

Progress Hse, Westwood Business Park, Westwood Way, Coventry CV4 8HS   (and 6500 centres)
☎ 0203 47003
ⓟ Ms Sue Martin, Corporate communications manager
Publications *RSA News*, termly; *Examinations Bulletin*, twice a year.
Remit To provide qualifications through examinations or assessment schemes for students, trainees, teachers, trainers and adults.

Awards given   RSA Certificates and Diplomas.
Objectives   The scope of the RSA Examinations Board extends beyond the schools (5–18) sector in the provision of a wide range of qualifications, mainly of a vocational nature; these are mostly in the administrative, business and secretarial occupational areas, but the Board has diversified in recent years in response to initiatives generated by NCVQ.
To ensure that qualifications meet the requirements of industry and commerce the Board and principal committees (including advisory committees) are structured to provide representation from providers and from users together with additional representatives to give specialist advice. Schemes are under continuous review to ensure that they satisfy the needs of students and trainees, and also of employers. Additionally, provisions are made for teachers' and trainers' qualifications to complement the student and trainee level provision.
Recent developments have resulted in major changes on the part of RSA and a greater degree of involvement in teaching and curricular issues – a growing trend away from formal examinations and greater use of continuous assessment; cooperation with GCSE groups in the certification of awards based on RSA units; the revision of the format for syllabuses, setting them out with stated objectives so that areas to be tested are clearly understood; greater use of assignments in the delivery of integrated vocational qualifications; the preparation of textbooks, teachers' manuals and practice materials to support the teaching of text processing schemes; a regular programme of workshops for teachers and trainers; meetings regionally on general or specific topics to allow for mutual feedback on the curricular and teaching aspects of RSA schemes; and the encouragement of new and varied developments through their certification on a non-standard basis.

16. Scottish Examination Board – SEB
Ironmills Rd, Dalkeith, Midlothian EH22 1LE
☎   031 663 6601
Ⓟ   Miss F.M. Mackay, higher administrative officer
Remit   The Board has the following duties: to make arrangements for and to conduct examinations each year for the award of certificates relating to secondary education; to award such certificates on such conditions approved by the Secretary of State for Scotland as the Board may impose; to advise the Secretary of State for Scotland on such matters relating to examinations for pupils receiving secondary education as the Secretary of State refers to them, or as the Board consider necessary; to give effect to such direction as the Secretary of State for Scotland may give to the Board under these

regulations as to the discharge by them of their functions.
Awards given   Scottish Certificate of Education (SCE) at standard/ordinary and higher grades; short courses are also certificated; Certificates of sixth form studies (CSYS).
Objectives   External examinations are offered at 16 plus (standard/ordinary grade), 17 plus (higher grade) and 18 plus (CSYS), based on nationally defined courses developed in conjuction with representatives of the Scottish Consultative Council on the Curriculum (SCCC) and finalised only after consultation with interested bodies in the education sector. The whole structure of school examinations in Scotland is currently undergoing change. Standard grade (a parallel development to GCSE in England and Wales) is being phased in between 1986 and 1993, as a replacement for ordinary grade which is to be discontinued in most subjects in 1991 or 1992, while higher grade and CSYS syllabuses and examinations are being revised in order to achieve all-through certification. Short courses, based on teaching/learning units of 20 to 40 hours' duration are now also available in a range of curricular areas.

17. Southern Examining Group – SEG
Stag Hill Hse, Guildford, Surrey GU2 5XJ
☎   0483 503123
Ⓟ   Chief executive
The constituent boards of SEG are:
Associated Examining Board, Stag Hill Hse, Guildford, Surrey GU2 5XJ   (Tel. 0483 506506)
Oxford School Examinations Board, Ewert Hse, Ewert Place, Banbury Road, Oxford OX2 7BZ   (Tel. 0865 54291) and three district offices: 8th Floor, 23–29 Marsh St, Bristol BS1 4BP   (Tel. 0272 273434)
Eastleigh Hse, Market St, Eastleigh, Hampshire SO5 4SW   (Tel. 0703 644811)
Beloe Hse, 2–10 Mount Ephraim Rd, Tunbridge Wells, Kent TN1 1EU   (Tel. 0892 35311)
Publications   Annual report; regulations and syllabuses
Remit   GCSE assessment
Awards given   GCSE

18. Southern Universities Joint Board for School Examinations – SUJB
Cotham Rd, Bristol BS6 6DD   (and about 400 regional centres)
☎   0272 736042
Ⓟ   Mr D.W. Bennett, Assistant secretary
Remit   The Board is a constituent member of the Midland Examining Group for GCSE. It also accepts entries from its Home Centres for GOSSEC AL and AS level examinations.
Awards given   GCSE
Objectives   The Board participates in developments regarding public examinations for pupils aged 14–18 and, in particular, innovation concerned with GCSE assessment.

19. University of Cambridge Local Examinations Syndicate – UCLES

Syndicate Buildings, 1 Hills Rd, Cambridge CB1 2EU
☎ 0223 61111   ⓣ 940127
Ⓕ 0223 460278
Ⓟ Ms Susannah Thomas, Information officer
Publications   GCSE News, for overseas schools following the international GCSE.
Remit   The Syndicate provides an assessment service in the United Kingdom and internationally, offering examinations and qualifications at various levels of education and training.
Awards given   GCSE; A and AS levels (including modular courses); EFL and TEFL qualifications; Cambridge Information Technology; Graded Objectives in French, Science, CDT and Mathematics; Records of Achievement. Certificate in Arabic and Arab studies.
Objectives   The Syndicate is committed to the continuing development of its provision, to meet the needs of teachers ad students, and in response to educational initiatives by government and other agencies. Currently the Syndicate is engaged in many developments in the United Kingdom, for example, Standard Assessments for the National Curriculum (as a partner Board in MEG), Records of Achievement (14–19) and modular A and AS levels. Internationally, developments include the International General Certificate of Secondary Education (IGCSE) and extensive English as a Foreign Language provision. The service provided by the Syndicate depends, among other things, on thorough cooperation between the Syndicate and teachers and other curriculum developers, for example in the design and delivery of assessments. There are many channels for consultation, ranging from discussions within one of the Syndicate's committees, where the interests of all parts of the education system are represented, to the teachers' conferences organised regularly by the Syndicate. The Syndicate's Council for Examination Development (contact: Dr Ron Malone, Director) is responsible for investigating and developing new assessments. The Council is currently, for example, developing tests of aptitude in critical reasoning skills. The Syndicate's International Consultancy and Training Services Department (David Gleave, Director) provides assessment expertise to support educational development projects in many different parts of the world, working closely with the staff of national education ministries and international agencies. This department also runs training programmes in examination administration for such personnel.

20. University of London School Examinations Board – ULSEB

Stewart Hse, 32 Russell Square, London WC1B 5DN
☎ 071 636 8000   ⓣ 291 813 ULSEB
Ⓕ 071 631 3369
Ⓟ Mr A. R. Stephenson, MA, Secretary
Publications   Regulations and syllabuses ; statistics; subject reports; past Question Papers (catalogue on written application).
Remit   The development of syllabuses and schemes of assessment mainly for secondary school pupils, students in further education, and private candidates; the conducting of these examinations based on these syllabuses and the award of appropriate nationally accredited certificates.
Awards given   GCE O level (overseas); GCE Advanced Level; GCE Advanced Supplementary Examination; Certificate of Attainment (Graded Tests); GCSE (as part of LEAG).
Objectives   ULSEB has been at the forefront of the development of public examinations, primarily for 16–18 year-olds in the United Kingdom and overseas for 150 years. It provides an assessment service to a wide range of students in full and part-time education in more than 140 countries. The Board is both innovative and responsive to national changes as determined by the DES. Users of the results of the examinations conducted by ULSEB, LEAs, and those who teach the students are full participants in the work of the Board. The development aspect of the Board's work is supported by a team of staff concerned with research and evaluation. Recent innovations have included the development of Advanced Supplementary Examinations, a pilot modular A level, and Graded Tests in English, Numeracy and Literacy.

21. University of Oxford Delegacy of Local Examinations

Ewert Hse, Banbury Rd, Oxford OX2 7BZ (and 1350 regional centres)
☎ 0865 54291   ⓣ 83617UODLEG
Ⓕ 0865 510085
Ⓟ James Pailing, Secretary to the Delegates
Publications   Annual report; regulations and syllabuses.
Remit   Expertise is currently being extended and developed at the Delegacy to meet the new demands for trainees and students in the industrial and educational worlds. Validation can be accorded to courses which meet the rigorous demands set by the Delegacy. Certification may be offered where trainees or students demonstrate specified achievements in an assessment scheme. Expert advice on assessment is offered by the Delegacy through its wholly owned company, Oxford International Assessment Services Limited.
Awards given   A level Certificates; AS level Certificates; the Oxford Examination in English as a Foreign Language (Preliminary and Higher levels); GCSE (as part of SEG)
Objectives   The Delegacy provides 36 A level and 21 AS level examinations for schools and colleges, within the United Kingdom and overseas. The Delegacy is a partner in SEG. It provides examinations for the GCSE. SEG offers more than 80 syllabuses and assessment patterns designed

by groups of specialist practising teachers. The Delegacy also conducts the Oxford Examination in English as a Foreign Language at both Preliminary Level (with a junior counterpart for younger students) and a Higher level. These test practical, non-literary English; test real-life English usage; use authentic materials; aim to be as enjoyable as possible; provide relevance to students' lives; give students an interesting opportunity to display their varied skills; are available worldwide in more than 600 countries; are held 3 times a year; are available on special request. Linked to the Oxford Delegacy of Local Examinations is the following project.

1   Oxford Certificate of Educational Achievement (OCEA).
Ⓟ   Ms Anne Matthews, Head Records of achievement and validation, OCEA Management and Development Unit, The Martin High School, Link Rd, Anstey, Leics LE7 7EB   (Tel. 0533 366027)
■   To develop and implement a Record of Achievement based on a set of principles which focus on: teaching; learning and assessment; recording and reporting; the organisation and management which underpin all of these. The aims of OCEA also include: the development of assessment in ways which support curriculum developement; the integration of assessment into the learning process; the greater involvement of students in their own learning; the provisions of a record which recognises a broad range of achievements and experiences.
The emphasis throughout the project has been on the development of the processes of recording achievement across the curriculum. Initiated in 1982, OCEA was one of the RoA developments to receive DES funding through a 3-year educational support grant. It was piloted in the 4 LEAs of Coventry, Leicestershire, Oxfordshire and Somerset between 1985 and 1987.
▼   OCEA newsletter

22. Welsh Joint Education Committee – WJEC
246 Western Ave, Cardiff CF5 2YX

☎ 0222 561231   Ⓕ 0222 551544
Ⓟ   Mel J. Jones, Examinations secretary
Remit   To research, design and implement syllabuses for the use of schools and colleges for examinations at ages 16 and 18. In addition, to develop and evaluate appropriate INSET programmes to raise teacher-awareness about the application of the various curricula.
Awards given   GCE A and AS levels; GCSE; Certificate of Education; Certificate in Agriculture; Joint Certification: CGLI/WJEC and RSA/WJEC; Certificate in Office Skills.
Objectives   The WJEC is a consortium of 8 Welsh LEAs and acts as an examining and certification agency which enjoys very close links with its LEAs and the schools and colleges of Wales. As a result, it responds to the needs of pupils in Welsh schools. For example, the major curriculum initiative for slower learning children, the Certificate of Education, was developed by an LEA, and adopted by the WJEC at that Authority's request, to be offered as an examination to schools in the whole of Wales and, latterly, England. However, the WJEC participates fully in its curriculum and assessment remit as a national examining board at 16 plus and 18 plus by working with the English and Northern Ireland examining groups for the GCSE and the GCE boards; for example, the WJEC works closely with NEA, JMB, RSA and CGLI. Current curriculum development is based upon areas of concern to teachers as highlighted by their representatives on the WJEC Examination and Assessment Committee and its Subject and Curriculum Panels, by the approaches to Examination Officers, and more formally through the Joint Comittee's membership of national organisations. Approaches are made through the Examinations Secretary. The WJEC is currently involved in developmental work and research in Records of Achievement, INSET evaluation, differentiation in teaching programmes, Science, Technology and Humanities.

Section 4

Curriculum Initiatives from Subject Groups

Curriculum Handbook

This section contains details of major organisations concerned with specific subjects or specialisms as opposed to having a general whole curricular interest. It, therefore, includes well-established organisations with permanent staff, but also smaller, but important, associations. These latter are sometimes difficult to contact because their very nature means that officials change from year to year and tend to work from homes or workplaces. Inevitably, therefore, some will have been missed because it has proved impossible to contact them.

It is difficult to suggest a solution to this problem. On the one hand it is important that small-scale interest groups should proliferate and have space to be active or comparatively inert as circumstances change. But in order to be effective, they do need to be accessible to outsiders. Perhaps some kind of umbrella organisation might be developed to look after their interests and provide a clearing house for information. Singly, they could not support a permanent secretariat; collectively, this might be feasible if some Institution were to take an initiative.

Because of the specific nature of the remit of most of these organisations, many are particularly active in Research and Development work. Not all of their activities may be defined neatly in terms of projects, but the selection included is an attempt to give a flavour of their work as well as to list the specific entries.

1. Association for Language Learning – ALL

Marton, Rugby CV23 9RY (and approximately 30 regional centres in England, Scotland and Wales)
☎ 0926 632335
Ⓟ Ms C. Wilding, Secretary general
Publication *Language World*, quarterly news sheet; journals (twice a year) *Language Learning Journal, Francophonie, German Teaching, Vida Hispanica, Tuttitalia, Russistika, Dutch Crossing.*
Contribution Consultation; raising theoretical curricular questions; organising meetings and courses; producing discussion papers; organising an annual conference (entitled 'Language World') each March, attended by more than 1000 delegates from UK and abroad
Objectives The ALL is a newly constituted organisation which arises from the amalgamation of the bodies heretofore working under the umbrella of the Joint Council of Language Associations: the Modern Languages Association; the British Association for Language Teaching; the Associations of Teachers of German, Italian, Spanish and Portuguese, Russian, and Dutch. ALL aims to offer support and services to language teachers in schools, further, higher, and adult education. By responding to requests for advice from a variety of sources including DES and Examination Boards it is able to influence policy and decisions

regarding languages in education. Within its membership there is the whole range of expertise and enquirers can be put in touch with appropriate persons. An important development in the field of assessment in modern languages has been the Graded Objective Tests, and new syllabuses for GCSE and A level. As the new Association develops it is anticipated that it will establish working parties for research and publications to respond to the needs of members and education in general.

2. Association for Science Education – ASE

College Lane, Hatfield, Hertfordshire AL10 9AA (and 19 regional centres)
☎ 0707 267411 Ⓕ 0781–266532
Ⓟ Dr. D. Moore, General secretary
Publication *School Science Review,* quarterly; *Primary Science Review,* termly; *Education in Science,* 5 times per year.
Contribution Consultation; provision of resource material; organising meetings and courses; producing discussion papers
Projects and curriculum initiatives
1 Initiatives in Primary Science: an Evaluation (IPSE) (primary age group).
▼ Reports/evaluations; resource materials; discussion documents
2 SATIS 16–19 (Science and Technology in Society) (1987–90, 16–19 age group).
▼ Resource materials
3 EARLY SATIS (1989–92, primary and early secondary age groups).
Objectives The association's major contribution to curriculum development is through the medium of its journals. Members submit articles on aspects of science education and current concerns; these are then published to the general membership. Through its committee structure, the association establishes a wide range of working parties on aspects of science education. Outcomes from these working parties are published through the journals or in separate in-house publications. Meetings and workshops on curriculum issues are held in after-school hours or at weekends and are organised regionally in all of the 19 regions. The annual meeting, which is held at a different university each year over a four-day period in January, provides an enormous range of exhibitions of publications and equipment, and a forum for discussion on many aspects of curriculum matters. Current attendance is in the order of 5,500.

3. Association for the Teaching of the Social Sciences – ATSS

PO Box 461, Sheffield S1 3BF
☎ 0244 683011
Ⓟ Mr Stuart Lunn, Secretary
Publications *Social Science Teacher,* 3 times a year
Contribution Consultation; raising theoretical curricular questions; provision of resource materials; organising meetings and courses; producing discussion papers;

producing assessment materials
Projects and curriculum initiatives
1 Sociology A and AS levels (ongoing, 16–18 age group).
Policy documents; discussion documents
Comment ATSS concentrates on the coursework/project elements.
2 Social science/integrated humanities (ongoing, 11–16 age group).
■ To assist GCSE developments, especially modular programmes
▼ Policy documents; discussion documents
3 Cross-curricular themes (ongoing, 11–16 age group).
■ Policy documents; discussion documents
Objectives This is the professional association for teachers of sociology and social science in schools and further education. In addition, it also has close links with professional social scientists and teacher trainers in HE, and fully consults with other related subject bodies in the social sciences and humanities via umbrella organisations such as FACTASS and COSTA. The association is particularly involved in promoting the interests of sociology teachers at A, AS and GCSE levels, and in promoting the contributions of social science and integrated humanities to 5–16 education. Increasingly, the association has taken on the role of coordinating general social science approaches to cross-curricular themes in the areas of equal opportunities, environmental education, political and economic awareness, PSE, information technology and community studies.
The roles of the association are to provide a support network of advice and learning resources to teachers in this general field; to foster and disseminate curriculum development within the social sciences; to consult with interested parties and produce discussion documents and curricular guidelines; to sponsor the major journal on social science teaching and run a national conference on related topical issues, together with a series of sixth form conferences; and to provide regular advice based on our members' views to policy-making bodies such as HMI, NCC and SEAC. At present, the Association is particularly involved with promoting social science input into the national curriculum, particularly through cross-curricular themes and dimensions.

4. Association of Advisers in Craft, Design and Technology – AACDT
124 Kidmore Rd, Caversham, Reading RG4 7N1B
☎ 0734 470615
Ⓟ Mr R.H. Welsh, Honorary secretary
Contribution Consultation; raising theoretical curricular questions providing resource material; organising meetings and courses; producing discussion papers
Objectives The AACDT is the professional organisation representing all advisers and inspectors responsible for CDT in LEAs in Britain. It has produced a policy paper on CDT

and a number of guidelines and discussion documents. It has a strong regional base and is consulted regularly by HMI, SEAC, NCC and other major policy making bodies. The association has produced, in consultation with the Health and Safety Executive, guidance notes on matters related to safety in schools. The association in actively engaged in the development of the national curriculum.

5. Association of Law Teachers – ALT
Department PSA2, Sheffield City Polytechnic, Sheffield S1 1WB
☎ 0244 720911 Ⓣ 54680
Ⓕ 0244 758019
Ⓟ Mr P. Harris, Secretary
Publications *The Law Teache*r, 3 times per year; *ALT Bulletin,* 3 times per year
Contribution Consultation; raising theoretical curricular questions; proving resource materials; organising meetings and courses
Objectives Representation on professional and examining bodies; frequent conferences for teachers of law in schools.

6. Association of Teachers of Mathematics – ATM
7 Shaftesbury St, Derby DE3 8YB (and 30 local branches)
☎ 0332 46599
Ⓟ Ms G. Hatch, Honorary secretary
Publications *Mathematics Teaching*, 4 times a year, *Micromath*, 3 times a year
Contribution Consultation; raising theoretical questions; provision of resource material; organising meetings and courses; producing discussion papers; producing assessment materials
Projects and curriculum initiatives
1 ATM GCSE validated by SEG (1985, 14–16 age group).
▼ Reports/evaluations; policy documents; discussion documents
2 Conference on the national curriculum jointly with MA, ASE & NATE (1989, 5–11 age group).
▼ Reports/evaluations
3 Monitoring the introduction of the national curriculum jointly with MA, ASE & NATE (1989–, 5–11 age group).
▼ Policy documents; discussion documents
4 Logo Microworlds' software pack (1987–9, 5–16 age group).
▼ Reports/evaluations; resource materials; discussion documents
Objectives The ATM exists to: support teachers in developing more child-centred approaches to teaching mathematics; create a network of teachers, through local branches and the journals, who can share and extend ideas about the teaching of mathematics; provide, as a result of members' activities, a supply of attractive and innovative publications to support the activities of others; demonstrate through the provision of children's workshops the power of an active approach to mathematics learning; help

members evaluate and respond to government and other central initiatives such as the national curriculum; and to provide an annual conference at which ideas can be shared and further developed.

7. British Association of Advisers and Lecturers in Physical Education – BAALPE

Nelson Hse, 3–6 The Beacon, Exmouth, Devon EX8 2AG (and 12 regional centres)
☎ 0395 263247
Ⓟ Mr G.M. Edmundson, General secretary
Publications *Bulletin of Physical Education*, quarterly
Contribution Consultation; raising theoretical curricular questions; provision of resource material; organising meeting and courses; producing discussion papers; producing assessment materials
Projects and curriculum initiatives
1 Physical education 5–16: attainment targets (1988–90, 5–16 age group).
▼ Discussion documents
2 Physical Education for children with special educational needs (1987–9, 5–16 age group).
▼ Books; resource materials
3 Gymnastics for secondary schools (1986–8, 11–16 age group).
▼ Books; resource materials
4 Physical Education 5–16: key stages of attainment (1989–90, 5–16 age group).
▼ Discussion documents
Objectives The association is innovative and responds to the needs of its members and other agencies. Marketing curriculum materials and resources has become a regular occurrence and the Safety Booklet is well used in the Courts of Law throughout the land. Working groups are commissioned by BAALPE's Council and individuals with special expertise represent the association on many national governing bodies and schools associations. Individual members are, through their institution or local authority, regularly involved in assessment of pupils and curricula. This expertise is then channelled into published material to assist quality control.
The Association works in regular partnership with the many other PE and sport related associations.

8. British Council of Physical Education – BCPE

Liverpool Institute of Higher Education, Woolton Rd, Liverpool L16 8ND
▼ 051 722 7331
Ⓟ Mr Fred Hirst, secretary
Publications Through its constituent organisations
Contribution Consultation; raising theoretical curricular questions; provision of resource material; organising meetings and courses; producing discussion papers; producing assessment materials
Projects and curriculum initiatives

1 Interim working group on PE in the national curriculum (ongoing, 5–18 age group).
▼ Reports/evaluations; policy documents; discussion documents
2 BCPE subcommittee as working party on assessment and examinations (ongoing, 5–18 age group).
▼ Reports/evaluations; policy documents; discussion documents; joint documentation with governing bodies of sport for the GCSE
Objectives BCPE has the task of acting as a formal group for policy discussion and implementation for its member associations. It has ongoing dialogue with the DES and HMI on curriculum developments. It is in close contact with the Sports Council and other bodies which have an interest in the work of PE in schools.

9. Centre for World Development Education – CWDE

Regents College, Inner Circle, Regents Park, London NW1 4NS
☎ 071 487 7410 Ⓕ 071 487 7545
Ⓟ Mr Hamish Aitchison, Education officer
Publications *Checklist*, quarterly; *Resources Catalogue*, annual.
Contribution Consultation; provision of resource material; organising meetings and courses; producing discussion papers; publication of educational materials
Projects and curriculum initiatives
1 The primary school in a changing world (1986–9, 5–11 age group).
■ To produce a handbook for primary teachers
▼ Books
2 Sugar Pack (1987–9, 14–16 age group).
■ To produce an economics activity pack
▼ Resource materials
3 Choices in development (1988–92, 14–16 age group).
■ To produce a series of sheets on development issues, eg water, trade, aid, tourism, literacy, etc.
▼ Resource materials
4 Human needs (1989–92, 5–11 age group).
■ To produce a series of resource packs for primary schools on, for example, health
▼ Resource materials
Objectives The Centre for World Development Education is an independent educational agency which promotes education in Britain about world development issues and Britain's interdependence with developing countries. Its special concern, through the work of its education department, is to support teachers in teaching with a global development perspective. It does this in several ways.
CWDE publishes a Resources Catalogue which is updated every year. It contains over 400 items – handbooks, books, leaflets, packs, simulation games, computer software and audio-visual material – specifically on world development themes from a wide range of sources, to provide differing perspectives

on the issues involved. Most of the material is designed for use in the classroom. The Resources Catalogue is free on request. CWDE offers a range of inputs to teacher in-service training courses – workshops for infant and primary, 9–13, GCSE, and computing. For details write to the Education officer at CWDE.

CWDE has extensive files of up-to-date material on a wide range of development themes and on many of the developing countries, together with lists of useful addresses and contacts. This information is available to teachers to help in the planning of courses, and to pupils for project or course work. In addition, the education department offers help to teachers on curriculum planning.

10. Christian Education Movement and Professional Council for Religious Education – CEM and PCFRE

Royal Buildings, Victoria St, Derby DE1 1GW (and 8 regional centres)
☎ 0322 296655
℗ Mr Colin Jackson, Publications director
Professional communication channels
Re Today, termly; *British Journal of Religious Education*, termly
Contribution Consultation; raising theoretical curricular questions; provision of resource material; organising meetings and courses; producing discussion papers; producing assessment materials
Projects and curriculum initiatives
1 RE values (DES funded) (1988–91, 14–16 age group).
■ To establish content and methodology concerning beliefs and values in RE for years 4 and 5 in the secondary school.
▼ Reports/evaluations; resource materials.
Objectives The PCFRE is a membership organisation functioning with the support of the Christian Education Movement, a charity bringing together LEA, church, school and individual interests in education and in religious education in particular. CEM/PCFRE has contributed substantially to the development of the religious education curriculum since it was formed in 1965, and publishes the only magazine and journal specialising in religious education. PCFRE makes formal representation to the DES on behalf of teachers of religious education, and holds national and regional conferences on professional matters including curriculum development. It has a particular interest at present in the assessment of religious education against the criteria determined in the Local Agreed Syllabus for Religious Education and in the context of the National Curriculum.

11. Classical Association – CA

c/o Dr M. Schofield, St John's College, Cambridge CB2 1TP
☎ 0223 338644
℗ Dr Malcolm Schofield, Honorary secretary

Publications *Greece and Rome*, 2 issues a year
Contribution Consultation
Objectives The Classical Association fosters the study of the classical world in a number of ways: by promoting scholarly research, principally through its journal: by creating opportunities both at its annual conference and in the activities of its 30 or so branches for classicists to meet and explore their subject; in the educational sphere it is invited to nominate members of SEAC, NCC and COSTA; its journal, G*reece and Rome* is designed to interest teachers and sixth formers; and it offers funding for schools branches events and bursaries to individual students.

12. Council for Education in World Citizenship

Seymour Mews Hse, Seymour Mews, London W1H 9PE
☎ 071 935 1752
℗ Director

13. Council for Environmental Education – CEE

School of Education, University of Reading, London Rd, Reading RG7 3JE
☎ 0734 318921
℗ Information officer
Publications Newsheet, 10 times a year; Annual review of environmental education
Contribution Consultation; provision of resource material; organising meetings and courses; producing discussion papers; producing assessment materials; provision of information; training in relation to curriculum development in the formal and youth sector
Projects and curriculum initiatives
1 Influencing the national curriculum (1987–90, all phases).
▼ Reports/evaluations
2 Training in relation to curriculum development and environmental education (1988–90, all phases).
▼ Reports/evaluations; resource materials
3 Resourcing curriculum development (ongoing, all phases).
▼ Resource materials
4 Research into evaluation and profiling of education experiences in relation to environmental education (1990–1, all phases).
▼ Reports/evaluations; resource materials; models including appropriate software training material
Objectives The CEE has campaigned for adequate provision of environmental education within the national curriculum, and as part of the whole curriculum. This has entailed the formation of groups drawn from its member organisations and LEA partners to make representation and detailed comment to the Subject Working Groups set up to report on the core and foundation subjects. CEE is also working directly with the NCC, reporting on environmental education as a cross-curricular theme within the national curriculum.

In order to facilitate this process, CEE is involved in the development of teacher education techniques and materials which address areas such as the nature of environmental education, its relationship with core and foundation subjects and the whole curriculum, handling controversial issues and problem-solving, and the development of school policies and curriculum management. CEE resources this area through the provision of information including an extensive data base and library of materials, and the production of resource sheets on a variety of topics.

CEE proposes to develop and evaluate techniques and approaches for profiling pupils' experiences in relation to environmental education delivered in a cross-curricular context.

14. Council of Subject Teaching Associations – COSTA

15 Courthill Terrace, Love Lane, Rochester, Kent MEI 1TN
☎ 0634 826357   Ⓕ 0634 830501
Ⓟ Mr A.R. Hall, Honorary Secretary
Contribution Consultation; organising meetings and courses; exchange of papers between constituent associations
Projects and curriculum initiatives
1 Directory of In-Service Training contacts in subject associations (1988–90, all phases).
▼ Directory
Objectives The COSTA was established in February 1972 with the following aims: to provide an effective means of involving subject teaching associations in decision and policy making at national and regional levels; to provide a means of communication between associations about their activities, methods of organisation and economic planning; to provide a forum of discussion of matters of common interest; and to take common action, where appropriate, on behalf of member associations, without thereby committing member associations as a whole, and protecting the right of any constituent association to act individually or to record a dissenting view.

15. Economics Association

Maxwelton Hse, 41/43 Boltro Rd, Haywards Heath, West Sussex RH1 1BJ (and 16 regional centres)
☎ 0444 455084
Ⓟ Mrs Carole Dyer, Administrative officer
Publications *Economics*, quarterly
Contribution to curriculum development. Consultation; raising theoretical curricular questions; provision of resource material; organising meetings and courses; producing discussion papers
Projects and curriculum initiatives
1 Primary economic awareness (1988–90, 5–13 age group).
▼ Resources materials
2 Economic understanding in non-advanced FE (1988–9, 16–19 age group and adult).
▼ Reports/evaluations

3 Survey of computer usage in economics and business education (1989, 11–19 age group).
▼ Reports/evaluations
4 Economic understanding in adult education (1986–7, post-compulsory phase).
▼ Reports/evaluations
Objectives The Economics Association is the major subject association for economics, economic understanding and broad business education. Through an annual conference and an extensive programme of local activities across the UK, support and curriculum developments are promoted. A Development Officer has been appointed to further promote the local branch network and to help extend the role of the Association.
Current priorities include economic understanding in the national curriculum and promoting developments in the post-16 curriculum. The Association is a respected voice for economics education and is widely consulted by HMI, SEAC, NCC and other bodies. The association was instrumental in pioneering economic understanding in the school curriculum through its Economic Education 14–16 Project (1976–87).
Its quarterly journal, *Economics*, helps to disseminate developments and to provide a forum for members.

16. Educational Institute of Design, Craft and Technology

852 Melton Rd, Thurmaston, Leicester LE4 8BN
☎ 0533 640083
Ⓟ Executive secretary

17. English Association

The Vicarage, Priory Gdns, London W4 1EA
☎ 081 995 4236
Ⓟ Dr Ruth Fairbanks Joseph, Secretary
Publications *English*, 3 times a year; *Essays and Studies*, annual; *Year's Work in English Studies*, annual
Contribution Organising meetings and courses
Objectives The object of the English Association is to promote understanding and appreciation of the English language and its literature. The Association's activities include sponsoring a number of publications and organising annual sixth-form conferences. The English Association was founded in 1906 by a small group of English teachers and scholars; among them were F.S. Boas, A.C. Bradley and Sir Israel Gollancz. It took a leading part in the movement to develop English studies in schools, while encouraging advanced studies in further and higher education. Today the association is an international organisation with branches at home and overseas.

18. Geographical Association – GA

343 Fulwood Rd, Sheffield S10 3BP (and 65 regional branches)
☎ 0742 670666
Ⓟ Mr D. Burtenshaw, Joint honorary secretary, Education; Mr P.S. Fox, Joint

THE GEOGRAPHICAL ASSOCIATION

The Geographical Association is one of the most progressive and up-to-date subject teaching associations of national standing. With over 8000 members and 70 branches throughout the UK it keeps its members informed of developments through its journals and magazines.

GEOGRAPHICAL WORK IN PRIMARY AND MIDDLE SCHOOLS
(new, revised edition) Edited by David Mills (312 pages)
A comprehensive handbook full of practical ideas for teaching geography to the 5-13 age range: sections on: field studies; drama; numeracy; school journeys; microcomputers; weather studies and many more topics.
£10.45 (members) £15.60 (non members)

MANAGING THE GEOGRAPHY DEPARTMENT
Edited by Patrick Wiegand (248 pages)
An essential handbook for teachers with responsibility for departmental management, with chapters covering the role of head of department; developing team spirit; working with Advisers and HMI; managing resources; curriculum development and innovation; reports, case studies and many other items.
£15.75 (members) £23.51 (non-members)

TEACHING ECONOMIC UNDERSTANDING THROUGH GEOGRAPHY
Edited by Graham Corney (over 300 pages)
This publication draws on the experience of the Geography, Schools and Industry Project, and includes guidelines for curriculum planning, examples of units of work, and guidelines to help LEA advisers and others to organise INSET activities, and initial teacher education courses.
Details of price from The Geographical Association.

Details of all types of membership and publications from:
THE GEOGRAPHICAL ASSOCIATION, DEPT. TT, 343 FULWOOD ROAD, SHEFFIELD, S10 3BP

honorary secretary, publications and communications
Publications *Geography*, quarterly; *Teaching Geography*, quarterly; *GA News*, quarterly; *Primary Geographer*, 3 times a year
Contribution Consultation; raising theoretical curricular questions; provision of resource material; organising meetings and courses; producing discussion papers; National Educational Resources Information Service (NERIS)
Projects and curriculum initiatives
1 Geography in the national curriculum (ongoing, all phases).
▼ Reports/evaluations; books; resource materials; policy documents; discussion documents
2 Primary geographer (ongoing, 4–13 age group).
▼ Resource materials
3 National Education Resources Information Service (NERIS) (ongoing, all phases).
▼ Resource materials
4 Geographical Association Topics: Energy (GATE) (ongoing, all phases).
▼ Reports/evaluations; resource materials
Objectives The GA, founded in 1893, is a subject teaching association of national and international standing. It has about 8000 members and 70 branches in England, Wales

and Northern Ireland. Its Council, Standing Committees, Section Committees, Working Groups and Working Parties are all active in responding to matters affecting teachers of geography in schools and colleges.
The association is working to safeguard and extend recognition of Geography's contribution to education at all levels, and in particular as a foundation subject in the National Curriculum. It has been particularly active in this respect and produced a discussion paper entitled 'Geography in the National Curriculum' prior to the setting up of the DES Working Group, as well as commenting on links between Geography and the core subjects, other foundation subjects and cross-curricular themes.
Through its regular journals, *Geography* and *Teaching Geography*, and the Newsletter, it keeps its members informed of research, world changes and problems, practical ideas for geography in the classroom, new curricular developments, uses of new technology and reviews of new publications and resources. *Primary Geographer* was launched in 1989, to help teachers meet the new demands of the national curriculum in infant, primary and middle schools. The association also produces a variety of professional and specialist publications.
A conference is held annually in London after

Easter, with lectures and workshops as well as an extensive exhibition of new books, visual aids, computer software and other materials for geography and related areas. The finals of the Worldwide Quiz take place during the annual conference. This is organised for under-16 year olds to test in a light-hearted and enjoyable manner that area of general knowledge which might be expected to be background for most pupils by the time they leave school.

GA branches, spread widely across the country, organise varied programmes, including INSET courses, conferences and careers conventions, to meet the needs of local teachers and sixth form students.

19. Geologists' Association – GA
Burlington Hse, Piccadilly, London W1V 9AG (and 10 local groups)
☎ 071 434 9298
Ⓟ Honorary general secretary
Publications *Proceedings of the Geologists' Association*, 4 times a year; *GA Circular*, 6 times a year; Directory, revised every other year; Guides, 1–2 a year
Contribution Raising theoretical curricular questions; provision of resource material; organising meetings and courses
Projects and curriculum initiatives
1 Writhlington coal measure study (ongoing).
■ To investigate insect fossils found in Writhlington coal measure
▼ Reports/evaluations; policy documents
2 Code for coring (ongoing).
To produce a code of conduct for those using portable drills
3 Science of earth (ongoing)
▼ Resource materials
Comment This project is funded with ATG for the GCSE.
4 Regional Guides (itineraries) (ongoing).
▼ 25 regional guides
Objectives The GA exists to promote Geology as an interest for amateurs through publication in straightforward, non-technical language. It also teaches through field excursions, in urban areas as well as the countryside.
Buildings in city streets and towns are a focus of attention, as are churchyards and cemeteries.
Conservation work of a wide range is funded by use of a curry fund. 3000 tons of coal shale were purchased from Writhlington for careful study. Local museums have been help, and 'codes of conduct' for geology have been produced by the GA. Science of earth booklets for GCSE projects were a joint GA–Teachers of Geology initiative.

20. Historical Association – HA
59A Kennington Park Rd, London SE11 4JH (and 80 regional centres).
☎ 071 735 3901
Ⓟ Ms Madeline Styles, Association secretary
Publications *The Historian*, quarterly;

Teaching History, quarterly; *History*, 3 times a year; pamphlets.
Contribution Consultation; organising meetings and courses; producing discussion papers; producing assessment materials
Projects and curriculum initiatives
1 History in the curriculum (ongoing, 5–16 age group).
▼ Reports/evaluations; discussion documents
2 Advanced certificate/diploma in the teaching of history (ongoing, 5–16 age group).
▼ Policy documents
3 Young historian Scheme (ongoing, 14–16 age group).
▼ Books
Objectives The Historical Association is the major subject teaching association for history teachers, and membership is open to all with an interest in history. It was founded in 1906 and its principal aim is to further the study and teaching of history at all levels. It publishes *History*, *Teaching History*, the annual bulletin of historical literature, and a magazine sent free to members, *The Historian*. The HA has a very wide range of publications including 'Teaching of History' series, occasional papers, and Young Historian GCSE projects. It organises conferences and meetings for teachers including a special series on history in the national curriculum.

21. Institute of Biology – IOB
20 Queensbury Place, London SW7 2DZ
☎ 071 581 8333   Ⓕ 071 823 9409
Ⓟ Education officer
Publications *Biologist,* 5 times a year *Journal of Biological Education*, quarterly
Contribution Consultation; organising meetings and courses; producing discussion papers
Objectives IOB is a professional body representing all biologists in the UK. Its main contribution to development of the curriculum lies in the area of responding to consultation documents.

22. Institute of Home Economics Ltd
Aldwych Hse, 71–91 Aldwych, London WC2B 4HN
☎ 071 404 5532
Ⓟ Honorary secretary

23. Institute of Linguists Educational Trust
24a Highbury Grove, London N5 2EA
☎ 071 359 7445/6386
Ⓟ General secretary

24. Institute of Mathematics and its Applications – IMA
Maitland Hse, Warrior Square, Southend-on-Sea, Essex SS1 2JY
☎ 0702 612177   Ⓕ 0702 612610
Ⓟ Miss Catherine Richards, Secretary and Registrar
Publications *Bulletin*, 8 times a year *Teaching Mathematics and its Applications*, 4

times a year newsletter; 5 other research journals

Contribution Consultation; raising theoretical curricular questions; provision of resource material; organising meetings and courses; producing discussion papers

Objectives The IMA aims to promote mathematics at all levels and in any way possible. The Institute's Council frequently provides informed and authoritative comment on educational policy statements and other educational initiatives. In doing so it draws upon the experience and expertise of members who are directly involved in education and also members from industry, commerce and government. The Institute has an education group which organises conferences, workshops and other activities for members and non-members. This group also produces a newsletter three times a year. The Institute has a schools liaison scheme for teachers who wish to be affiliated to the education group.

25. Institute of Physics – IoP
47 Belgrave Square, London SW1X 8QX
☎ 071 235 6111
Ⓟ Education officer

26. Integrated Humanities Association
43 Blake Rd, Stapleford, Nottingham NG9 6HP
Ⓟ Mr G. Fowler

27. Joint Association of Classical Teachers – JACT
31–34 Gordon Square, London WC1H OPY
☎ 071 387 0348
Ⓟ Ms Lorna Kellett, Executive secretary
Publications *Bulletin*, termly; *JACT Review*, twice a year,; *Omnibus*, twice a year; *Minibus*, twice a year.
Contribution to curriculum development. Consultation; raising theoretical curricular questions; provision of resource material; organising meetings and courses; producing discussion papers
Projects and curriculum initiatives
1 Classics 5–13 – the contribution Classics can make to the core curriculum (1988–90, 5–13 age group).
▼ Resource materials
2 Reading Greek (ongoing, 16–18 age group).
▼ Books
3 Examination syllabuses in Greek, Ancient History and Classical Civilisation (ongoing, 16–18 age group and adult).
▼ Examination syllabuses and papers
Objectives JACT was founded in 1962 in the belief that classical studies has something of irreplaceable value to contribute to the education of all pupils. It feels that the future of the subject depends on the quality of teaching and on the ability of teachers to reinterpret the traditional discipline in terms appropriate to the present. In addition to its regular publications, it appoints working

parties and committees for specific purposes (eg curriculum, aural and visual aids) and sponsors new syllabuses. It provides an information service for teachers at all levels, promotes local activities and organises summer schools in Greek, Latin and Classical Civilisation for beginners and other students.

28. Mathematical Association – MA
259 London Rd, Leicester LE2 3BE
☎ 0533 703877
Ⓟ Mr Alan Ward, Executive secretary
Publications *Mathematical Gazette*, quarterly; *Mathematics in Schools*, 5 times a year; *Struggle*, termly; *Mathematics round the country*, termly; Newsletter, termly
Contribution Consultation; raising theoretical curricular questions; provision of resource material; organising meetings and courses; producing discussion papers; producing assessment materials; validation of awards
Projects and curriculum initiatives
1 Diploma in Mathematical Education 5–13, (ongoing, 5–13 age group).
▼ Reports/evaluations; resource materials; policy documents; discussion documents
2 Diploma: low attainers in mathematics (ongoing, all phases).
▼ Reports/evaluations; resource materials; policy documents; discussion documents
3 Diploma for heads of secondary departments (ongoing, secondary phase).
▼ Reports/evaluations; resource materials; policy documents; discussion documents
Objectives The MA serves those interested in mathematics and the teaching of mathematics in the following ways: through journals (4 for teachers and 2 for pupils); through a termly newsletter; through regular reports on various aspects of the teaching of mathematics; through conferences organised by the Association; through the validation of diplomas; through representation on national bodies; and through occasional publications and as a forum for advice.

29. Music Advisers National Association
Avon House North, St James Barton, Bristol BS99 7EB
☎ 0272 290777
Ⓟ Secretary

30. National Association for Design Education – NADE
Kirby Hill, Plawsworth, Chester-le-Street, Durham DH2 3LD
☎ 091 371 1236
Ⓟ Mr David Buchan, Honorary general secretary
Publications *NADE journal*, once or twice a year; *NADE Newsletter*, 3 or 4 times a year
Contribution Consultation; raising theoretical curricular questions; organising meetings and courses; producing discussion papers
Projects and curriculum initiatives
1 Developments in the primary field –

conference (1988, primary phase).
▼   Reports/evaluations
2   Design education and the national
curriculum – conference (1988, all phases).
▼   Reports/evaluations
3   Assessment and its implications –
conference (1988, all phases).
▼   Reports/evaluations
4   Computers in art and design –
conference (1988, all phases).
▼   Reports/evaluations
Objectives   NADE is a voluntary
organisation representing teachers as well as
some members of design-related professions.
Interested in education at all age levels and in
curriculum development, most members are
teachers/lecturers in art and design, CDT, or
home economics in primary, secondary,
further or higher education. It is the only
organisation active in promoting design and
technology education across the curriculum
and as a problem-centred curriculum subject
in its own right. NADE publishes a journal and
a newsletter containing articles and reports
relating to these matters. Usually 2 or 3
conferences are organised annually in
different parts of the country including an
AGM in November.
NADE is consulted by official bodies (eg
SEAC, RIBA and examination boards) and
maintains regular contact with the DES and
the Design Council Education Section. It has
been well-placed in contributing to the
development of design and technology in
connection with the national curriculum
proposals and has presented oral as well as
written evidence to the Working Group in that
subject area. In addition, written responses
have been submitted to reports issued by the
working Groups in English, science and
mathematics.
NADE is at present involved in an initiative to
establish a new association which will cater
for teachers of design and technology when
the new subject becomes established as part
of the national curriculum.

31. National Association for Education in the Arts – NAEA
13 Back Lane, South Luffenham, Oakham,
Leicestershire LE15 8NQ
☎   0780 721115
℗   Ms Linad Cummins, Secretary
Publications   Take-up series (once or twice
a year)
Contribution   Raising theoretical curricular
questions; organising meetings and courses;
producing discussion papers
Objectives   The NAEA was founded in 1983
to promote and advance the understanding,
practice and status of the arts in education. By
the arts, the association means dance, drama,
music, the visual arts, literature and the
media. Although the arts are diverse in their
traditions and practices within the context of
education there is a strong case for close
collaboration on matters of common concern.
NEAE works for close relations between those

with different interests within arts education, to
influence education decision-making at all
levels and to provide a forum in which
members may share experience and
exchange views and information.

32. National Association for Environmental Education – NAEE
West Midlands College of HE, Gorway,
Walsall WS1 3BD
☎   0922 31200
℗   Mr Philip Neal, General secretary
Publications   *Environmental Education*,
termly
Contribution   Consultation; provision of
resource materials; organising meetings and
courses; producing discussion papers
Projects and curriculum initiatives
1   Planning and implementing the
environmental curriculum in primary and
secondary schools (1986–7, 5–18 age group).
▼   Reports/evaluations
Objectives   The NAEE is the association of
teachers, lecturers and other concerned with
education and the environment. Its members
work in all types of schools, colleges,
polytechnics and universities. They include
representatives of all the disciplines involved
in environmental education from both the
sciences and the humanities.
The Association has produced 'A Statement of
Aims' setting out the objectives of
environmental education at all levels in detail
and it also produces journals, newsletters, a
series of practical teachers' guides and other
publications. National conferences are held
regularly, to which come educationalists and
leading speakers on national and worldwide
environmental problems. Members are
encouraged to help in study conferences or
working parties to carry out research,
construct syllabuses or suggest practical
teaching methods.
In addition the association, either on its own
account or through the Council for
Environmental Education, continually presses
for financial or other help for environmental
education in schools through the DES,
examination boards and LEAs. It is particularly
concerned to encourage teacher training in
environmental education. The association acts
as a channel for outside bodies to help
teachers of environmental education with
information and materials.

33. National Association for Outdoor Education
National Advice and Information Centre,
Doncaster Metropolitan Institute of Higher
Education, High Melton, Doncaster DN1 3EX
℗   Director

34. National Association of Language Advisers
Curriculum Development Centre, Church
Lane, Princes Plain, Bromley, Kent BR2 8LD
☎   081 462 6229

Ⓟ Honorary secretary

35. National Association of Mathematics Advisers

Education Department, Northampton Hse,
Northampton NN1 2HX
☎ 0604 236248
Ⓟ Secretary

36. National Association for the Teaching of English – NATE

Birley Street Annexe, Fox Lane, Sheffield S12 4WY
☎ 0742 390081
Ⓟ Mr Martin Senior, Development officer
Publications *English in Education*, termly;
Newsletter, termly
Contribution Consultation; raising
theoretical curricular questions; provision of
resource material; organising meetings and
courses; producing discussion papers;
producing assessment materials
Projects and curriculum initiatives
1 English assessment: writing – what can
be assessed? (1989–90, 5–16 age group).
▼ Reports/evaluations
2 English 12–16: developing resources
(1988, 12–16 age group).
▼ Books; resource materials
3 English language and gender issues
(ongoing, all phases).
▼ Books; resource materials; policy
documents; discussion documents
4 English multicultural issues (ongoing, all
phases).
▼ Resource materials; policy documents;
discussion documents
Objectives NATE provides a support
service for teachers of English including an
information service, regular publications,
national and regional conferences, local
branch activities, and a national voice.
Working parties operate regularly to formulate
policy, reappraise curricula, and prepare
resources for various age groups and areas of
interest, such as assessment, language and
gender, drama, IT, and multicultural matters.

37. National Association of Language Advisers – NALA

Curriculum Development Centre, Church
Lane, Princes Plain, Bromley, Kent BR2 8LD
☎ 081 462 6229
Ⓟ Mr Jeffrey G. Lee, Honorary secretary
Publications *NALA Newsletter*, twice a
year; Journal, twice a year
Contribution Consultation; organising
meetings and courses; producing discussion
papers
Projects and curriculum initiatives
1 Diversification of first foreign languages:
national survey (1989–90, secondary phase).
▼ Reports/evaluations
2 Foreign language assistants: NALA and
Central Bureau Working Group (ongoing,
secondary phase).
▼ Books; discussion documents
3 Equipping the languages classroom for

the 1990s (1987–9, secondary).
▼ Books
4 National curriculum submission to
subject working group (1989, secondary).
▼ Discussion documents
Objectives NALA counts among its 200 or
so members the vast majority of LEA
advisers, inspectors and advisory teachers
working in the field of foreign languages, as
well as others in allied fields of activity.
As an association, NALA operates both
nationally and regionally, holding an annual
course and termly meetings in each of the six
regions. It responds to consultative policy
documents from DES, HMI, NCC, SEAC, etc.
There are close working links with CILT, the
Central Bureau, JCLA, foreign institutes and
embassies, as well as with HMI through
meetings nationally and regionally and
through jointly mounted INSET.
In the field of assessment NALA has played a
key role in the development of graded
objectives, GCSE national criteria, GCSE
modular and Mode 3 initiatives and in testing
at 18 plus. NALA members serve as
consultants/representatives on various bodies
responsible for curriculum development,
examinations and assessment.
NALA working groups have produced
handbooks on 'Foreign languages in the
curriculum to 16', 'Using the foreign language
assistant', 'The scheme of work', 'The role of
the head of department', and, most recently,
'Equipping the languages classroom for the
1990s'. NALA regional groups promote
collaborative projects, often of a cross-
curricular nature within, for example, TVEI
extension and Records of Achievement.
NALA members have a responsibility for
curriculum development as part of their duties
within LEAs. This includes (dependent upon
precise status) monitoring and evaluation,
provision and management of INSET and,
where appropriate, specific curriculum
projects and production of resources. They
may facilitate and manage secondment of
teachers assigned to curriculum development
work either as an LEA initiative or within a
national context. Close contact is maintained
with publishers and language teachers'
associations. NALA is thus responsible for
developing LEA curricular policies and helping
teachers to implement these within an overall
national framework for modern languages
teaching.

38. National Association of Teachers of Home Economics

Hamilton Hse, Mabledon Place, London
WC1H 9BJ
☎ 071 387 1441   Ⓕ 071 383 7230
Ⓟ General Manager

39. National Congress on Languages in Education and Training NCLE

21 Webster Gdns, London W5 5NA
☎ 081 567 6159
Ⓟ Mr T. Cooper, Secretary
Publications *NCLE Newsletter*, intermittent

Contribution   Raising theoretical curricular questions; organising meetings and courses; producing discussion papers.
Projects and curriculum initiatives
1   Company foreign language policy in mainland Europe (1988–9, adult).
▼   Proceedings of NCLE conferences
2   Realising the UK's linguistic resources in response to the National Curriculum (1989–90, secondary phase).
Objectives   NCLE is an organisation for professional language associations, educational boards and institutions and other groups and units in education, commerce and industry. It provides a framework which enables language specialists of all interests to pool experience and to undertakes joint research beyond the parameters of their individual subject areas.
NCLE seeks to provide, through conferences and research, factual evidence as a basis for policy-making in language teaching and training and to create a forum for the discussions of future needs and actions.
It embraces English as a mother tongue, English as a foreign language, the languages of minority communities, applied linguistics and modern foreign languages.

40. National Society for Education in Art and Design – NSEAD

7A High St, Corsham, Wiltshire SN13 OES
☎   0249 714825   ℱ   0249 716138
℗   Mr John Steers, General secretary
Publications   Newsletter, 6 times a year; *Journal of Art and Design Education,* termly; information booklets
Contribution   Consultation; raising theoretical curricular questions; provision of resource material; organising meetings and courses; producing discussion papers
Projects and curriculum initiatives
1   Introducing computers in art, craft and design (1987–9, 11–18 age group).
▼   Books
2   GCSE art and design (1988–9, 14–16 age group).
▼   Discussion documents
3   Maskwork (1989–90, 5–16 age group).
▼   Resource materials
Objectives   NSEAD exists to promote and defend art, craft and design education and the professional interests of those engaged in it. It is the only educational organisation which is able to draw on the expertise of members from all sectors of education from primary schools to the universities in this specific subject area. It has both formal and informal contacts throughout its field, including links with all official bodies, major associations and organisations in this subject area in the UK. It provides a major national and international forum for the dissemination of information, ideas, practical developments and research findings in art, craft and design education.

41. Nature Conservancy Council (Earth Science Division) – NCC-ESD

Northminster Hse, Peterborough, Cambridgeshire PE1 1UA

☎   0733 40345
℗   Administrative officer, Earth science division
Publications   *Earth Science Conservation,* twice yearly
Contribution   Provision of resource materials, including field guides and fact sheets
Projects and curriculum initiatives
1   Earth science fieldwork in the secondary school curriculum (1987–8. 11–16 age group).
▼   Book (teachers' manual of the same name)
2   The making of modern Britain (1988–91, 11–16 age group).
▼   A series of 15 booklets, in preparation
Objectives   The Nature Conservancy Council is the government body which promotes nature conservancy in Great Britain and its work is based on the identification and protection of sites of special scientific interest and the management of national nature reserves. The safeguard of geological and geomorphological sites is part of the NCC's statutory responsibility and this work is coordinated by its Earth Science Division. A range of publications has been developed by the Earth Science Division, many of which are of value to earth science teachers.

42. Physical Education Association – PEA

Ling Hse, 162 Kings Cross Rd, London WC1H 9DH
☎   071 278 9311
℗   Ms Joan Milton, Information officer
Publications   *British Journal of Physical Education,* quarterly.
Contribution   Raising theoretical curricular questions; provision of resource material; producing discussion papers; producing assessment materials
Projects and curriculum initiatives
1   Health related fitness (ongoing, all phases).
Comment   This project is run jointly with HEA.
Objectives   The Physical Education Association of Great Britain and Northern Ireland keeps members informed of developments in assessment of children and the curriculum in the area of physical education through its quarterly publication. The journal is read not only by members but by a high proportion of physical educationists. The Association also runs conferences from time to time on assessment. A recent example is a conference on Assessment and Profiling in 1989 which attracted over 100 members. A conference report is obtainable from the association.
PEA has been involved in the setting up of an interim working party for physical education in the national curriculum. Part of its work will be to consider the role and nature of assessment of PE within the national curriculum.

43. Politics Association – PA

16 Gower St, London WC1E 6DP (and 5 regional centres)

☎ 071 323 1131
ⓟ Mr Geoffrey Prout, Chairman
Publications *Talking Politics*, termly;
Grassroots, termly
Contribution Consultation; raising
theoretical curricular questions; provision of
resource material; organising meetings and
courses; producing discussion papers
Projects and curriculum initiatives
1 Political Education in the National
Curriculum (1989–90, 5–16 age group).
▼ Books; resource materials; policy
documents
Objectives The Politics Association is the
professional teachers' association in the UK
concerned with the promotion of the study and
teaching of politics (both the theory and the
practice). It organises a major annual
conference in September each year and
meetings for teachers in regional centres
around the country. It also organises day
conferences for sixth form students of Politics
and General Studies in London, Manchester,
Oxford, Sheffield and Leicester, as well as the
annual Revision Course (1 week) at the
University of Manchester (April). The Politics
Association Resources Bank (PARB) provides
written, audio and video resources for
teachers and students. The association is able
to offer advice/assistance to groups of
teachers, advisers, and LEAs on all aspects of
Political Education.

44. Religious Education Council – REC

St Martin's College, Lancaster LA1 3JD
☎ 0524 63446
ⓟ Dr Brian Gates, Chairperson
Contribution Consultation; raising
theoretical curricular questions; producing
discussion papers
Projects and curriculum initiatives
1 Religious education, values and worship
(1988–9, 5–18 age group).
▼ Reports/evaluations
2 RE teachers: supply for the 1990s (1988,
5–16 age group).
▼ Reports/evaluations
Objectives The REC is involved in
consultations on RE school provision, about
the expectations of the faith communities, and
about government resourcing. It makes
representations to the DES, HMI, and LEAs
on conditions of RE provision and future
needs.

45. Royal Society

6 Carlton House Terrace, London SW1Y 5AG
☎ 071 839 5561 ⓕ 071 930 2170
ⓟ Ms Jill A. Nelson, Education officer
Publications Ad hoc reports on educational
issues
Contribution Raising theoretical curricular
questions; producing discussion papers
Objectives The Royal Society is concerned
with policy for science education at all levels.
It focuses on the science curriculum, on

assessment of performance, on the supply
and training of teachers, and on resources.

46. Royal Society of Chemistry – RSC

Burlington Hse, Piccadilly, London W1V OBN
☎ 071 437 8656 ⓣ 268001
ⓕ 071 437 8883
ⓟ Dr N. V. Reed, Schools liaison officer
Publications *Chemistry in Britain*, monthly;
Education in Chemistry, 6 times a year
Contribution Consultation; raising
theoretical curricular questions; provision of
resource material; organising meetings and
courses; producing discussion papers
Projects and curriculum initiatives
1 industry study tours (ongoing, 11–18 age
group).
▼ Reports/evaluations
2 Chemical egg races (1986–91, 7–18 age
group).
▼ Resource materials
3 Core content for post 16 chemistry
courses (1986–9, 16–18 age group).
▼ Policy documents
4 School publication service (ongoing,
11–18 age group).
▼ Books; resource materials
Objectives The Royal Society of Chemistry
is the professional qualifying body for
chemistry in the United Kingdom with a
membership of over 40,000. Its charter
requires it to foster and encourage the growth
of chemical science by the dissemination of
chemical knowledge. As such, the Society is
regularly consulted by the DES, NCC, SEAC
and other major policy-making bodies.
The Society regularly enters into consultations
with interested parties about curriculum policy-
making, the production of discussion
documents and guidelines, and the running of
meetings and courses. Within the Society the
Education Division coordinates the activities
with respect to education. The Division has 9
regions and 5 subject groups with interests in
the curriculum, assessment, tertiary
education, chemical research, and
educational techniques. The education
department of the Society has a range of
activities targeted at schools including one-
day symposia for teachers, free careers
literature and posters, chemical egg races,
and organising the International Chemistry
Olympiad team for the UK.

47. Standing Conference on Schools' Science and Technology

1 Birdcage Walk, London SW1H 9JJ
☎ 071 222 7899
ⓟ Secretary

48. United Kingdom Council for Music Education and Training – UKCMET

13 Back Lane, South Luffenham, Oakham,
Leicestershire LE15 8NQ
☎ 0780 721115

Curriculum Handbook

Ⓟ   Ms Linda Cummins, Secretary
Publications   Newsletter, termly
Contribution   Consultation; raising
theoretical curricular questions; organising
meetings and courses; producing discussion
papers; producing assessment materials
Projects and curriculum initiatives
1   Standing committee on the school
curriculum (ongoing, all phases).
▼   Discussion document (National
curriculum for music)

2   Standing committee on examinations
and assessment in music (ongoing, 5–18 age
group).
▼   Discussion documents
Objectives   UKCMET advises the Secretary
of State and NCC on issues concerning the
music curriculum and on aspects of music.
education which concern other areas of the
curriculum. It also advises the Secretary of
State, HMI, and SEAC on matters concerned
with examinations and assessment in music.

Section 5

Curriculum Initiatives from Groups Concerned with the Whole-School Curriculum Development

Curriculum Handbook

This section contains details of major organisations which have an interest in the whole curriculum in schools. They vary from, at one end, groups which are primarily interested in schools and their curricula to, at the other end, groups which exist for other, specific reasons (for example, religious bodies), but have a very real interest in what is taught and learned in schools.

Some of the organisations in this section are large, but there are also very small, but important, associations which are inevitably difficult to contact. Some of these depend on voluntary officers who change from year to year, and operate from their homes or workplaces. One wonders how the National Curriculum Council manages to contact all the bodies they are statutorily required to consult. If an umbrella organisation, as suggested in the introduction to section 4, were to be developed, it could help with these associations too.

Because of their varied nature, the organisations in this section play very different, active roles in the curriculum debate. Some of them run or sponsor major Research and Development projects, but quite a large proportion play an essentially reactive role, responding to national discussion papers and initiatives. Although they all share an interest in the curriculum as a whole, they work in contrasting ways.

1. Advisory Centre for Education – ACE
18 Victoria Park Square, Bethnal Green, London E2 9PB
☎ 081 980 4596
Publications *ACE Bulletin*, 6 times a year; information sheets; occasional publications.
Objectives : ACE is funded by charitable donations and revenue raised from sales of ACE publications. It is entirely independent of central and local government and offers free advice and support to parents of children in state-maintained schools. ACE works for a more open and more responsive education service; one that values all children irrespective of ability, and which seeks to work in a genuine partnership with pupils and parents.

2. Arts Council
105 Piccadilly, London W1V OAU
☎ 071 629 9495   ⓣ 9312102069 AC G
ⓕ 071 355 4389

3. Assistant Masters and Mistresses Association – AMMA
7 Northumberland St, London WC2N 5DA
☎ 071 930 6441 and 071 782 0160
ⓕ 071 782 0070
ⓟ Ms Joyce Baird and Mr. Peter Smith, Joint secretaries
Publications *Report*, 9 issues a year; Update, broadsheet
Contribution Consultation: raising theoretical curricular questions; organising meetings and courses

Objectives AMMA is a teachers' organisation of over 130,000 members in all types of educational establishments, both maintained and independent, ranging from infants through primary and secondary to tertiary, sixth form and further education colleges. There are 109 branches conterminous with LEA boundaries. The association is consulted by major policy-making bodies including DES, HMI, SEAC, NNC, and is represented on Examining Boards and Groups. AMMA regularly organises conferences on educational issues and, through its publications keeps members informed of current curriculum developments.

4. Association for all Speech-impaired Children – AFASIC
347 Central Markets, Smithfield, London EC1A 9NH
☎ 071 236 3632
ⓟ Ms Norma Corkish, director
Publications Newsletter, 3 times a year
Contribution Consultation: organising meetings and courses
Objectives The AFASIC is concerned to ensure that children with speech and/or language disorders can benefit from mainstream education and the national curriculum. It responds, therefore, to government proposals, contributes where possible to Working Parties, initiates teacher training, and organises meetings to discuss relevant issues.

5. Association for the Education and Welfare of the Visually Handicapped
St Vincents School, Yew Tree Lane, West Derby, Liverpool L12 9HN
☎ 051 228 9968
ⓟ Mrs S. Clamp, secretary

6. Association of Career Teachers – ACT
Hillsboro, Castledine St, Loughborough, Leicestershire LE11 2DX   (and 2 regional centres)
☎ 0509 214617
ⓟ Miss R. Yaffe, General secretary
Publications Report, quarterly
Contribution Consultation: raising theoretical curricular questions; organising meetings and courses; producing discussion papers

7. Association of Commonwealth Teachers
42 Camborne Ave, London W13 9QZ
☎ 081 567 3221
ⓟ Mr C.J. Thamoram, General secretary

8. Association of Educational Psychologists
3 Sunderland Rd, Durham DH1 2LH
☎ 091 384 9512
ⓟ Ms Ann Baumber, Honorary secretary

9. Association of Workers for Maladjusted Children – AWMC

Red Hill School, East Sutton, Maidstone, Kent ME17 3DQ (and 7 regional centres)
☎ 0622 843104
℗ Mr A.J. Rimmer, General secretary
Publications *Maladjustment and Therapeutic Education*, 3 times a year
Contribution Consultation; raising theoretical curricular questions; organising meetings and courses. Nature of contribution of the organisation. AWMC is a cross-disciplinary organisation. As such it is not in a position to engage in formal contributions to curriculum. However, many members do so in their professional capacities.

10. Board of Deputies of British Jews

Woburn Hse, Upper Woburn Place, London WC1H OEP
℗ Mr Stuart Polak, Education officer

11. British Association for Early Childhood Education – BAECE

111 City View Hse, 463 Bethnal Green Rd, London E2 9QY (and 53 regional centres)
☎ 071 739 7594
℗ Mrs Barbara Boon, Secretary
Publications *News from BAECE*, 3 times a year
Contribution Consultation; raising theoretical curricular questions; provision of resource material; organising meetings and courses; producing discussion papers
Projects and curriculum initiatives
1 Questionnaire to all nursery schools in England and Wales: 'Nursery schools: centres of excellence' (1988–89, 3–5 age group)
▼ Currently being collated
2 The 4 year-old in the classroom (1986–7, 4 year-olds)
▼ Report/evaluation
3 Can early entrants catch up? (1990–1, 7 year-olds).
▼ Still at the pilot study stage
4 Competencies and skills in relation to age and maturity (1989–90, 3–8 age group).
▼ Discussion documents
Objectives BAECE (formerly the Nursery School Association) was established in 1923 and is concerned with the welfare and education of young children. It undertakes research, publishes advisory material for teachers, nursery staff and parents, and arranges national conferences and seminars. Regular programmes of meetings are held in 53 local branches in England, Ireland, Scotland and Wales.
The Association is concerned with the quality and standard of educational provision for children from 0 to 9 years, and is increasingly consulted by national committees and enquiries and asked to provide evidence on current educational issues. Members are involved in action research on curriculum and assessment of children, particularly in the development of skills and competencies, and in representing the association on national committees.

12. British Association for Commercial and Industrial Education

16 Park Crescent, London W1N 4AP
☎ 071 636 5351
℗ Mr R.W. Lyne, Secretary

13. British Association of Teachers of the Deaf – BATOD

Icknield High School H.I.U., Riddy Lane, Luton, Bedfordshire LU3 2AH (and 7 regional centres)
☎ 0582 596599
℗ Ms Sandra Dowe, Honorary secretary
Publications *The Journal of the British Association of Teachers of the Deaf*, 5 times a year.
Contribution Consultation: raising theoretical curricular questions; provision of resource material; organising meetings and courses; producing discussion papers; involvement in teacher training for the mandatory qualification for teaching the deaf (based at Birmingham University)
Projects and curriculum initiatives
1 Response to NCC (1988, 5–16 age group).
■ To respond to the national curriculum science proposals
▼ Report/evaluation
2 Response to NCC (1988, 5–16 age group).
■ To respond to the national curriculum mathematics proposals
▼ Report/evaluation
3 Response to NCC (1989, 5–16 age group).
■ To respond to the national curriculum English proposals
▼ Report/evaluation
4 The national curriculum implications for hearing-impaired children: a national conference (1989, 5–16 age group).
■ A one day conference to consider the implications of the national curriculum with regard to the special educational needs of hearing-impaired children
▼ None
Objectives The association promotes the education of all hearing-impaired children, young persons and adults, whatever their degree of hearing loss or educational potential. It is concerned with initial and further training of teachers of the deaf as a means of ensuring that pupils/students are served by teachers who have studied their needs and can give them access to the full national curriculum.

14. British Council of Churches Religious Education Consultative Group of Committee for Relations with People of Other Faiths – CRPOFREG

Inter-Church Hse, 35–41 Lower Marsh, London SE1 7RL
☎ 071 620 4444 ℉ 071 620 0719
℗ Rev Vlinton Bennett, Executive secretary
Publications *Discernment*, quarterly

Contribution Consultation: provision of resource material; producing discussion papers
Projects and curriculum initiatives
1 Educational principles in religious education (1985–6, all ages).
▼ Policy documents
2 School worship (1986–9, all ages).
■ To produce resources for worship in education
▼ Books, discussion documents
Objectives The Group's main contribution is in the policy area, with particular emphasis on the teaching of RE, within the multi-faith context. It is able to comment on DES circulars and on draft legislation from a specifically Christian point of view. Members include people employed by LEAs and HE institutions as well as by Church agencies. The Group is prepared to advise SACREs if requested. It is also able to produce a limited number of resources which are tested before publication.

15. British Dyslexia Association – BDA
98 London Rd, Reading, Berkshire RG1 5AU (and 77 regional centres)
☎ 0734 668271 Ⓕ 0734 351927
Ⓟ Ms Jean Augur, Education officer
Publications *Dyslexia Contact*, twice a year
Contribution Consultation; organising meetings and courses; producing discussion papers
Projects and curriculum initiatives
1 BDA Diploma for teachers of those with special learning difficulties (on-going, all ages).
▼ Syllabus
Nature of contribution of the organisation
The association is presently working on: criteria for examination allowances for children with literacy problems; early identification of children with literacy problems; and assessment of children's literacy problems.

16. British Institute of Management – BIM
Management Hse, Cottingham Rd, Corby, Northants NN17 1TT (and 9 regional centres)
☎ 0536 204222 Ⓕ 0536 201651
Ⓟ Ms Elsa Davies, Education liaison manager
Publications *Management News*, 10 times a year
Contribution Consultation; organising meetings and courses; producing discussion papers; membership of national working groups
Projects and curriculum initiatives
1 BIM management challenge (management education) (annually, 6th Form and FE age groups).
▼ Resource materials
2 Management awareness (pilot in 1989, 11–16 age group).
▼ In preparation
Objectives BIM is the major management

organisation in the country. It is interested in those aspects of the education system which are of relevance and interest to Britain's managers. As well as the development of education management practice, BIM seeks to influence curricular development through consultation and collaboration with local and national government on new and developing initiatives. It also works with other groups in encouraging education business partnerships involving a variety of activities. BIM's major national competition, 'Management Challenge', provides a sophisticated learning tool based on business decisions for sixth form and FE students. BIM has over 70,000 members in 103 local Branches throughout the United Kingdom. The majority of these Branches engage in education liaison activities which support the work of schools. Some of this activity focuses on school and college government as many BIM members are governors.

17. British Youth Council
57 Chalton St, London NW1 1HU
☎ 071 387 7559/5882
Ⓟ Mr N. Sloggie, Secretary general

18. Campaign for the Advancement of State Education – CASE
The Grove, 110 High St, Sawston, Cambridge CB2 4HJ
☎ 0223 833179
Ⓟ Ms Sue Hodgson, Honorary secretary
Publications *Parents and Schools*, 3 times a year
Contribution Consultation; raising theoretical curricular questions; organising meetings and courses; producing discussion papers.
Projects and curriculum initiatives
1 The National Curriculum (5–16 age group).
▼ Briefing Paper
2 Complaints procedures under the 1988 Education Act (5–16 age groups).
▼ Briefing paper
Objectives The Campaign is concerned to improve by all possible means the provision and quality of state education. Much of the work over recent years has consisted of responding to government requests for consultation concerning the introduction of the national curriculum and changes in the management of schools.

19. Careers Research and Advisory Centre – CRAC
Sheraton Hse, Castle Park, Cambridge CB3 OAX
☎ 0223 460277 Ⓣ 94011229 CRAC G
Ⓕ 0223 311708
Ⓟ Mr John Rushton, Projects Manager
Contribution Consultation; raising theoretical curricular questions; provision of resource materials; organising meetings and courses; producing discussion papers.
Projects and curriculum initiatives
1 Learning for a changing world (1983, 12–16 age group).

■   A curriculum development project to
develop cross-curricular skills in teachers.
▼   Report/evaluation; resource materials;
policy documents.
2   Education and training programmes (ongoing, 10–18 age group).
■   To establish sound management
structures which provide insights and
understanding of adult and working life. This is
a series of projects.
▼   Reports/evaluations
3   CRAC insight programmes (on-going,
post-18 age group).
■   To improve student understanding of
business enterprise by short courses for
students and INSET for staff. This is the
leading national industry–education link
project.
▼   Reports/evaluations; resource materials
4   Enterprise in higher education (on-going,
post-18 age group).
■   To develop staff skills in encouraging
enterprise in general and particularly in areas
such as group work and problem-solving.
▼   Reports/evaluations, resource materials
Objectives   CRAC programmes are created
to assist LEAS and schools to carry through
good quality training initiatives. Companies
provide essential backing, assisting CRAC to
develop and deliver training projects which
become the blueprint for later repeat versions
which are run with local expertise.
CRAC provides responsive project
management of the whole process of staff
training in response to the ever-increasing
demand for INSET. Programmes support
individual development needs and aim to
integrate with other initiatives. In overall terms,
CRAC aims to develop: industry–education
relationship; curriculum relevance to adult and
working life; particular skills in management,
problem-solving and active learning
approaches. Methods include: concentration
on an activity-based approach,using small
teams; drawing on experienced support tutors
who help to reinforce the training message in
schools; a combination of training courses
with action-plans to achieve change.

20. Catholic Bishops' Conference of England and Wales [Department for Christian Doctrine and Formation]

39. Eccleston Square, London SW1V 1PD
☎   071 630 5101
ⓟ   Rev J.H. Stratton, Secretary
Contribution   Consultation; provision of
resource materials; producing discussion
papers.
Projects and curriculum initiatives
1   To enable Catholic schools to develop
their distinctive contribution for their pupils
(1988–, 5–16 age group).
■   To develop distinctive contributions,
particularly in religious, personal and social
education. This includes work on assessment
and Records of Achievement, through INSET
and teacher appraisal
▼   Resource materials
Objectives   The Department of Catholic

Education has been concerned to develop the
distinctive nature of Catholic schools, and
consequently has concentrated on the
production of guidelines for inservice
evaluation, and appraisal for Catholic schools.
It has also promoted a national RE
programme for schools.

21. Centre for Studies on Integration in Education – CSIE

4th Fl, 415 Edgware Rd, London NW2 6NB
☎   081 452 8642
ⓟ   through the Centre
Publications   Booklets; survey reports and
factsheets; details available on request
(please enclose SAE)
Contribution   Consultation; provision of
resource materials; organising meetings and
courses; producing discussion papers
Objectives   The Centre works to help raise
public, professional and political awareness
about the issue of integration in education and
to promote good practice in schools and
LEAs. It is concerned with the full range of
children and young people with disabilities or
those with difficulties in learning, and
promotes increased parental involvement in
their education.
It works by: producing and selling booklets,
survey reports and factsheets; collecting
information from LEAs, schools, colleges,
universities, parents and parent groups,
voluntary organisations, Government
Departments and from overseas; organising
national and regional conferences and other
meetings; offering a free advice service on law
and changing practices; working directly with
parents and people with disabilities; helping to
put in touch those running effective integration
with those who wish to do the same; working
with other organisations; producing evidence
for committees of enquiry; giving public talks
to a wide variety of audiences; acting as
consultants to LEAs, press and media and
voluntary organisations.

22. Centre for the Study of Comprehensive Schools – CSCS

University of York, Heslington, York YO1 5DD
(and 3 regional centres)
☎   0904 433240
ⓟ   Ms Liza Griffiths, Information officer
Publications   *All-in-Success*, termly
Contribution   Consultation; raising
theoretical curricular questions; provision of
resource material; organising meetings and
courses; producing discussion papers;
producing occasional publications offering
small curriculum development funding.
Projects and curriculum initiatives
1   Parent–school partnership – broadsheet
15 (ongoing, 11–18 age group).
▼   Reports/evaluations; discussion
documents; examples of school practice
2   Schools in the market place –
broadsheet 17 (ongoing, 11–18 age group).
▼   Discussion documents; examples of
school practice
3   Implementing technology across the

curriculum – broadsheet 18 (ongoing, 11–18 age group).
▼ Reports/evaluations; books; discussion documents; examples of school practice
4 The environmental challenges; problems and solutions – broadsheet 19 (ongoing, 11–18 age group).
▼ Discussion documents; examples of school practice
5 Expressive arts – broadsheet 26 (ongoing, 5–18 age group).
▼ Discussion documents; response to ERA
Objectives CSCS is a membership organisation, set up in 1981 by a group of teachers and industrialists who were concerned to improve the quality of comprehensive schools by the collection and dissemination of interesting school practice across the whole of school life. By opening up these practices to a wider public, CSCS has created a national database of interesting practice, produces a wide range of Broadsheets and publications and offers a programme of conferences, courses and seminars, and has established a regional organisation covering most of the UK.
CSCS provides a service to schools and LEAs in 4 main areas. *Cash*: the CSCS small-scale curriculum award scheme makes development grants of up to 1,000 available to individual schools. *Support*: CSCS members receive the journal, *All-in-Success* and Broadsheets in the form of teachers' guides on a range of contemporary issues from TVEI to relations with the media. *Consultancy*; CSCS has set up a consultancy service to help in the inservice training aspects of school management. The Centre can provide speakers, INSET packages and a variety of consultancy services. *Service*: at a time of rapid change there is need for a service which allows teachers to exchange information on a variety of different subjects and courses, on curriculum issues and on different approaches to organisation and management. CSCS Information Service provides an opportunity for this exchange.

23. Commission for Racial Equality – CRE
Elliot Hse, 10/12 Allington St, London SW1E 5EH (and 4 regional centres)
☎ 071 828 7022 Ⓕ 071 630 7606
Ⓟ Mr R.A. German, Principal education officer
Publications *New Community*, 4 times a year
Contribution Consultation; provision of resource materials; organising meetings and courses; producing discussion papers
Projects and curriculum initiatives
1 Report of a formal investigation into the teaching of English as a second language in Calderdale LEA (1985–6, 5–18 age groups).
▼ Report/evaluation
2 From the cradle to school – an account of the race relations aspects of under-fives provision (1986–9, under-fives age group).
▼ Discussion documents

3 Education Code; a race relations code of practice (1988–9, all ages)
▼ Policy documents
4 Governors' Broadsheet on education for a multi-ethnic society (1989, all ages).
▼ Discussion documents
Objectives CRE's interest in education is defined by their duties under the Race Relations Act of 1976 which specifies that the organisation should work towards the elimination of racial discrimination, and the promotion of equality of opportunity and good race relations. To that end CRE supports individual complaints and embarks on formal investigations with regard to allegations of discrimination in schools and colleges; it engages in promotional work with a whole range of organisations concerned to ensure that course content and the materials used are appropriate for education for life in a multi-ethnic society. It promotes and funds research, currently: (a) an ethnographic study into the experiences of black children in nursery and primary schools, and (b) racial harassment in selected schools in 2 LEAs. CRE funds bodies like the Working Group Against Racism in Children's Resources, and makes contributions to the work of such bodies as the Anti-Racist Teachers' Network. It also funds publications like 'The World in a City' and 'World Religions: a Handbook for Teachers'. It also advises on equal opportunity policies and is represented at conferences organised by LEAs in particular. Its contribution to curriculum is by way of asserting certain general principles that should be observed, and in responding to DES consultative documents and enquiries by subject bodies. Its concerns with assessment are similarly expressed.

24. Confederation of British Industry – CBI
Centre Point, 103 New Oxford St, London WC1A 1DU
☎ 071 379 7400
Ⓟ Mr M. Hunt, Secretary

25. Curriculum Association – CA
School of Education, The Open University, Walton Hall, Milton Keynes MK7 6AA
☎ 0908 274066
Ⓟ Professor Bob Moon, Chairperson
Publications *The Curriculum Journal*, termly.
Contribution Consultation; raising theoretical curricular questions; organising meetings and courses; organising an annual international conference.
Objectives The Curriculum Association has a national membership of LEA officers and advisers, teachers from all types of schools and tutors from further and higher education. There are a number of overseas members and the annual conference always has international contributors. Links exist with similar bodies in USA, Canada and Australia, and overseas contacts are fostered. Many regions have established local groups, ten of

which exist at present, with others in the process of being formed. *The Curriculum Journal* is the association's journal and is published by Routledge.

Apart from the annual national conference, the local groups run many one-day and half-day conferences on issues related to the curriculum and assessment. The association has responded in consultation with the various bodies proposing developments within schools and colleges and has several times taken the initiative of linking with other associations in the mounting of conferences. Conference proceedings sometimes result in published books. The Curriculum Association has funded or part-funded small-scale research projects in schools and generally supports teachers in such work. The Association welcomes any contact with those who are working with learners, the curriculum and assessment.

26. The Engineering Council

10 Maltravers St, London WC2R 3 ER   (and 19 regional centres)
☎ 071 240 7891   Ⓕ 071 240 7517
Ⓟ Dr J.K. Williams, General education executive
Publications   *Engineering Council Newsletter*, twice a year
Contribution   Consultation; raising theoretical curricular questions; provision of resource material; organising meetings and courses; producing discussion papers; producing assessment materials; statements with other organisations for national publication and dissemination.
Projects and curriculum initiatives
1   Eastern Region Teacher Education Consortium (ERTEC) (1989–94, 5–16 age groups).
▼   Reports/evaluations; resource materials; policy documents; discussion documents
2   Neighbourhood engineers (on-going, 5–16 age group).
▼   Reports/evaluations; resource materials; policy documents; discussion documents
3   Problem solving (on-going, 5–12 age group).
▼   Reports/evaluations; resource materials; policy documents; discussion documents
Objectives   The Engineering Council on a national level, and regionally through the 19 Engineering Council Regional Organisations (ECROs), offers support to schools, FE and HE institutions across all subject areas. It also offers general managerial support. This support includes resources and activities (for example, work experience and work shadowing). The Council is concerned with equal opportunities and broadening access to all post-16 education.

27. Equal Opportunities Commission – EOC

Overseas Hse, Quay St, Manchester M3 3HN (and 2 regional centres)
☎ 061 833 9244
Ⓟ Education and Training Unit

Publications   *Network*, twice yearly to equal opportunities officers in LEAs
Contribution   Consultation; provision of resource material
Objectives   The Commission's recent strategy has been to move out of schools into the area of the school and work interface and the training of youth and adult women. However, the recently established Education and Training Unit is still monitoring the implications for schools of the Education Reform Act of 1988 in respect of gender issues. It is also responding to the consultation over the national curriculum.

28. Free Church Federal Council – FCFC

27 Tavistock Square, London WC1H 9HH
☎ 071 387 8413   Ⓕ 071 383 0150
Ⓟ Rev Professor H.N. Marratt, educational consultant
Publications   *Free Church Chronicle*, 3 times a year; *FCFC Education Committee documentation*, 3 times a year
Contribution   Consultation; raising theoretical curricular questions; organising meetings and courses; producing discussion papers.
Objectives   FCFC contributes in the following ways: representation to DES on all DES publications, statements and circulars on the whole curriculum, and on draft regulations; representation to the Churches' Joint Education Policy Committee; membership of the Religious Education Council, and its Working Parties on assessment, teacher training and supply, and the syllabuses for religious education; publication of statements on church schools, school worship, and religious education; attendance at relevant courses, conferences and working parties, for example, on General Teaching Council, assessment and testing and multi-cultural education; representations to the NCC and SEAC discussions; keeping a watching brief on treatment of minority groups in a pluralistic society; and representation on LEA education committees.

29. Health Education Authority – HEA

Hamilton Hse, Mabledon Place, London WC1H 9TX
☎ 071 631 0930   Ⓕ 071 387 0550
Ⓟ Ms Lynda Finn (Manager: Young People's Programme).
Publications   *Health Education Journal*, quarterly; *Health Education News*, bi-monthly; Health Education for Young People; a guide to projects and resources, occasionally
Contribution   Raising theoretical curricular questions; provision of resource material
Projects and curriculum initiatives
1   Health skills dissemination project: a whole school approach to lifeskills and health education (on-going, all ages).
■   To disseminate staff and curriculum development training materials and courses and classroom materials developed in the HEC project, 'integration of lifeskills teaching

and health education'
▼ Reports; resource materials
2 16–19 dissemination project (on-going, 16–19 age group).
■ To support and disseminate work produced by the HEA 16–19 project
▼ Resource materials
3 Health education for slow learners project (1984–7, all ages).
■ To trial and revise a training programme for teachers on the development of health education for pupils with mild and moderate learning difficulties
▼ A book, *Parents, Schools and Community: Working together in health education*
4 TACADE (formerly, Teachers Advisory Council for Alcohol and Drug Education) (on-going, all ages).
■ The production of materials relevant to education about alcohol and drugs; provision of training courses for a range of professional groups; provision of advice, information, support and consultancy to any individual, group or organisation requiring help concerning the issue of health or drugs
▼ Resource materials; training manual; curriculum guide
Objectives The Young People's Programme aims: to develop and support provision of health education for young people in schools, colleges, and in other settings such as the Youth Service and the Youth Training Scheme; to initiate and support curriculum and staff development projects concerned with strategies for teaching and coordination of health education within schools and colleges; to support pastoral programmes through the development of materials and training for tutors; to encourage the coordination and development of health education regionally; to encourage HEA projects to support each other and to exchange good practice in research, development, dissemination, and evaluation; to foster links between the Health Education Authority, LEAs and Health Authorities, with a view to furthering health education for young people; to provide a resource in terms of local support for health educators; to support school governors in their increasingly important role in the curriculum; to encourage the support and involvement of parents and the community in health education; to link with, and mutually support, other HEA activities, especially those related to young people; and to encourage publicity of HEA activities, nationally and internationally.

30. Home and School Council – HSC
81 Rustlings Rd, Sheffield S11 7AB
☎ 0742 662467
Ⓟ Mrs B. Bullivant, Honorary secretary
Publications Booklets, termly
Contribution The publication of booklets of information for parents
Objectives HSC was formed by the 3 Associations, ACE, CASE and NCPTA. It acts as a forum for these 3 bodies to meet together, but its main function is to publish

booklets on aspects of home–school relations. A new, or fully-revised, booklet is published each term. General enquiries on home–school relations may be addressed to the Secretary (please enclose SAE).

31. Industrial Society
48 Bryanston Square, London W1
☎ 071 262 2401
Ⓟ Ms Julia Cleverdon, Director of education

32. Institute of Careers Officers – ICO
27A Lower High St, Stourbridge, West Midlands DY8 1TA
☎ 0384 376464   Ⓕ 0384 440830
Ⓟ Mr J.M. Hartland, Director
Publications *The Careers Officer*, quarterly
Contribution Consultation
Objectives The central focus of the ICO is the needs of young people within Careers Education and Guidance. It works, through consultation, to ensure that the crucial place of Careers Education and Guidance in the national curriculum is recognised.

33. Joint Unit for CPVE and Foundation Programmes
46 Britannia St, London WC1X 9RG
☎ 071 278 3344   Ⓕ 071 278 9460
Ⓟ Ms S. Fifer, Head of Unit
Publications *Focus* (CPVE only), termly; Scheme/Moderator update (as needed)
Contribution Consultation; raising theoretical curricular questions; organising meetings and courses; producing discussion papers; producing assessment materials
Projects and curriculum initiatives
1 Certificate of Pre-Vocational Education (CPVE) (on-going, 16–18 age group). Pre-vocational education includes all the elements of the curriculum. The Joint Unit oversees the national programme, and accredits the awards.
▼ Reports/evaluations; publicity; handbooks
2 Foundation programmes (on-going, 14–16 age group).
■ These are designed to link with the subjects of the National Curriculum and provide a basis for CPVE study.
▼ Discussion documents; publicity; handbooks
Objectives Both CPVE and Foundation programmes provide an externally accredited framework for the development of pre-vocational education in schools and colleges. Students are helped to see the relevance of their work to their future in employment, training or further education. They are encouraged to negotiate their programmes of study with their teachers, and the formative review and assessment process is an important part of each course. Summative reporting of skills developed reflects the principles of Records of Achievement. The programmes have encouraged the development of new teaching and learning styles as well as a range of cross-curricular assignments. Institutions undertaking the

programmes are required to produce a detailed submission which is then reviewed on a continuing basis, both through scheme self-evaluation, formal resubmission, and regular moderator visits. In many LEAs, the programmes are being used as vehicles for the implementation and delivery of TVEI extension.

34. National Association for Gifted Children – NAGC

1 South Audley St, London W1Y 5DQ
☎ 071 499 1188/9
Ⓟ Mr John Welch, Education director
Publications *Looking to their future*, yearly; *Gossip Column*, termly
Contribution Consultation; raising theoretical curricular questions; organising meetings and courses; producing discussion papers; producing research papers.
Projects and curriculum initiatives
1 Survey of LEAs in England and Wales (1989, 5–18 age groups).
■ To investigate the national provision for gifted children and their special education needs
▼ Report/evaluation
Contribution NAGC exists to assist by all possible means children with outstanding gifts and talents to fulfil their potential. Its activities include mutual support, exchange of ideas and experiences and arranging activities for children, as well as more formal work in research, INSET and Parent–Teacher cooperation. There are local branches throughout the country. At a national level, NAGC organises conferences for parents, educators and child welfare agencies. It makes representations about needs to Government and LEAs. It informs and encourages support from industry, commerce, the arts and the professions.

35. National Association for Pastoral Care in Education – NAPCE

Education Department, University of Warwick, Coventry CV4 7AL
☎ 0203 523810
Ⓟ Mr David Lambourn, Development Officer, NAPCE
Publications *Pastoral Care in Education*, 4 times a year
Contribution Consultation; raising theoretical curricular questions; organising meetings and courses; producing discussion papers; representations to those national bodies influencing/determining the curriculum, eg. HMI, DES, NCC
Projects and curriculum initiatives
1 Sex education (1–15 age group).
▼ Discussion documents
2 Child abuse
■ To investigate ways of helping child abuse victims through personal and social education, special education needs, and citizenship education

▼ Books
3 Teacher appraisal (9–15 age group).
■ To work on policies and support for appraisal of teachers in junior and secondary schools
▼ Policy documents
4 PSE in the primary school (1–8 age group).
▼ Books
Publications The association focuses upon Pastoral Care and upon Personal and Social Education (PSE), and views these as whole-school issues, neither separated from the curriculum, nor limited to being simply a part of it. Within a whole-school approach, NAPCE members have focused upon particular areas, the most recent including: school discipline; PSE in the Primary School; child abuse; juvenile crime; sex education; teacher appraisal; assessment; records of achievement. NAPCE welcomes members from a wide geographical and subject base, and approaches on any aspect of curriculum development and school organisation, whether from teachers, researchers, or other interested groups.

36. National Association for Primary Education – NAPE

60 Willett Way, Petts Wood, Kent BR5 1QE
☎ 0689 29971
Ⓟ Ms Jill Thompson, Honorary secretary
Publications *New Childhood*, 3 times a year
Contribution Consultation; raising theoretical curricular questions; provision of resource material; organising meetings and courses; producing discussion papers; producing policy statements
Projects and curriculum initiatives
1 Parents rolling conferences (1987–91, primary phase)
▼ Reports/evaluations
2 Resourcing of primary education (primary phase)
▼ Policy documents
3 Under- 5s in infant classes (1987–8, infant phase).
▼ Policy documents
4 Retraining of secondary teachers for primary work (1986–7, primary).
▼ Policy documents
Objectives NAPE exists to promote an interest in young children from birth to 13, emphasising partnership, best practice and the status and importance of primary education. It produces policy documents on pertinent issues of concern relating to young children, contributing to discussion and judgement that will promote positive decision-making on the experiences primary children should have in their formal years of education. Its links with government and media have enhanced its profile and resultant contributions to primary education. Its concept of partnership aims to inform all interested parties of how children best learn, through understanding of curriculum initiatives.

37. National Association for Remedial Education – NARE

NARE Central Office, 2 Lichfield Rd, Stafford, Staffordshire ST17 4JX   (and 54 regional centres)
☎ 0785 46872
Ⓟ Mr C. Gallow, Office manager
Publications *Support for Learning*, quarterly; *NARE Newsletter*, 3 times a year
Contribution Consultation; raising theoretical curricular questions; provision of resource materials; organising meetings and courses; producing discussion papers; producing assessment materials; publication of books and guidelines. Nature of contribution of the organisation. NARE responds to curriculum initiatives through its quarterly journal, its newsletter, its publications (details of which are to be found in the NARE booklist) and its annual courses. Through its curriculum sub-committee it responds to DES papers, and executive members attend relevant meetings. NARE is a member of SENNAC (Special Educational Needs National Advisory Council).

38. National Association of Advisory Officers for Special Education – NAAOSE

32A Pleasant Valley, Saffron Walden, Essex CB11 4AP
☎ 0799 21257
Ⓟ Mr Christopher Dyer, Honorary secretary
Contribution Consultation; raising theoretical curricular questions
Objectives NAAOSE exists as a means of keeping LEA advisers and inspectors for Special Educational Needs in touch with each other. Through regional meetings and by dissemination of information from its national officers, it seeks to make informed responses to curriculum issues and other matters of educational concern to the NCC, to DES, and others.It does not, as an association, directly set up curriculum initiatives; that is the function, at LEA level, of its membership. It acts, however, as an information exchange and, via regions, as a support and encouragement to individual advisers and inspectors.

39. National Association of Governors and Managers – NAGM

81 Rustlings Rd, Sheffield S11 7AB
☎ 0742 662467
Ⓟ Mrs B. Bullivant, Honorary secretary
Publications *NAGM News*, termly
Contribution Consultation; organising meetings and courses; producing discussion papers; producing resources to inform and train governors of schools
Objectives NAGM responds to enquiries from DES and SEAC on governors' attitudes to curriculum and assessment. It trains governors, for example, on their role vis-à-vis the curriculum, assessment, and appraisal, but it leaves professional matters to the professionals.

40. National Association of Headteachers – NAHT

1 Heath Square, Boltro Rd, Haywards Heath, West Sussex RH16 1BL
☎ 0444 458133   Ⓕ 0444 416326
Ⓟ Mr Arthur De Caux, Senior assistant secretary, education
Publications *Head Teachers Review*, 3 times a year; *NAHT Bulletin*, 6 times a year
Contribution Consultation; raising theoretical curricular questions; organising meetings and courses; producing discussion papers; producing guidance documents for members.
Objectives NAHT produces a series of publications to assist its members in the performance of their professional duties. These include the following: guidance and commentary on all education acts; information and commentary on other relevant matters; NAHT Council Memoranda – advice documents on a whole range of practical matters connected with the management and running of a school; discussion papers; curriculum booklets. The NAHT is run by a National Council supported by a committee structure. This structure includes 3 education committees: curriculum and assessment; training development and support; school management. There are also committees on: professional and legal matters; salaries, pensions and conditions of service; membership and organisation. Finally there are advisory committees by phase (primary, secondary, middle), and for special educational needs, and numerous working parties when appropriate.

41. National Association of Inspectors and Educational Advisers – NAIEA

The Old Grammar School, Broadway, Letchworth, Herts. SG6 3PP
☎ 0462 677030
Ⓟ Mr M.J. Gifford, General secretary

42. National Association of Youth and Community Education Officers – NAYCEO

Cross Park, Ringmore, Kingsbridge, Devon TQ7 4HW
☎ 0548 810238
Ⓟ Mr John Tate, Executive secretary
Contribution to curriculum development Producing discussion papers
Projects and curriculum initiatives
1 Political education.
▼ Policy documents
2 HIV and AIDS
▼ Policy documents
3 Environmental issues
▼ Policy documents
4 Special needs
▼ Policy documents
Objectives NAYCEO is continually seeking ways and means of furthering the two concepts of social and community education.

It is fully aware of the need to keep abreast of the many issues with which present-day society is confronted.To assist the association to achieve these two objectives, it publishes Policy Statements representing the consensus view of its membership. Similarly, by publishing discussion papers, it hopes to facilitate further debate within the Association and with those other organisations concerned with social and community education and with whom the Association has contact.

43. National Autistic Society
276 Willesden Lane, London NW2 5RB
☎ 081 451 3844
Ⓟ Mrs M. White

44. National Children's Bureau
8 Wakley St, London EC1V 7QE (and 10 local groups)
☎ 071 278 9441 Ⓕ 071 278 9512
Ⓟ Ms Gillian Pugh, Head of the Under Fives Unit
Publications *Concern*, quarterly
Contribution Consultation; raising theoretical curricular questions; provision of resource material; organisation meetings and courses; producing discussion papers
Projects and curriculum initiatives
1 Curriculum in the early years (ongoing, 3–7 age group).
▼ Resource materials
Objectives The National Children's Bureau's Under Fives Unit is a national centre for advice, guidance and information on current practice, thinking and research in the under fives field. It aims to raise awareness of the needs of young children; to improve policy and service provision across education, social services, health and the voluntary sector; and support the raising of professional standards. The Unit is funded by the DES and the Department of Health.
The Unit's publications include a training pack, 'Working with children: developing a curriculum for the early years' (edited by Mary Jane Drummond, Margaret Lally and Gillian Pugh), research summaries, bibliographies, and the report of an INSET course, 'An integrated approach to the National Curriculum in the early years'. The Unit has an extensive programme of conferences and workshops, and can offer consultancy and inservice training on curriculum and assessment in the early years.

45. National Council for Special Education – NCSE
1 Wood St, Stratford-upon-Avon, Warwicks CV37 6JE (and 50 regional centres)
☎ 0789 205332
Ⓟ Ms Sally Harvey, Assistant general secretary
Publications *Special Education – Forward Trends*, quarterly; a newsletter; *Research Exchange*, twice a year; occasional papers
Contribution Consultation; raising

theoretical curricular questions; provision of resource materials; organising meetings and courses; producing discussion papers
Projects and curriculum initiatives
1 GRIST: a professional study
■ To investigate the availability of funds and courses for the further professional study of teachers working in the area of special educational needs
2 CQSE
■ A qualification in collaboration with NCSE for teachers of children with special educational needs
Objectives NCSE exists to further the education and welfare of all those who are in any way handicapped, children and adults with any form or degree of special educational need. It is not a pressure group, and cannot undertake to represent anyone with a grievance. Membership is open to all and there are some 50 regional branches which organise conferences and courses. The Council publishes a newsletter, a journal, *Special Education*, and a *Research Exchange* twice yearly, as well as reports, papers and reviews.

46. National Council for Teacher-centred Professional Development – NCTPD
Somerset Education Centre, Park Rd, Bridgwater, Somerset TA6 7HS
☎ 0278 432721
Ⓟ Mr Keith Martin, Secretary
Publications *Centrepost*, 6 times a year
Contribution Consultation; raising theoretical curricular questions; provision of resource material; organising meetings and courses; producing discussion papers.
Projects and curriculum initiatives
1 BP/British Council/NCTPD Travel Scholarship (1986–8, for teachers of pupils of all ages).
■ To support overseas study, primarily in USA, Scandinavia, China and Hong Kong
▼ Reports/evaluations; books; resource materials; policy documents; discussion documents
2 NCTPD development project (1989–91, for teachers of pupils of all ages).
■ To ensure that the Council accommodates to a changing range of membership and evolving role developments
▼ In preparation
3 What do we do? (1988–90, for teachers of pupils of all ages).
■ To facilitate the exchange and collation of profiles of ways of working with members
▼ In preparation
Objectives NCTPD is an educational networking organisation which seeks to represent the professional development interests and concerns of its membership. This membership includes teachers, professional development centre leaders, LEA professional development coordinators, LEA advisers/inspectors, and other colleagues whose key concern is the development of teachers. NCTPD is particularly innovative in its approach to INSET and curriculum review

National Council for Teacher-centered Professional Development

Hon. Secretary: Keith Martin, Somerset Education Centre, Park Road Bridgwater, Somerset, TA6 7HS. Tel: (0278) 432721

The National Council for Teacher-centered Professional Development aims to:

★ *Establish, maintain and improve communications as equal partners between those involved in the support of teacher centered professional development.*

★ *Provide for the professional development of members and others and in particular facilitate and support the provision of national courses and conferences.*

N.C.T.P.D. arranges courses for its members on a regional basis, holds an annual national conference and is an experienced national consultancy ready to help others by arranging relevant courses, offering advice and preparing INSET strategies. To all those engaged in the professional development of teachers. This is the organisation for you - Join us now!

strategies, and this is reflected in the annual conference which is open to non-members. It has a national executive committee derived from an active regional structure spanning England, Wales, Northern Ireland and the Irish Republic. It is regularly involved in consultation with DES.
NCTPD maintains contact with colleagues abroad. It also collaborates with many other organisations, and this has resulted in the establishment of short-term travel scholarships, support for countries setting up teachers' centres, the development of resources and educational visit arrangements for visitors from other countries as well as feedback to its own members.
In essence, the NCTPD assists the development and assessment of children and curricula by seeking to promote and support professional development and curriculum enquiry with schools and colleges, with a particular focus on training the trainers.
NATPD offers guidance to any teachers who are seeking to establish a collaborative local network for mutual support or professional development purposes.

47. National Deaf Children's Society
45 Hereford Rd, London W2 5AH
☎ 071 229 9272/4
℗ Mr Harry Cayton, Director

48. National Institute for Careers Education and Counselling – NICEC
Hertford Campus, Hatfield Polytechnic, Balls Park, Hertford SG13 8QF
☎ 0992 558451
℗ Mr A.G. Watts, Director

49. National Society's Religious Education Centre – NSREC
23 Kensington Square, London W8 5HN
☎ 071 937 4241
℗ Mr A. Brown, Director
Publications *Crosscurrent*, termly; *Together*, 9 times a year.

Contribution Consultation; provision of resource material; organising meetings and courses; producing discussion papers.
Projects and curriculum initiatives
1 Islam in textbooks (1989–92, 5–16 age groups).
■ To investigate the content of RE, geography, and history textbooks with regard to content about Islam.
▼ In preparation
2 RE and special educational needs (1988–, 5–16 age groups).
▼ In preparation
Objectives The National Society is committed to support for, and development of, religious education at all levels in both Church and LEA schools. It offers, for reference, a wide range of materials, including more than 13,000 books and 5,000 audio-visual aids which can be used by teachers in the classroom. The Church of England's Board of Education Curriculum Advisory Group meets at the Centre to reply to DES statements and also to prepare its own statements. These are available on request.
The Chichester Project on teaching Christianity in the secondary school has its headquarters at the Centre, and the Shap Working Party on World Religions in Education distributes its annual mailing from the Centre.

50. National Union of Teachers – NUT
Hamilton Hse, Mabledon Place, London WC1H 9BD (and 10 regional centres)
☎ 071 388 6191 ⓕ 071 387 8458
℗ Ms Catherine Matheson, Assistant editor
Publications *NUT Education Review*, twice a year.
Contribution Consultation; raising theoretical curricular questions; organising meetings and courses; producing discussion papers.
Projects and curriculum initiatives
1 UK/USA Micro-electronics Seminar (1985, all ages).
■ Practising teachers, principals, teacher trainers and other educational computing specialists worked together for a week in order to analyse the state of educational computing in Great Britain and the United States, to establish recommendations for policy and practice, and to carry out innovative projects stimulating new growth in educational computing
2 Towards equality for girls and boys: guidelines on countering sexism in schools (1989, all ages).
■ To produce a pack designed for everyday, practical use by teachers, student teachers, teacher trainers and those doing research on gender equality
▼ Resource materials
3 NUT guidelines on anti-racism in education (1989, all ages).
■ To support teachers in anti-racist educational practice and to suggest ways of gaining the support of parents, governors, and the local community in developing a whole-school anti-racist policy

▼ Booklet
4 National testing and assessment
conferences (1988–9, all ages)
■ To explore the issues involved in the new
system of national testing and assessment
Objectives The NUT responds to each of
the government's working party reports on the
National Curriculum and assessment, and to
the statutory orders as published by the DES.

51. The Nuffield Foundation
Nuffield Lodge, Regents Park, London NW1
4RS
☎ 071 722 8871
Ⓟ Mr J.P. Cornford, Director

52. Nuffield–Chelsea Curriculum Trust–NCCT
King's College, 552 King's Rd, London SW10
OUA
☎ 071 376 5895
Ⓟ Mr Dieter Pevsner, Publications manager
Contribution Consultation; raising
theoretical curricular questions; provision of
resource material; organising meetings and
courses; producing assessment materials.
1 Nuffield co-ordinated sciences project
(1986–9, 15–16 age group).
▼ Books; resource materials
2 Nuffield science year 9 (1988–90, 14 age
group).
▼ Books; resource materials
3 Nuffield assessment in science
(1987–90, 11–16 age group).
▼ Books
4 Nuffield secondary mathematics
(1987–90, 11–16 age group).
▼ Books; resource materials
5 Nuffield primary SPACE science
(1988–91, 5–11 age group).
▼ Books; resource materials
6 Nuffield modular science (1989–92,
13–16 age group).
Objectives NCCT is an educational charity,
created in 1979 out of the Science and
Mathematics Teaching Projects of the Nuffield
Foundation. It is unique in having been set up
specifically to advance and improve the
teaching and learning of science, mathematics
and related subjects in schools. It is unique
also in that its curriculum developments
embrace every possible kind of work: it
mounts research; it formulates aims for new
curricula; it tests draft materials with working
teachers in school classrooms; it commissions
editors, writers, and illustrators to prepare
every aspect of the books and other materials
for publication. The commercial publishers are
selected for their commitment to the work of a
particular project, and the Trust is self-funding
since receipts from the publishers finance
further research and development.
The reasons for the Trust's work are clear:
there is a national shortage of science and
mathematics teachers and a national shortage
of entrants to higher education in both
subjects. The publications of the Trust, by
combining the expertise of academic
researchers, teacher trainers, and
schoolteachers, improve the quality of what

teachers do and of how children learn.
Nuffield materials have transformed science
and mathematics teaching by emphasising the
need for children to learn by exploring and
experimenting, not simply by learning facts.
This approach is now so widely accepted that
the processes of science and mathematics
have been formally incorporated, alongside
factual knowledge, into the new criteria for the
GCSE and subsequently into the national
curriculum.

53. Professional Association of Teachers – PAT
St James's Court, 77 Friar Gate, Derby DE1
1BT
☎ 0332 372337 Ⓕ 0332 290310
Ⓟ Miss Jackie Miller, Assistant general
secretary
Publications *Professional Teacher*, termly
Contribution Consultation; raising
theoretical curricular questions; producing
discussion papers

54. Quaker Peace and Service – QPS
Friends Hse, Euston Rd, London NW1 2BJ
☎ 071 387 3601 Ⓕ 071 388 1977
Ⓟ Mr Tom Leimdorfer, Education adviser
Publications *QPS Reporter and Resources
Sheet*, quarterly
Contribution Consultation; provision of
resource materials; organising meetings and
courses
Projects and curriculum initiatives
1 Conflict resolution and mediation
techniques (ongoing, 5–18 age group, and
adult).
▼ Reports/evaluations; books; resource
materials
2 Human Rights education (ongoing,
11–18 age group).
▼ Discussion documents
3 East/West perspectives in education
(ongoing, 11–18 age group).
▼ Resource materials; discussion
documents
4 Issues of peace and war; pacifiism;
Quakerism (ongoing, 11–18 age group).
▼ Books; resource materials
Objectives The QPS Education Advisory
Programme offers: advice on resources,
methodology and possible ways of coping with
problems on topics related to world
development and environmental issues,
human rights education, conflict resolution,
the social skills required for greater personal
awareness and affirmation, and the basis of
the Quaker peace testimony; one-day or half-
day inservice courses which can focus on
techniques of conflict resolution, mediation
and problem-solving (relating such techniques
to the school curriculum as a whole) or on
specific issues relating, for example, to
Northern Ireland, South Africa, Sri Lanka, the
Middle East, Latin America, East–West
relations, environmental problems, sharing the
world's resources, disarmament, the work of
the United Nations; visits to schools to give
talks, initiate discussions or facilitate
workshop-type sessions with teachers and/or

pupils. No fees are charged, though donations towards expenses are appreciated.

55. Royal Association for Disability and Rehabilitation – RADAR

25 Mortimer St, London W1N 8AB
☎ 071 637 5400
Ⓟ Policy officer, employment
Publication *Bulletin*, monthly; *Contact*, quarterly
Objectives RADAR makes no formal contribution to curriculum development. It is, however, able to supply single copies of items that may be requested, while teachers may purchase any of the books and other publications from the current publication list. In 1989, RADAR launched a new book on self-care and independence training for physically disabled children. For more details on the book, 'Passivity to empowerment', please contact the Education officer.

56. Royal National Institute for the Blind – RNIB

Rushton Hall School, Kettering, Northants NN14 1RR
☎ 0536 710506
Ⓟ Mr R. Orr, Headteacher
Contribution Consultation; raising theoretical curricular questions; provision of resource material; organising meetings and courses; producing discussion papers; producing assessment materials.
Projects and curriculum initiatives
1 Precursors to the national curriculum for profoundly handicapped blind children (1989–90, 5–12 age group).
■ To work on general development of the curriculum for profoundly handicapped blind children
▼ Reports/evaluations; policy documents; discussion documents
Objectives RNIB Rushton Hall works with LEA personnel, social workers, and other special schools to provide a specialist service to multiply handicapped blind children and their families in a residential setting. The management of rare disorders, the fostering of optimum development, providing a structured environment for establishing emotional stability, the furtherance of language acquisition, self-help skills and mobility and facilities for dual sensory disabilities – deaf/blind – physiotherapy, hydrotherapy, are all features of this provision. Staff are ready to advise visitors, visit children in other schools, address staff groups, and run day courses at Rushton. Five teams, each with a qualified teacher of the blind, provide 38 weeks of full boarding with waking night cover. They are continually devising strategies to cope with the varied needs of their client group drawn from all parts of the country.

57. Royal Society for Mentally Handicapped Children and Adults – MENCAP

MENCAP National Centre, 123 Golden Lane, London EC1Y 0RT

☎ 071 253 9433
Ⓟ Mr F. Heddel, Director, Education, training and employment

58. Secondary Heads Association – SHA

130 Regent Rd, Leicester LE1 7PG
☎ 0533 471797   Ⓕ 0533 471152
Ⓟ Mr John Sutton, General secretary
Publications *Headlines*, 3 times a year
Contribution Consultation; raising theoretical curricular questions; provision of resource material; producing discussion papers; producing assessment materials. Nature of contribution of the organisation. SHA represents the great majority of heads and deputy heads of secondary schools in the United Kingdom. As leaders of secondary education, the Association's members take a close interest in all matters relating to the school curriculum. They make a significant contribution to national discussions on the subject by participating in consultation with the relevant organisations (eg NCC, SEAC) as well as with the DES. In addition the Association produces regular information for members and publications for a wider market covering various aspects of curriculum development.

59. Society of Education Officers – SEO

21-27 Lambs Conduit St, London WC1N 3NJ (and 9 regional centres)
☎ 071 831 1973   Ⓕ 071 831 2855
Ⓟ Mr Dennis Hatfield, CBE, General secretary
Publications *New Education Officer*, termly
Contribution Consultation; organising meetings and courses; producing discussion papers
Projects and curriculum initiatives
1 Schools curriculum award (ongoing, 5–18 age group).
Objectives SEO is a forum for discussion for all education officers in local government.

60. Technical and Vocational Education Initiative – TVEI

236 Grays Inn Rd, London WC1X 8HL   (and 10 regional centres)
☎ 071 278 0363
Ⓟ TVEI enquiry point x 4055
Publications *Insight*, termly
Objectives TVEI aims to provide young people with learning opportunities which will equip them for the demands of working life in a rapidly changing society. TVEI seeks to influence the education of 14–18 year-olds in 5 explicit ways: by making sure the curriculum uses every opportunity to relate education to the world of work, by using real examples if possible; by making sure that young people get the knowledge, competencies and qualifications they need in a highly technological society which is itself part of Europe and the world economy; by making sure that young people get direct opportunities to learn about the nature of the economy and

the world of work, through work experience, work shadowing, projects in the community and so on; by making sure that young people learn how to be effective, solve problems, work in teams, and be enterprising and creative, through the ways in which they are taught; by making sure that young people have access to initial guidance and counselling, and then continuing education and training, and opportunities for progression throughout their lives.

61. Thinking Skills Network – TSN
Hertfordshire Achievement Project, St. Audrey's School, Travellers Lane, Hatfield, Herts. AL10 HSQ
☎ 0707 263396
ⓟ Ms Marjorie Needham, Chairperson
Publications *Thinking Skills Network Newsletter*, twice a year
Contribution Consultation; raising theoretical curricular questions; organising meetings and courses; producing discussion papers.
Projects and curriculum initiatives
1 Somerset project: learning how to learn (ongoing, 10–18 age group and adult).
▼ Reports/evaluations; books; resource materials
2 Oxfordshire project: learning how to learn (ongoing, 10–18 age group and adult).
▼ Reports/evaluations; resource materials
Objectives TSN acts as a focal point for those people concerned with the development of thinking skills in children. The objective is to disseminate information about specific curriculum initiatives, to create a register of interested practitioners in the different fields of thinking skills programmes, to create interest groups across the different educational sectors and to encourage discussion and research.

62. Trades Union Congress – TUC
Congress Hse, Great Russell St, London WC1B 3CS (and 10 regional centres)
☎ 071 636 4030 ⓣ 268328 TUC G
ⓕ 071 636 0632
ⓟ Ms Carol Shgerriff, Assistant secretary, education.
Publications *TUC Bulletin*, monthly; *TUC Education Briefing*, twice a year.
Projects and curriculum initiatives
1 Learning about trade unions (jointly with Education for Economic Awareness) (ongoing, 14–18 age group).
▼ Reports/evaluations; resource materials
Objectives The TUC produces materials for the use of teachers at school and FE level.

They are intended to be used in studies of the world of work and in learning about trade unions. It has also produced a short video on the role of trade unions, which has pause points for discussion, so that it can be used as a complete item or in a series of lessons. There is also a workbook suggesting active learning methods of introducing the concept of trade unions into the classroom. The TUC also provides advice on such issues as work experience. The TUC's particular concern in the curriculum is that all pupils, regardless of ability, have a knowledge and understanding of the world of work including trade unions.

63. Understanding British Industry – UBI
Sun Alliance Hse, New Inn Halll St, Oxford OX1 2QE (and 5 regional centres)
☎ 0865 722585 ⓕ 0865 723488
ⓟ Mrs Jan Hussey, Information officer
Publications *UBI Update*, 10 times a year
Contribution Consultation; raising theoretical curricular questions; provision of resource materials; organising meetings and courses; producing discussion papers.
Projects and curriculum initiatives
1 Teacher placement service
▼ Reports/evaluations; resource materials
2 Management workshops (ongoing)
3 INDTEL – initial teacher education (ongoing)
▼ Reports/evaluations; resource materials; discussion documents
4 Modern languages in industry (ongoing, 14–16 age group).
Objectives UBI has 3 aims: to improve understanding of industry, commerce and wealth creation among teachers of secondary school pupils; to help teachers to influence school curricula and examinations, bringing the lessons taught in school more into line with the needs of adult life; and to improve understanding of the education system among people in industry and business.

64. Voluntary Council for Handicapped Children – VCHC
8 Wakley St, London EC1V 7QE
☎ 071 278 9441 ⓕ 071 278 9512
ⓟ Ms Philippa Russell, Principal officer, or, Ms Sheila Gatiss, Development officer
Publications *Concern*, quarterly
Contribution Organising meetings and courses; producing discussion papers
Objectives VCHC is a voluntary organisation involved in discussion, training and research on all aspects of special educational needs.

Section 6

Curriculum Initiatives in Local Education Authorities

Curriculum Handbook

This section contains details of the Education Authorities of Great Britain. It might be anticipated that this would be the most homogeneous section of the book, but this would probably be a wrong assumption. Apart from great variations in size and composition, these Authorities operate under different education systems. The National Curriculum, for example, is not the curriculum of Great Britain.

It is clearly difficult for Education Authorities to be specific about projects and curriculum initiatives, as their priorities are, at least in part, decided on a yearly basis by the DES. Also, there is no obvious dividing line between a specific project and what might be considered the normal work of the Authority; such a division is much clearer for HE institutions. Thus it is understandable, but regrettable, that some Authorities declined to give details of this part of their work.

Inevitably, the role of these Authorities will be changing in the next few years as more power is devolved to schools. Quite what will be their role in the future is still to be determined.

1. Inner London Education Authority

London Boroughs have appointed Chief education officer in Camden, City of London, Greenwich, Hackney, Hammersmith and Fulham, Islington, Kensington and Chelsea, Lambeth, Lewisham, Southwark, Tower Hamlets, Wandsworth, and Westminster. See following entries.

2. Barking and Dagenham

Town Hall, Barking, Essex IG11 7LU
☎ 081 592 4500
Ⓟ Chief education officer

3. Barnet

Town Hall, Friern Barnet, London N11 3DL
☎ 081 368 1255
Ⓟ Chief education officer

4. Bexley

Town Hall, Crayford, Kent DA1 4EN
☎ 081 303 7777   Ⓕ 0322 529344
Ⓟ Chief education officer
Projects and curriculum initiatives
1 Languages into industry project (1989–90, secondary age group).
▼ Discussion documents
2 Arts curriculum project (1988–91, primary and secondary age group).
▼ Discussion documents
3 Business information service (1988–91, secondary age group).
▼ Discussion documents

5. Brent

Centre for Staff Development, Brentfield Rd, London NW10
☎ 081 963 0735
Ⓟ Chief education officer
Projects and curriculum initiatives
1 I can do that! (1989, primary phase).
■ The production of a primary science handbook for teachers, based on the national curriculum.
2 Brent Record of Learning and Achievement (ongoing, primary phase).
▼ Reports/evaluations; books; resource materials; policy documents; discussion documents
3 Equal opportunities (ongoing, primary phase).
■ To produce booklets for teachers concerned with aspects of equal opportunity
▼ Reports/evaluations; books
4 Mathematics (ongoing, secondary phase).
▼ Books; resource materials

6. Bromley

Town Hall, Tweedy Rd, Bromley, Kent BR1 1SB
☎ 081 464 3333   Ⓕ 081 464 5066
Ⓟ Chief education officer
Projects and curriculum initiatives
1 Bromley school self-evaluation (1988–92, all age groups).
■ To enable schools to develop a realistic school (institution) development plan by a process of self-evaluation and regular review
Ⓣ 4 General Inspectors and a Working Group of headteachers from primary, secondary, and special schools.
▼ Separate introductory booklet; more detailed background booklet and resource materials appropriate to the phase.
Comment The scheme was devised by the Working Group. It provides practical help and advice as well as detailing the essential principles which should guide institutions when they put together a development plan. The emphasis is on planning and action – identifying individual and group responsibilities as well as time scales – based upon sound self-evaluation and review. The format allows a great deal of flexibility and creativity and avoids a rigid, formal approach.
2 Bromley Screening Pack (1986–90, primary and secondary).
■ To enable teachers to confirm their concerns about the performance of children at both ends of the learning spectrum
Ⓣ Project director, Chief Inspector, members of the Inspectorate, advisory teachers and selected teachers.
▼ A loose-leaf pack containing 2 Mathematics sections (for the more able and those with learning difficulties), and 2 Readability sections (information and assessment texts).
Comment Further research and piloting in the areas of language, motor skills and learning skills will enable the remaining sections of the pack to be published by June 1990. The project is an example of a resource developed jointly by trainers (Thames Polytechnic), assessors (Bromley Inspectorate and practitioners), and practising teachers. In addition to confirming concerns about a child's learning, the operation of the pack will help teachers to develop their skills of observation and identification.

3 Bromley Inspectors' Review of schools and colleges: first cycle (1988–90, all age groups).
■ To assist the LEA and governors to fulfil their responsibilities for the curriculum and management in the light of ERA, by developing regular and comprehensive reviews
Ⓣ Chief Inspector, 14 General Inspectors
▼ Schools handbook; colleges handbook; committee reports; review reports and evaluation documents
Comment This project is an attempt to develop a regular, objective and developmental review process which will report to a wide audience, indicate strengths and weaknesses, and growth points for the future. It includes subjective reporting and objective data collation. Areas such as team development, training needs, information dissemination and management processes are also covered.

7. Camden
Crowndale Offices, 216–220 Eversholt St, London NW1 1DE
☎ 071 278 4444 Ⓕ 071 860 1536
Ⓟ Director of education

8. City of London
Clements Hse, 14–18 Gresham St, London EC4 2EJ
☎ 071 606 3030
Ⓟ Chief education officer

9. Croydon
Taberner House, Park Lane, Croydon, Surrey CR9 1TP
☎ 081 686 4433 Ⓕ 081 760 5603
Ⓟ Chief education inspector
Projects and curriculum initiatives
1 National Oracy Project (1988–93, primary and secondary).
▼ Reports/evaluation
2 Primary teaching project (1988–91, primary and secondary).
▼ Reports/evaluations; resource materials; discussion documents
3 Project Trident (ongoing, secondary).
▼ Policy documents
4 Social responsibility (1988–92, secondary).
▼ Reports/evaluations; discussion documents

10. Ealing
Hadley Hse, 79–81 Uxbridge Rd, London W5 5SU
☎ 01 579 2424
Ⓟ Chief education officer

11. Enfield
PO Box 56, Civic Centre, Enfield EN1 3XQ
☎ 081 366 6565
Ⓟ Director of education
1 Special needs programme (1987–92, all phases).

■ To review current provision and procedures for meeting pupils' special educational needs, and to identify and build upon good practice; to review the provision of services from other authorities and placement of pupils outside the LEA.
▼ Books; policy documents; discussion documents
Comment The initiative covers all stages of education from pre-school to FE. It involves mainstream, special schools and units and colleges. A Statement of Principles has been produced and task groups are investigating areas such as integration, current provision in special schools and units, and a coordinated advisory and support service for special educational needs.

12. Greenwich
Riverside Hse, Beresford St, London SE16 6DF
☎ 081 855 3161
Ⓟ Director of education

13. Hackney
Edith Cavell Bldg, Enfield Rd, London N1 5AZ
☎ 071 254 9882
Ⓟ Director of education

14. Hammersmith & Fulham
Cambridge Gr, Banda Hse, Ground fl, London W6
Ⓟ Director of education

15. Haringey
48 Station Rd, Wood Green, London N22 4TY
☎ 081 975 9700
Ⓟ Chief education officer

16. Harrow
Civic Centre, Harrow, Middlesex HA1 2UW
☎ 081 863 5611
Ⓟ Chief education officer
Projects and curriculum initiatives
1 Graded assessment in middle and high schools (1989–92, secondary age group).
■ To enable middle and high schools to work together across the phases on assessment and record keeping
Ⓣ A teacher from each of the 5 schools, advisory headteacher and subject adviser
▼ Resource materials
Comment The bulk of the money is being spent on release teachers for INSET. It is intended that the project's methods of assessment and record keeping will inform other subject areas in schools and provide examples of well tested good practice.
2 Language development in data base work (1989–90, primary age group).
■ To look at language development in all aspects of data base activities both on and off the computer. It is intended to observe all pupils but to concentrate especially on lower attaining pupils

T Advisory headteacher, coordinator for special needs, 3 IT advisory teachers, 3 learning support teachers, 2 teachers from each school.
▼ In preparation
3 Making sense of primary technology (1989, 5–7 age group).
■ To help primary teaches with Key Stage 1 of the design and technology aspects of the national curriculum
▼ Resource materials
4 Pilot for design and technology education in the national curriculum (1989–95, 11–14 age group).
■ To develop a strategy for implementing design and technology for 11–14 year olds.
▼ Reports/evaluation; resource materials; discussion documents
5 Designer craftspeople in schools (1988–89, all age groups).
▼ Discussion documents
6 Personal, social and health education (1986–93, 8–adult age group).
■ To develop and support implementation of curriculum initiatives in personal, social and health education
T LEA adviser and PSHE coordinator
▼ Books; resource materials; policy documents
7 Integration of pupils with learning difficulties into mainstream schools (1990, all age groups).
■ To evaluate current part-time and full-time initiatives taking place to integrate pupils with learning difficulties into mainstream schools; to make recommendations and proposals for future resourcing and INSET
T One seconded teacher
▼ Discussion documents
Comment A major part of the project will be the setting up of a group of special and mainstream teachers to work collaboratively on the identification of issues.
8 A programme of acts of worship 1987–90, 5–16 age group).
■ To pilot a scheme whereby pupils meet on occasions for acts of worship in faith groups as part of an overall assembly programme. The faith group worship happens as seldom or as often as the school feels appropriate. On the designated day all pupils meet in faith (but not denominational) groups, or as a group with no particular faith orientation, and the worship is led by members of the community. On all other days, pupils meet together in normal school groups
T Headteacher, advisory teacher, 8 teachers from first, middle and high schools and 6 members of the Harrow Interfaith Council
▼ Report/evaluation: resource materials
9 A data base of places of worship (1988–90, 5–18 and adult age groups).
■ To create a data base giving details of all places of worship within the Borough of Harrow.
T Advisory teacher, 1 member of TVEI team, a high school teacher, the head of library reference services, and 6 members of the Harrow Interfaith Council.

▼ Detailed handbook of religious education
10 Cross accreditation of coursework for GCSE (1988–91), 14–16 age group).
T Director (Kings College, London), cross-curricular team from a school, adviser, advisory headteacher
▼ Reports/evaluation

17. Havering
Mercury House, Mercury Gdns, Romford RM1 3DR
☎ 0708 766999
Ⓟ Director of educational services

18. Hillingdon
Civic Centre, Uxbridge, Middlesex UB8 1UW
☎ 0895 50530   Ⓕ 0895 934224
Ⓟ Chief education officer

19. Hounslow
Civic Centre, Lampton Rd, Hounslow, Middlesex TW3 4DN
☎ 081 570 7728
Ⓟ Director of education

20. Islington
Barnsbury Complex, Barnsbury Pk, London N1 1QF
☎ 071 607 6080   Ⓕ 071 607 6080
Ⓟ Chief education officer

21. Kensington & Chelsea
Town Hall, Hornton St, London W8 7NX
☎ 071 937 5464   Ⓕ 071 937 0038
Ⓟ Director of education

22. Kingston upon Thames
Directorate of Education, Guildhall, Kingston upon Thames, Surrey KT1 1EU
☎ 081 546 2121
Ⓟ Chief education officer
Projects and curriculum initiatives
1 Records of Achievement (1985–88, 11–18 age group).
■ Kingston LEA is part of a consortium of 5 London Boroughs working with AEB to pilot and extend the South East Record of Achievement (SERA)
Ⓟ Advisory teacher for ROA and LEA Inspector
▼ Reports/evaluations; books; resource materials; policy documents; discussion documents
Comment The project is being extended to include 16–19 age group and pupils with special education needs.
2 Maths and TVEI (1988–90, 14–18 age group).
■ A joint support activity involving the London Boroughs of Harrow, Ealing, Hillingdon, Kingston upon Thames and Richmond upon Thames together with the London Institute of Education
T LEA Inspectors, TVEI project leaders, advisory teachers and seconded teachers
▼ Resource materials (being prepared)
3 Participation on national primary LOGO

use in mathematics project (1989–91, 7–11 age group).

■ An inter-borough consortium with Richmond upon Thames to explore the effects of continued use of LOGO on young children's learning in mathematics. It supports work already undertaken in the LEA concerning use of LOGO

T NCET/MESU coordinators, LEA advisers, advisory teachers and classroom teachers

Comment This project is funded by NCET, the Nuffield Foundation and Chester College.

4 IT in English (1988–90, 11–18 age group).

T 2 LEA Inspectors, senior advisory teacher for IT, and seconded teacher

▼ Reports/evaluations

23. Lambeth
Lambeth Town Hall, Brixton Hill, London SW2 1RW
☎ 071 274 7722
Ⓟ Chief education officer

24. Lewisham
1 Aitken Rd, Catford, London SE6
☎ 081 697 8166
Ⓟ Director of education

25. Merton
Education and Recreation Department, Crown Hse, London Rd, Morden, Surrey SM4 5DX
☎ 081 543 2222   Ⓕ 081 543 7126
Ⓟ Chief education officer
Projects and curriculum initiatives
1 Environmental Education Centre (Snuff Mill) (ongoing, primary).
■ To encourage development work in environmental education including ecological studies, local history and nature trails.
T 1 project officer and links with advisory and other teachers
▼ Reports/evaluations; resource materials; policy documents
2 Profiling, Recording and Observation of Competencies and Experience at the Start of School (PROCESS) (ongoing, 3–6 age group).
■ To support and develop everyday observations of young children learning in the classroom, involving parents, teachers, nursery assistants and LEA inspectorate and advisory staff in liaison with Roehampton Institute of Higher Education
▼ Resource materials; policy documents; workbooks
3 British Petroleum management training project (ongoing, primary–secondary cross-phase).
Headteacher management training in conjunction with British Petroleum executive training scheme
T 2 seconded teachers and senior staff from other LEAs
▼ Reports/evaluations
4 Special needs integration (ongoing, secondary).
■ To develop strategies for integrating pupils from special schools into mainstream

classes
▼ Reports/evaluations; policy documents; discussion documents

26. Newham
379–383 High St, Stratford, London E15 4RD
☎ 081 534 4545
Ⓟ Chief education officer
Projects and curriculum initiatives
1 Teamwork project (ongoing, primary and secondary age groups).
■ To develop the management of the school curriculum
▼ Reports/evaluations; discussion documents
2 IT in primary schools (1988–90, 5–11 age group).
▼ Reports/evaluations; discussion documents
3 Special needs integration (ongoing, primary and secondary age groups).
▼ Reports/evaluations; resource materials; policy documents; discussion documents
4 Profiling and Records of Achievement (1987–90, secondary age group).
▼ Reports/evaluations; discussion documents

27. Redbridge
Lynton House, 255–259 High Rd, Ilford, Essex IG1 1NN
☎ 081 478 3020
Ⓟ Director of educational services

28. Richmond upon Thames
Regal Hse, London Rd, Twickenham TW1 3QB
☎ 081 891 1411
Ⓟ Director of education

29. Southwark
19 Grange Rd, London SE1 3BE
☎ 071 237 4551
Ⓟ Director of education

30. Sutton
The Grove, Carshalton, Surrey SM5 3AL
☎ 081 770 5000   Ⓕ 01 770 6545
Ⓟ Chief education officer
Projects and curriculum initiatives
1 South East Records of Achievement (SERA), in conjunction with Bexley, Kingston, Merton, Surrey and AEB (ongoing, 5–19 age group).
▼ Reports/evaluations; resource materials; policy documents; school manual and guidelines

31. Tower Hamlets
Town Hall, Patriot Sq, London E2 9LN
☎ 081 980 4831
Ⓟ Chief education officer

32. Waltham Forest
Municipal Offices, High Rd, Leyton, London E10 5QJ

☎ 081 527 5544
Ⓟ Chief education officer
Projects and curriculum initiatives
1 Attainment and assessment in religious education (1989–90, 5–16 age group).
■ To develop attainment targets and assessment methods related to the LEA Agreed Syllabus
Ⓣ SACRE, 15 co-opted teachers and head teachers and 10 pilot schools
▼ Reports/evaluations; policy documents

33. Wandsworth
Town Hall, Wandsworth High St,
London SW18 2PU
☎ 081 871 6000
Ⓟ Director of education

34. Westminster
City Hall, 64 Victoria St, London SW1E 6QP
☎ 071 828 8070
Ⓟ Director of education

35. Avon
PO Box 57, Avon Hse North, St James Barton, Bristol BS99 7EB
☎ 0272 290777   Ⓕ 0272 251174
Ⓟ Chief education officer
Projects and curriculum initiatives
1 Mathematics in the national curriculum (1989–90, primary).
■ To develop curriculum support materials for key stages 1 and 2
Ⓣ Editor, mathematics adviser, 6 advisory teachers
▼ Resource materials
2 Telling our stories (1989–90, primary and secondary).
■ To encourage autobiographical writing in English and 9 other mother tongues
Ⓣ Editor, FE lecturer
▼ Books
3 Controversial issues and farming (1989–90, secondary).
■ To develop audio and video materials and booklets about farming in conjunction with the North Somerset Agricultural Society and B.B.C. Radio Bristol
▼ Books; resource materials
4 The earth in space (1989–90, primary and secondary).
■ To develop approaches to science in the national curriculum with an emphasis on Attainment Target 16
▼ Books; resource materials

36. Barnsley
Berneslai Close, Barnsley S70 2HS
☎ 0226 733252
Ⓟ Chief education officer

37. Bedfordshire
County Hall, Bedford MK42 9AP
☎ 0234 228327
Ⓟ Chief education officer
Projects and curriculum initiatives
1 Developing quality control and quality assurance systems in colleges of further education (1987–90, post 16 age group).

■ A joint LEA/college initiative designed to increase accountability and responsibility of delivery teams in colleges
▼ Reports/evaluations; resource materials
2 Development of customised training for industry (1989–91, post 16 age group).
■ To test new approaches to training using DACUM systems and linking results to National Vocational Qualifications
▼ Reports/evaluations
3 Implementing the Education Reform Act in further education (1988–89, post 16 age group).
▼ 4-page bulletins

38. Berkshire
Shire Hall, Reading RG7 9XE
☎ 0734 875444   Ⓕ 0734 750360
Ⓟ Chief education officer
Projects and curriculum initiatives
1 Berkshire Arts initiative (1988–92, 3–19 age group).
■ To develop all aspects of arts education in the context of the national curriculum
▼ Policy documents; discussion documents; 'Assessment and evaluation in the Arts 10' from Berkshire Arts, Fox Hill, Pon Moor Road, Bracknell, Berkshire RG12 4AY
2 Project bridgebuilder (1988–90, 5–16 age group).
■ To develop curriculum bridges, ie links to and with the community, and adult to adult communication skills
▼ Reports/evaluations; discussion documents
3 Planning for school and staff development (1988–92, 3–18 age group).
■ To develop strategic planning strategies
▼ Guidelines for school development plans 3–50, and Planning for school and staff developments: working papers 2–50, both from School In-service Section, Education Offices
4 Learning through action (1986–91, 5–16 age group).
▼ Approaches to Learning through Action from Project Director, Newtown Primary School, School Rd, Reading

39. Birmingham
Education Department, Margaret St, Birmingham B3 3BU
☎ 021 235 2550   Ⓕ 021 233 4685
Ⓟ Chief education officer
Projects and curriculum initiatives
1 Community education (ongoing, 3 plus age group).
■ To promote self-esteem in local communities with a major emphasis on pre-school workers and support for parents
Ⓣ Led by Dr R.M. Atkinson (senior adviser)
▼ Policy documents, discussion documents
2 Health education (ongoing, 3 plus age group).
■ A Birmingham-wide initiative to support a Health for Life strategy; major emphasis on preventative approaches
Ⓣ Led by Mr J. Harvey (general adviser, health education)

▼   Policy documents, discussion documents
3   Management of children's behavioural problems and emotional needs (ongoing, 3 plus age group).
■   To draw together, in the south area of the LEA, headteachers, the Health Authority and the National Primary Centre
Ⓣ   Contact Sue Bordwell (021 428 1167)
▼   Policy documents, discussion documents.
4   Design Dimensions (1989–92, 5 plus age group).
■   A cross-curricular project linking up with the Design Dimension Trust.
Ⓟ   Contact John Bakewell, General adviser, English
▼   Policy documents, discussion documents

40. Bolton
PO Box 53, Paderborn Hse, Civic Centre, Bolton BL1 1JW
☎   0204 22311
Ⓟ   Chief education officer

41. Bradford
Provincial Hse, Tyrrel St, Bradford BD1 1NP
☎   0274 752111
Ⓟ   Chief education officer
Projects and curriculum initiatives
1   STAR project (1988–90, 7-year-olds).
■   A pilot scheme to develop SATs for 7-year-olds, including bilingual SATs
▼   Reports/evaluations; resource materials
2   LEA Economic Awareness (1989–91, 5–16 age group).
■   A pilot project involving a pyramid of schools to look at the planning, delivery, continuity and progression of the curriculum .
▼   Resource materials
3   A-level enhancement project (ongoing, 16–18 age group).
■   To work cooperatively with 4 other northern LEAs in the building of core skills and enrichments into A level in 15 major subjects; this is part of an overall LEA developmental framework for post-16 education
▼   Reports/evaluations; books; resource materials; policy documents
4   Curriculum-based assessment development project (ongoing, 5–18 age group).
■   To develop teacher skills in national curriculum assessment
▼   Resource materials; policy documents

42. Buckinghamshire
County Hall, Aylesbury HP22 6EH
☎   0296 395000   Ⓕ   0296 383367
Ⓟ   Chief education officer
Projects and curriculum initiatives
1   Diversification of first foreign language (1989–93, 12–16 age group).
■   To increase the number of pupils studying a language other than French as their first foreign language, and to assess the implication of the introduction of such a change
Ⓣ   1 coordinator and seconded advisory teachers

▼   Reports/evaluations
2   Buckinghamshire grade objectives in modern languages (ongoing, 11–16 age group).
■   The continuing development and evolution of the GOML scheme, encouraging the clearer setting of short term targets for language learning. Recent developments emphasise integrated skill, task or assignment-based approaches and the integration of assessment into the day-to-day teaching and learning process
Ⓣ   Advisory teachers, seconded teachers and teachers
▼   Resource materials
3   Assignment-based approaches to foreign languages learning (ongoing, 14–18 age group).
■   To develop flexible approaches to assignment design in foreign language teaching
▼   Reports/evaluations; resource materials
4   Buckinghamshire Observation Procedure (BOP) (1989–90, reception class).
▼   Resource materials; video
5   Curriculum development – Swann project (1988–94, 5–18 age group).
■   To implement the recommendations of the Swann Report and the national curriculum. While curriculum review and development inevitably form the major part of the work, this is placed in the wider contexts of school management and the community
6   Economic awareness project (1989–90, 5–19 age group).
■   To develop an outline for a 5–19 entitlement for economics and industrial understanding. Detailed work in schools includes the conducting of curriculum auditors and provision of INSET.
Ⓣ   1 advisory teacher and teachers
▼   Policy documents; discussion documents
7   Primary guidelines in art and design (1989–90, 5–12 age group).
▼   Resource materials

43. Bury
Athenaeum Hse, Market St, Bury BL9 0BN
☎   061 705 5000
Ⓟ   Chief education officer
Projects and curriculum initiatives
1   Secondary records of achievement (1988–95, 11–18 age group).
■   To develop records of achievement for the 11–18 age group in all LEA establishments.
Ⓣ   1 consultant, 1 LEA adviser
▼   Reports/evaluations; resource materials; policy documents; discussion documents
2   Primary Records of Achievement (1989–91, 3–11 age group).
■   To develop Records of Achievement for the primary age group
Ⓣ   1 consultant, 1 LEA adviser
▼   Policy documents
3   Special needs, record keeping and Records of Achievement (1988–91, 3–18 age group).
■   To look at the position of special needs in the development of Records of Achievement

T   2 consultants, 1 LEA adviser
▼   Profiles and records are being tried out
4   Personal and social education (1988–89, 11–18 age group).
■   To develop a coherent programme of PSE for schools and the LEA. To show schools how to conduct a PSE audit of the subject curriculum
▼   Resource materials; policy documents
5   Primary teachers into industry (ongoing, primary phase).
Comment   A 5-day course followed by INSET in schools, involving 20 teachers and industrialists from 20 companies.
6   Teachers into industry (1989–90, 11–18 age group and adults).
Comment   An 11-day course followed by INSET in schools, involving 16 high school teachers, 18 college lecturers and industrialists.
7   Marketing education (1989–90, secondary age group).
■   To use industry as a resource
Comment   For heads and deputies from high schools and trainers from industry.
8   Summerseat Residential Special School – Leavers curriculum development (ongoing, 14–16 age group).
T   1 teacher and a range of AOTs
9   Story friends (ongoing, infant age group).
■   To use adults from the local community to partner children in story sharing on a one to one basis
▼   Discussion documents
10   Nursery story tape (1989–90, nursery age group).
■   A pilot project to provide a resource bank of children's literature and tapes for use at home with nursery age children
▼   Discussion documents
11   TVEI extension (1988–94, 14–18 age group).
■   A major initiative to give young people a wider and richer education to support them in life in which work is a part
▼   Reports/evaluations; resource materials
12   Nursery assessment procedure (1987–90, nursery age group).
■   To make use of teacher observation
▼   Resource materials
13   World studies (1987–90, 4–19 age group).
T   3 seconded teachers, 1 adviser
▼   Reports/evaluations; resource materials; discussion documents; news bulletin

44. Calderdale

Northgate Hse, Halifax, West Yorkshire HX1 1UN
☎   0422 357257
Ⓟ   Chief education officer
Projects and curriculum initiatives
1   Evaluation of the ESG-funded primary science and technology scheme (1988–90, primary phase).
▼   Reports/evaluations

45. Cambridgeshire

Castle Court, Shire Hall, Castle Hill, Cambridge CB3 0AP

☎   0223 317990
Ⓟ   Chief education officer
Projects and curriculum initiatives
1   To review and recommend practical approaches to the National Curriculum (1989–91, all phases).
▼   Books; resource materials; discussion documents
2   Learning now – an introduction to the National Curriculum (1988–89, all phases).
▼   Books

46. Cheshire

Education Department, County Hall, Chester CH1 1SQ
☎   0244 602424
Ⓟ   Chief education officer

47. Cleveland

Woodlands Rd, Middlesbrough, Cleveland TS1 3BN
☎   0642 248155
Ⓟ   County education officer

48. Cornwall

Education Department, County Hall, Truro TR1 3BA
☎   0872 74282
Ⓟ   Chief education officer
Projects and curriculum initiatives
1   Learning together programme.
■   To develop an early learning programme of games and activities to encourage partnership between home and school
▼   Contact Dawn Bishop, Primary Resource Centre, Basset Road, Camborne, Cornwall TR14 8SL (0209 710158).
2   Integrated learning through topic work (primary phase).
■   To develop integrated learning through topic work in primary schools throughout Cornwall
▼   Contact Olga Collier, Dalvenie House, County Hall, Truro, Cornwall TR1 3BA (0872 74282)
3   4-year-olds in school (4–5 age group).
■   An analysis of policy and practice for the education of 4-year-old children in infant reception classes
▼   Contact Joy Kell, Primary Resources Centre, Pondhu House, Penwinnick Road, St. Austell, Cornwall (0726 65952)
4   Roseland project (9–13 age group).
■   To foster and evaluate primary and secondary curriculum continuity in the Roseland area of Cornwall
▼   Contact Olga Collier (as above)
5   TVEI extension (ongoing).
▼   Contact Peter Butts, Trevithick Centre for TVEI in Cornwall, Poll, Redruth, Cornwall TR15 9RD (0209 714280)

49. Coventry

New Council Offices, Earl St, Coventry CV1 5RS
☎   0203 833333   Ⓣ   265451
Ⓕ   0203 831620
Ⓟ   Chief education officer
Projects and curriculum initiatives

1   Community education (ongoing, all age groups).
■   To focus on community approaches to the curriculum
▼   Resource materials
2   Multi-faith approaches to RE (ongoing, all age groups).
▼   Resource materials
3   Asian dance (1988–90, secondary phase).
▼   Videotape; pupil guide on Asian dance
4   Bilingual assessment (1989, secondary phase).
▼   Discussion papers
5   Active lifestyles project (1984–91, 14–23 age group).
▼   Reports/evaluations; policy documents
Comment   This is a Sports Council National Demonstration Project.
6   The special needs action programme (ongoing, all age groups).
■   To give support to teachers in mainstream schools
▼   Reports/evaluations; books; resource materials
7   Gender, Equality in TVEI (1989–90, secondary and FE age groups).
■   To develop, support and disseminate positive action strategies
▼   Books
8   Staff development: women teachers (1987–9, all age groups).
■   To target professional development of women teachers across all levels and phases of education
T   4 teachers, 2 advisers
▼   Resource materials
9   Advanced diploma in education: management in schools (ongoing, all age groups).
▼   Books: resource materials.
10   Records of Achievement (ongoing, all age groups).
▼   Policy documents

50. Cumbria
5 Portland Sq, Carlisle CA1 1PU
☎   0228 23456
Ⓟ   Chief education officer
Projects and curriculum initiatives
1   Practical problem-solving 5–13 (1987–89, 5–13 age group).
■   To encourage a problem-solving approach to learning in all areas of the curriculum; to establish a framework for progression-skills, attitude, concepts and knowledge; to develop effective means of recording, assessing and evaluating the printed word; to produce guidelines for organisation and management of practical activities
T   Inspector/adviser, SATRO leader, 1 science/technology teacher
▼   Reports/evaluations; discussion documents
Comment   This is part of a national project involving a central team and other LEAs.
2   Records of Achievement in education, training and employment (1987–92, 4–19 age group).

■   To develop and pilot ROA systems throughout the phases of education; to develop coherent systems linking ROA to employment training including NROVA
T   LEA inspector/adviser, school/college coordinators
▼   Books; resource materials; policy documents; file format
Comment   This project is run in collaboration with Cumbria TEC.
3   Oracy across the curriculum 5–16 (1987–90, 5–16 age group).
■   To develop high-quality self-tutoring in-service materials with the focus of learning being by small group discussion
T   Seconded teachers, supported by LEA inspector/adviser
▼   Separate primary and secondary packages of video and booklet materials
4   Teacher and headteacher appraisal (1987–9, 5–19 age group).
■   To pilot work in the field of appraisal prior to the introduction of a national scheme; to develop, test and report on a scheme for a systematic and formative system of appraisal for teaching staffs in schools and its support documentation
T   1 (later, 2) seconded senior staff from schools plus full-time administrative assistant, all reporting to a working party
▼   4 handbooks; sample documentation; reports; a 3-tape video package with notes
Comment   Cumbria is 1 of 6 LEAs selected by the DES to pilot this work. It is based on the practical experience of introducing and implementing a developmental and supportive scheme of appraisal in 10 per cent of the schools in the LEA. These include nursery, primary, secondary, and special; the learning support service and FE are also involved.

51. Derbyshire
County Offices, Matlock DE4 3AG
☎   0629 580000   Ⓕ   0629 580350
Ⓟ   Chief education officer
Projects and curriculum initiatives
1   Derbyshire schools development project (ongoing, secondary phase).
■   To develop strategies for preventing disruption in secondary schools
T   Project leaders, County educational psychologist, Assistant director (schools), Chief adviser, Secondary adviser
▼   Reports/evaluations; policy documents; dissemination papers
2   Oracy (1987–90, primary and secondary phases).
■   To develop oral aspects of language in primary and secondary schools
T   English adviser, project leader
▼   Reports/evaluations; resource materials
3   Staff development (ongoing, primary and secondary phases).
■   To develop needs identification and collaboration staff development by clusters of schools
T   Adviser (staff development), 4 area coordinators for staff development
▼   Reports/evaluations; policy documents
4   TTNS in primary schools (ongoing,

primary phase).
■ To develop use of TTNS in primary schools through pilot projects
Ⓣ Adviser for IT, Head of the Software Centre, advisory teacher (IT, primary)
▼ Reports/evaluations; resource materials; discussion documents.

52. Devon
County Hall, Topsham Rd, Exeter EX2 4QG
☎ 0392 77977   Ⓣ 42467
Ⓕ 0392 272301
Ⓟ Chief education officer
Projects and curriculum initiatives
1 Satellite communication in distance learning (ongoing, all phases).
■ To develop the use of satellite communication in distance learning, for example with teachers and governors together and by children in world studies contexts. To develop interaction through satellites and telephonic apparatus. To encourage links with the EEC
Ⓣ LEA Adviser, advisory teacher, HE and secondary schools
▼ Reports/evaluations; film
2 Assessment in religious education (1989–92, 5–16 age group).
■ To develop assessment in religious education in conjunction with other South West LEAs
Ⓣ LEA adviser and advisory teachers, part-time project teachers and regional project officers
▼ Reports/evaluations
3 Devon Records of Achievement project (ongoing, secondary).
■ To authenticate school schemes and processes
Ⓣ LEA adviser and advisory teacher
▼ Reports/evaluations

53. Doncaster
Directorate of Educational Services, Princegate, Doncaster,
DN1 3EP
☎ 0302 735162
Ⓟ Chief education officer
Projects and curriculum initiatives
1 Learning through talking (1987–89, all phases).
■ To raise awareness about, and develop practice in, oracy; to offer guidelines and recommended approaches via a publication.
Ⓣ Advisor and advisory teacher
▼ Books; resource materials
2 Calculator Aware Number (CAN) Curriculum (1986–92, 6–11 age group).
■ Curriculum and associated staff development to take advantage of the availability of electronic calculators
Ⓣ Mathematics adviser, 3 advisory teachers, in association with former PRiME team members and other LEAs
▼ Reports/evaluations
3 Mechanics in action (1988–91, secondary phase).
■ To develop activities to support and enhance experience in mechanics elements in

'A' level mathematics courses and coursework of a practical nature in GCSE mathematics
Ⓣ Sheffield University staff, LEA seconded project officer, advisory teacher, mathematics adviser
4 Royal Institution Mathematics Master Classes (ongoing, middle/secondary phases). Curriculum enrichment for pupils of 12–13 years and linked staff development
Ⓣ Sheffield University staff, mathematics adviser, advisory teacher, headteacher, head of department and several teachers on a rota basis
▼ Programme outline

54. Dorset
County Hall, Dorchester, Dorset DT1 1XJ
☎ 0305 251000
Ⓟ County education officer

55. Dudley
Westox Hse, 1 Trinity Rd, Dudley, West Midlands DY1 1JB
☎ 0384 456000   Ⓕ 0384 452216
Ⓟ Chief education officer
Projects and curriculum initiatives
1 Computer hardware evaluation (ongoing, all groups).
■ Evaluation of a wide range of computer hardware and software applications
▼ Reports/evaluations
2 Dudley LEA Information Technology Policy (ongoing, all age groups).
▼ Policy documents
3 Interspan project (1989–90, secondary phase).
■ To establish electronic communications with schools in 3 European countries. There is the potential for all Dudley secondary school children to communicate by this means both cheaply and effectively
▼ Reports/evaluations; discussion documents
4 Easy access to computers on networks (ongoing, secondary phase).
■ To develop a philosophy for implementation with software
▼ Resource materials

56. Durham
County Hall, Durham DH1 5UJ
☎ 091 386 4411
Ⓟ Chief education officer
Projects and curriculum initiatives
1 Graded objectives scheme (1984–7, 11–13 age group).
■ To develop French teaching in respect of: Niveau Fundamental continuous assessment, involving self, peer and teacher assessment; and Niveau Moyen – talk-based continuous assessment with some mixed skills
Ⓣ LEA adviser, HE lecturer, seconded teachers
▼ Resource materials; assessment materials
2 Outdoor education review (1989, primary and secondary phases).
Ⓣ Advisers and LEA staff

▼ Policy documents; discussion documents
3 Records of Achievement (1986–91, primary phase).
▼ Resource materials; policy documents
4 Calculator Aware Number curriculum in primary education (CAN) (1986–91, primary phase).
▼ Report on 3 years of CAN in County Durham

57. East Sussex
Education Department, PO Box 4, County Hall, Lewes, East Sussex BN7 1SG
☎ 0273 475400
Ⓟ County education officer

58. Essex
Threadneedle Hse, Market Rd, Chelmsford CM1 1LD
☎ 0245 492211 Ⓕ 0245 492759
Ⓟ Chief education officer

Projects and curriculum initiatives
1 Positive approaches to pupil behaviour (1989–90, 11–16 age group).
■ The review of school management and organisation with a view to improving the antecedent conditions; the use of peer group support to enable teachers to identify ways of improving pupil behaviour (ie teaching and learning strategies)
Ⓣ Project director, 0.5 FTE staff enhancement in each project school
▼ Resource materials; discussion documents
2 Essex assessment initiative (1988–90, 5–16 age group).
■ The preparation of staff development materials to support school-focused programmes of training in techniques of assessing, recording and reporting pupil achievement in readiness for the national curriculum programme of testing
▼ Discussion documents (1 pack for primary schools and 1 pack for secondary schools)
3 Essex Education Library Project (ongoing, 5–18 age group).
■ Primary and secondary schools have been asked to relate the provision and organisation of their learning resources to curriculum objectives and priorities in order to promote whole school participation and representation in matters of library policy
Ⓣ 2 advisory teachers, 3 inspectors, 1 officer, 1 adviser, 1 assistant county librarian

59. Gateshead
Civic Centre, Regent St, Gateshead NE8 1HH
☎ 091 477 1011
Ⓟ Chief education officer
Projects and curriculum initiatives
1 Primary science/technology/industry project (1988–9, 4–11 age group).
■ To give children an insight into the world of work through the manufacturing, testing and quality control procedures used in industry via the medium of science and technology

Ⓣ 1 adviser, 2 advisory teachers, 2 seconded teachers.
▼ Documents available. Resource materials – teachers' guides, pupils' books
2 MESU collaborative activities communications project (1988–90, 4–11 age group).
■ To extend the social and educational horizons of children in urban and rural environments, by enabling contrasting communities to communicate with each other and to share their experiences through the medium of electronic communications
Ⓣ 1 adviser, 1 advisory teacher
▼ Evaluation report to be completed at end of project
Comment This is an inter-LEA collaborative venture between Northumberland and Gateshead.
3 Teletext project (1989–90, 4–11 age group).
■ To encourage pupils and teachers in schools to use teletext as a resource in the development of their classroom-based work
Ⓣ 1 adviser, 1 advisory teacher
▼ Project structure and brief with resource pack
Comment Participating schools will use the Gateshead Bulletin system as the communications medium of the project.
4 NARNIA (1989, 4–11 age group).
■ To encourage teachers and pupils to use electronic communications as a resource for problem-solving and curriculum development in cooperation with other schools and services in the LEA
Ⓣ 1 advisory teacher, 1 teacher
▼ Teachers' guide and INSET resources. Songs written by pupils
Comment This project employs cross-curricular approaches.

60. Gloucestershire
Shire Hall, Gloucester GL1 2TP
☎ 0452 425457
Ⓟ Chief education officer
Projects and curriculum initiatives
1 Management of learning (ongoing, 11–19 age group).
■ To research student learning experiences and classroom management, in order to target key areas for development; to fund small institution/consortium-based development projects
Ⓣ 9 phase advisers and advisory teachers
▼ Reports/evaluations
2 Low attaining pupils in secondary schools (1987–90, 11–14 age group).
■ To raise the achievements and motivation of low-attaining 11–14 year-old pupils through a variety of cross-curricular school-based activities
Ⓣ 2 advisers and 1 seconded advisory teacher
▼ Reports/evaluations; resource materials
3 Gloucestershire Oracy Project (1988–90, 5–16 age group).
■ This is an offshoot of the National Oracy Project and is designed to encourage cross-curricular exploration of approaches to

learning through talking and listening. All materials are generated, piloted and evaluated in schools by practitioners
Ⓣ 5 advisers, 1 HE lecturer and 1 advisory teacher
▼ Reports/evaluations; resource materials; audio and video tapes
4 Project '92 (1989–92, 16–19 age group).
■ This is a Training Agency-funded Youth Development Project to develop 'managers of the future'. Able students are given protracted involvement with a firm or organisation and co-tutored by education and industry. Each participant is involved in enterprise and personal development activities, a personal action plan and a paid year in the firm
Ⓣ 1 advisory teacher
▼ Reports/evaluations; policy documents

61. Hampshire
The Castle, Winchester SO23 8UG
☎ 0962 841841
Ⓟ County education officer

62. Hereford and Worcester
Education Offices, Castle St, Worcester WR1 3AG
☎ 0905 763763   Ⓕ 0905 726665
Ⓟ Chief education officer
Projects and curriculum initiatives
1 Primary Science Matters (PRISM) (1989–90, primary phase).
■ To develop guidelines and materials to help primary teachers meet the expectations of the National Curriculum in science. The main thrust of the pack produced is to provide a comprehensive set of ideas and experiences for teachers to use in planning their work
Ⓣ Primary science and technology project leader, 3 advisory teachers
▼ Resource materials
2 Advanced Certificate/Diploma in the teaching of history (1989–91, all phases).
■ To provide a flexible approach to in-service work in history in a widely spread LEA; to help teachers respond effectively to the national curriculum and to support those without specialist training in history
Ⓣ LEA inspector, advisory teacher, 2 teachers
Comment The course is part-time and includes a distance-learning component. It is validated by the Historical Association.
3 Project pathways (ongoing, infant, primary and middle phases).
■ To develop a package to help schools choose, structure and evaluate their project/thematic work; to help school to take a holistic approach to learning in the light of the national curriculum
Ⓣ 2 LEA inspectors, 10 heads and deputies from first, primary and middle schools
▼ Resource materials
4 Business Orientated Resource Information System (BORIS) (1988–91, 14–19 age group).
■ The promotion, development and dissemination of support materials for the

teaching of business education
Ⓣ Advisory teacher, linking with advisory teachers from each of the 5 LEAs involved
▼ Resource materials
Comment The project is funded by the Supported Self-Study Unit of the Training Agency and is coordinated by the Centre for Business Education at Wolverhampton Polytechnic.

63. Hertfordshire
County Hall, Hertford SG13 8DF
☎ 0992 555827
Ⓟ County education officer

64. Humberside
County Hall, Beverley, North Humberside HU17 9BA
☎ 0482 867131   Ⓕ 0482 863684
Ⓟ Chief education officer
Projects and curriculum initiatives
1 Structuring thematic enquiry in the primary school (1984–88, primary phase).
■ To emphasise a whole school approach to planning and evaluating; production of materials offering planning support using an analytical framework ideally suited to national curriculum requirements
▼ Resource materials; policy documents; videos
Comment The videos and leaders' notes are the result of a 3-year strategy involving secondments to Humberside College of Higher Education.
2 Strategy for evaluating all INSET activities (1988–89, all phases).
■ A cross-phase working group has produced a strategy for evaluating all INSET activities; each school in the LEA has a trained INSET co-ordinator and the area of evaluation now has a high profile
Ⓣ Working group led by Senior Adviser (INSET), SEO (Curriculum), staff development services
▼ Policy documents ('Evaluation strategy for curriculum and staff development')
3 Guidelines and support materials for meeting special educational needs (1987–89, all phases).
Ⓣ Working group of senior practitioners led by Senior Adviser (SEN)
▼ Policy documents ('Meeting SEN in Mainstream')
4 Political and social education (1988-89, all phases).
Ⓣ Working group led by General Adviser for History.
▼ Policy documents
5 Pre-school curriculum (1984–5 and 1989–90, pre-school age group).
■ To produce and update the LEA pre-school guidelines
Ⓣ Working group of pre-school practitioners led by Senior Adviser (early years)
▼ Policy documents ('Working Together')

65. Isles of Scilly
Town Hall, St Mary's. Isles of Scilly TR21 OLW
☎ 0720 22537   Ⓕ 0720 22122

Ⓣ Assistant chief executive, general services

66. Isle of Wight
County Council Education Department, County Hall, Newport, Isle of Wight PO30 1UD
☎ 0983 823416   Ⓣ 8694291W
Ⓕ 0983 521817
Ⓟ Assistant county education officer
Projects and curriculum initiatives
1 Geography (1988–93, 14–16 age group, extending to 9–16).
■ The preparation of syllabus and teaching materials in order to implement a Mode 3 GCSE course common to all the island high schools
Ⓣ 1 seconded teacher with an inter-school support group
▼ Resource materials
2 Development of broad, balanced science programmes at Key Stage 3 (1989–90, 9–13 age group).
■ The development of broad, balanced science programmes at key stage 3 so as to foster common practices within the framework of a revised middle school (9–13) core science document setting out policy and practice
Ⓣ 2 seconded teachers working with LEA adviser and inter-school support group
▼ Books; policy documents
3 Economic awareness (1989–92, 5–19 age group).
■ A strategy to offer learning experiences within the whole curriculum to form part of the entitlement of every pupil throughout school life
Ⓣ 1 seconded teacher and support group
▼ Discussion documents
4 Curriculum support (1989–92, 16–19 age group).
■ The development of a programme of enrichment/enhancement units offered conjointly by schools and the College of Arts and Technology, open to all post-16 students. The units are designed to add breadth and depth to existing programmes of study, and will utilise associated supported self-study and open learning facilities being developed as part of the project

67. Kent
Springfield, Maidstone ME14 2LJ
☎ 0622 671411
Ⓟ County education officer
Projects and curriculum initiatives
1 Kent assessment and support project (ongoing, Key Stage 1 onwards).
■ Research and development to support the work of identified groups of teachers through strategies and materials for classroom based assessment. Specific areas of focus include: Records of Achievement (dissemination of LEA policy and production of summary record); primary profiles (development of a portfolio record to include national curriculum and other aspects of pupil development); research into developing good

practice in science and design technology in the national curriculum Key STAGE 3); maths and English (as above) in Key Stage 1; recording and reporting achievement (research into contextual factors affecting pupil and school performance through analysis of examination results at Key Stage 4 and monitoring progress of pupils at Key Stage 1)
Ⓣ 6 seconded project officers
▼ Reports/evaluations
2 'A' level history (1989–91, 16–18 age group and adults).
■ To develop the Cambridge History Project (Option 1: people, power and politics; Option 2: technology and society)
Ⓣ 2 seconded teachers, LEA adviser, 2 writing groups of teachers
▼ Resource materials (pupil and teacher materials; general background information; cluster group support materials; newsletter)
Comment   This project is jointly funded by the LEA, Cambridge University Local Examination Syndicate, and the Training Agency; it is based at the Kent History Centre.
3 Exploring sounds and themes (1988–9, Key Stage 1 and 2).
■ To develop and disseminate ideas for making music in primary schools
Ⓣ LEA inspector, staff development coordinator, 1 teacher, supported by working party of 21 class teachers
▼ Resource materials (box set of 18 music cards for use by school teachers with their children)
4 Arts in schools project (SCDC) (1984–88, primary and secondary phases).
■ To examine curriculum practice in the arts. The specific focus for Kent was the arts as perceived by the community (parents, governors, outside agencies).
Ⓣ 1 seconded coordinator, 3 secondary teachers, 8 primary teachers, supported by subject inspectors

68. Kirklees
Oldgate Hse, Oldgate, Huddersfield HD1 6QW
☎ 0484 422133   Ⓣ 94013537
Ⓟ Chief education officer
Projects and curriculum initiatives
1 Schools science development plan (1989, 9–16 age group).
■ To provide a planning framework for departments to work within when considering the mapping exercise moving from current provision to a programme that accommodates the national curriculum orders for science
Ⓣ 2 seconded teachers
▼ Policy documents
2 National curriculum INSET (1989, 5–6 age group).
■ A one week training course for teachers of 5–6 year-olds, to cover the 3 core subjects and cross-curricular issues as well as record keeping and teacher assessment.
Ⓣ 1 inspector, 1 lecturer, 1 advisory teacher
▼ Resource materials; discussion documents

3   ESG primary science and technology
(1986–89, 4–13 age group).
■   To develop primary science and
technology by team members working
alongside teachers in classrooms
▼   Resource materials; policy documents
4   Foreign languages (1989–90, 11–16 age
group).
■   To research, collate and develop ideas
and materials for more appropriate foreign
language learning experiences for those
pupils who do not currently study foreign
languages but will be required to do so by the
national curriculum
Ⓣ   1 inspector, 1 seconded teacher
▼   Reports/evaluations; policy documents
5   Foreign languages other than French
(1989–90, 11–16 age group).
■   To develop appropriate learning
materials and to review
methodologies and assessment techniques
with regard to learning languages other than
French
Ⓣ   1 inspector, 1 seconded teacher
▼   Reports/evaluations; policy documents

69. Knowsley
Huyton Hey Rd, Huyton, Merseyside L36 5YH
☎   051 480 5111
Ⓟ   Chief education officer

70. Lancashire
PO Box 61, County Hall, Preston PR1 8RJ
☎   0772 54868
Ⓟ   Chief education officer

71. Leeds
Education Offices, 110 Merrion Centre, Leeds
LS2 8DT
☎   0532 462856   Ⓣ   556237
Ⓕ   0532 421321
Ⓟ   Chief education officer
Projects and curriculum initiatives
1   Primary Needs Programme (PNP)
(ongoing, 3–11 age group).
■   A major programme of enrichment for
primary schools involving significant additional
staffing and resources
Comment   The project is being
independently evaluated by Leeds University
▼   Reports/evaluations.

72. Leicestershire
County Hall, Glenfield, Leicester LE3 8RF
☎   0533 656307   Ⓣ   0533 341478
Ⓕ   0533 656634
Ⓟ   Chief education officer
Projects and curriculum initiatives
1   TEVI Pilot (1983–8, 14–19 age group).
■   To enable all students to study a broad,
balanced, relevant and differentiated
curriculum; to support active learning by
students; to prepare students for adult and
working life; to value the full range of each
student's achievements; to prepare students
for a variety of courses and related
assessments; to improve 14–19 progression
▼   Reports/evaluations; resource materials;
policy documents; discussion documents
104

2   TVEI extension (1987–92, 14–19 age
group).
■   As for Project 1
▼   Reports/evaluations; books; resource
materials; policy documents; discussion
documents

73. Lincolnshire
County Offices, Newland, Lincoln LN1 1YQ
☎   0522 552222   Ⓕ   0522 512288
Ⓟ   County education officer
Projects and curriculum initiatives
1   Craft, design and technology –
secondary (ongoing, secondary phase)
■   To develop: A-level work; CDT in girls'
schools; unified schemes of work and to train
teachers
Ⓣ   3 teachers and 1 technician
▼   Reports/evaluations; books; resource
materials
2   Primary science and technology
(ongoing, primary phase).
■   To produce national curriculum guide for
primary science, tool kits and electricity kits
sponsored by local industry
Ⓣ   7 staff housed in a training centre
▼   Reports/evaluations; books; resource
materials
3   Mobile Technology Unit (ongoing, all
phases).
■   To take IT and new technologies to
schools, industry and the general public;
sponsored by local industry
Ⓣ   Advisory teacher, driver, and technician,
supported by the Microelectronic
Development Unit
▼   Reports/evaluations
4   Record of Achievement (ongoing,
secondary phase).
■   To develop a computerised software
package for record keeping
Ⓣ   3 teachers
▼   Computer software

74. Liverpool
14 Sir Thomas St, Liverpool L1 6BJ
☎   051 225 2760/2722
Ⓟ   Chief education officer
Projects and curriculum initiatives
1   City based Resources Unit (ongoing, all
age groups).
■   To relate school needs for source
materials to data available in city Technical
departments and agencies. To translate raw
data into a resource format accessible to
teachers and pupils, and manage its
dissemination to schools. To provide inservice
support to schools and teachers on practical
classroom applications and curriculum
contexts of source materials
Ⓣ   2 seconded teachers, LEA adviser and
members of city Technical departments
▼   Project outline and report
2   Business education (1988–93, 14–18
age group).
■   To develop, pilot and print resource
materials for business education across the
upper secondary age range. This initiative is
an attempt to establish a coherent strategy for

business education
T   1 seconded teacher, 8 teachers
▼   Resource materials
Comment   The project team also acts as a support network for teachers across the LEA. Work is prepared by the group, used in their schools, evaluated and written up.

75. Manchester
Crown Square, Manchester M60 3BB
☎   061 234 5000
Ⓟ   Chief education officer

76. Newcastle upon Tyne
Civic Centre, Barras Bridge, Newcastle upon Tyne NE1 8PU
☎   091 232 8520
Ⓟ   Chief education officer
Projects and curriculum initiatives
1   Teacher appraisal (1987–9, all phases).
▼   Reports/evaluations; books; resource materials
2   Primary technology (1987–9, 4–11 age group).
▼   Resource materials
3   Primary schools enquiry (1987–9, 4–11 age group).
▼   Reports/evaluations
4   Real connections project (1988–9, 4–18 age group).
▼   Reports/evaluations

77. Norfolk
County Hall, Martineau Lane, Norwich NR1 2DL
☎   0603 222146   Ⓕ   0603 222119
Ⓟ   County education officer
Projects and curriculum initiatives
1   National curriculum team (1989–94, 4–16 age group).
■   To focus on the interpretation, coordination and evaluation of the National Curriculum and assessment in a local context. First phase: to help with forward planning, school management plans, assessment and in the specific curriculum areas of science, technology and English. Second phase: to address the basic curriculum and assessment
T   8 teachers reporting to the Senior general adviser
▼   Resource materials
2   Norfolk Oracy project – dissemination phase (1990–1, 3–16 age group).
■   To develop classroom management of small group work 5–16, cross-curricular topic work 5–8, oracy across the curriculum 11–16 and to monitor and assess oracy 5–16.
T   4 advisory teachers
▼   Reports/evaluations; books; resource materials; discussion documents
3   Norfolk Educational Press (part of the TVEI extension programme) (1988–94, 14–18 age group).
■   To produce and publish curriculum resources and to function as an outlet for materials produced by the INSET Centre
▼   Reports/evaluations; booklets; resource materials

78. North Tyneside
The Chase, North Shields, Tyne and Wear NE29 0HW
☎   091 257 6621
Ⓟ   Chief education officer

79. North Yorkshire
County Hall, Northallerton DL7 8AE
☎   0609 780780
Ⓟ   County education officer

80. Northamptonshire
Northampton Hse, Northampton NN1 2HX
☎   0604 236241   T   312516
Ⓕ   0604 236188
Ⓟ   County education officer
Projects and curriculum initiatives
1   National curriculum implementation (1989–91, 5–16 age group).
■   To begin the delivery of the national curriculum in core subjects plus design and technology
T   1 inspector, 28 advisory teachers in teams of 4 (2 secondary, 1 middle, 4 primary).
▼   Reports/evaluations; policy documents
2   Northamptonshire Assessment and Recording of Achievement (NARA) (ongoing, 5–19 age groups).
■   To support assessment, recording and reporting in all Northamptonshire schools. It is undertaking work on: developing record of achievement practices; researching to develop IT support for Record of Achievement processes; preparing for national curriculum assessment through training early years teachers as trainers, raising teachers' awareness and developing IT support for assessment and recording; retaining overview and responsibilities for such things as CPVE and BTEC and developing liaison with other interested parties. Ultimately it will work towards preparing guidelines for assessment, recording and reporting
▼   Reports/evaluations; policy documents; discussion documents
3   Northamptonshire TVEI – equality of opportunity (1988–90, 14–18 age group).
■   To address equality of opportunity, gender, race and special needs, in a variety of ways. The broad strategy has been to complement and support LEA provision and developments. The guiding principle has been to seek to ensure inclusivity, and to tackle factors which effectively exclude individuals and groups from entitlement. TVEI has funded part- and full-time secondments; established a network comprising teachers, lecturers, careers officers, LEA officers and inspectors, and headteachers; arranged awareness-raising and specifically focused training events, seminars and workshops; and encouraged dissemination of information and ideas via occasional papers
▼   Resource materials; position statements; secondment report
4   Citizenship (1989–90, 11–18 age group).
■   To consider how best to develop and recognise active citizenship within a wide range of groups in the community (both local

and national), including school students, adults, and those in full employment as well as volunteers. In cooperation with Leicester University and Leicestershire LEA, a seconded head teacher of a comprehensive school is researching current practice in a number of LEA schools
▼ Reports/evaluations

81. Northumberland
County Hall, Morpeth, Northumberland NE61 2EF
☎ 0670 514343   ⓣ 537048
Ⓕ 0670 511707
Ⓟ Chief education officer
Projects and curriculum initiatives
1 Post-16 supported self-study project (ongoing, 16–18 age group).
■ To develop a range of A-level courses through this mode
Ⓣ Led by Mr Chris Boothroyd
▼ Reports/evaluations; resource materials
2 Rural schools project (1987–92, 4–9 age group).
■ To maintain and enhance the curriculum in rural first schools
Ⓣ Led by Ms Kath Tickell
▼ Reports/evaluations
3 Governor training course (1989–93, 4–18 age group).
■ To provide modular courses for governors in curriculum, management, budget, and LEA services
4 Middle school development project (ongoing, 9–13 age group).
■ A radical review of curriculum organisation and management in middle schools
Ⓣ Led by Mrs M. Hughes
▼ Resource materials; discussion documents

82. Nottinghamshire
County Hall, West Bridgford, Nottingham NG2 7QP
☎ 0602 823823   ⓣ 37485
Ⓕ 0602 817945
Ⓟ Principal education officer
Projects and curriculum initiatives
1 Information technology in schools and colleges (1988–92, all phases).
■ To develop the use of information technology across the curriculum
Ⓣ 16 seconded teachers
▼ Reports/evaluations; resource materials
Comment Schools work in groups to develop continuity and progression.
2 Primary science and technology (1987–9, 4–11 age group).
■ To support teachers in developing the science curriculum in primary schools; to develop a range of materials which meet the requirements of the national curriculum
▼ Reports/evaluations; resources materials
3 Nottinghamshire staff development project (ongoing, all phases).
■ To train a consultant for curriculum and staff development for every school and college in the LEA; to provide time for each institution to develop staff development

programmes
▼ Reports/evaluations; resource materials; discussion documents
4 TVEI extension (1989–97, 14–18 age group).
■ To enhance the 14–18 curriculum. This has implications for the way in which any course, subject or programme of study is taught in that it should develop: learning and teaching styles; technology across the curriculum; guidance and support; industry and community links; equal opportunities
▼ Discussion documents

83. Oldham
Old Town Hall, Middleton Rd, Chadderton, Oldham OL9 6PP
☎ 061 678 4202
Ⓟ Chief education officer
Projects and curriculum initiatives
1 Record of Achievement (1987–93, 11–16 age group).
■ To investigate how an operational system of accreditation might be introduced and how schools might be monitored and helped
Ⓣ 1 seconded teacher supported by the Profiling Group
▼ Reports/evaluations; policy documents
2 Joint support activity (1988–91, 11–16 age group).
■ To support applied science and technology for all in secondary schools; to examine use of existing material and the teaching and learning associated with them
Ⓣ 4 seconded teachers, 1 adviser
▼ Reports/evaluations; policy documents
Comment Supported by 4 LEAs and the Training Agency.
3 Colleague headteachers' support to primary schools and associate tutor scheme (1989–90, 5–11 age group).
■ Support for new headteachers in use of GRIDS self-evaluation and in the management of initial training in schools
Ⓣ Headteachers with partial secondment
▼ Reports/evaluations; policy documents
Comment A joint project with Manchester Polytechnic and Oldham LEA.
4 Caen-Oldham link (1989–93, 11–16 age group).
■ Teacher and pupil exchange
▼ Reports/evaluations
5 TVEI curriculum enrichment programme (ongoing, 16–18 age group).
6 NEA credit accumulation project (ongoing, 14–16 age group).
7 Support material for teaching GCSE Agriculture and Horticulture (ongoing, 14–16 age group).
■ To support GCSE syllabus in agriculture and horticulture and modules of agriculture and horticulture in modular science syllabuses
▼ Resource materials (booklets obtainable from David Kirkwood, Rossendale Groundwork Trust, New Hall Hay Road, Rawtenstall, Rossendale BB4 6HR)

84. Oxfordshire
Education Department, Macclesfield House, New Rd, Oxford OX1 1NA

☎ 0865 815185/815997
ⓕ 0865 791637
ⓟ County education officer

Projects and curriculum initiatives

1 Records of Achievement in middle, upper, secondary, special and post-16 institutions (1985–90, 11–18 age group and adult).

■ To promote a countywide collaborative exploration of how students can be more closely involved in the assessment of their progress so that they become better learners and more confident people; to develop documentation that supports this process and also meets the needs of other users

Ⓣ ROA working unit, advisory and support services

▼ Reports/evaluations; discussion documents

Comment There is an emphasis on school-based secondment.

2 The achievement project 1988 (ongoing, 5–18 age group).

■ To focus on under-achieving pupils, to find ways of encouraging and recognising achievement in all areas of learning and to stimulate greater awareness of the needs of under-achieving pupils

Ⓣ Director, deputy, 4 community link tutors based in project schools

▼ Reports/evaluations; discussion documents

Comment This project developed from the Oxfordshire version of the Lower Attaining Pupils' Project (LAPP) funded by the DES.

3 Oxfordshire Examination Syndicate Credit Bank (1986–90 – though Credit Bank will continue beyond this date, 14–19 – though wider applications possible).

■ To explore the modular curriculum and related criteria-driven assessment within a number of contexts; to develop modular courses as appropriate; to develop and disseminate INSET support and good practice; to bank modules and assessment examples; to develop recording and reporting systems appropriate to modular course assessment

Ⓣ 1 project leader, seconded teachers

▼ Reports/evaluations; resource materials; policy documents; discussion documents; teachers' handbooks; course syllabuses

4 Oxfordshire Skills Programme (ongoing, 5–18 age group).

■ To inform teachers' working knowledge of the cognitive skills underpinning effective learning; to focus on the style of teaching which encourage active thinking and stimulate creativity and critical awareness; to direct teachers' attention towards the importance of assessment as a device for formative guidance; to facilitate language development, particularly the language of thinking; to encourage teachers to see the opportunities for integrated approaches to learning across the whole curriculum; to invite consideration of a whole school approach to the development of skills in cognitive processes

Ⓣ 2 coordinators

▼ Books; discussion documents

85. Rochdale

PO Box 70, Municipal Offices, Smith St, Rochdale OL16 1YD
☎ 0706 47474
ⓟ Chief education officer

86. Rotherham

Education Office, Walker Place, Rotherham S60 1QT
☎ 0709 382121
ⓟ Director of education

87. St Helens

Century Hse, Hardshaw St, St Helens WA10 1RN
☎ 0744 24061
ⓟ Director of community education

88. Salford

Chapel St, Salford M3 5LT
☎ 061 832 9751   ⓕ 061 835 1561
ⓟ Chief education officer

Projects and curriculum initiatives

1 Careers education support programme (1989–93, 14–19 age group).

■ To identify and develop the contribution of core and foundation subjects to careers education; to encourage links with the Careers Service, and to investigate IT applications

Ⓣ Staff of 3 supported by a series of secondments

▼ Discussion documents; reports/evaluations to come

2 IT in the secondary mathematics classroom (1989–93, 14–16 age group).

■ A small scale pilot study in 5 schools using up to date hardware and software

Ⓣ Coordinated by the Mathematics adviser

▼ Reports/evaluations to come

3 Supported self study (1989–90, 14–19 age group).

■ To investigate potential approaches in a variety of contexts as part of a North West consortium

Ⓣ 1 advisory teacher

▼ Reports/evaluations and leaflet to come

4 Art and design in the primary school (ongoing, 3–11 age group).

■ To develop good practice in art and design linking into thematic and topic approaches to learning including language development and critical and historical studies

Ⓣ LEA adviser, 1 curriculum trainer

▼ Reports/evaluations; books; policy documents

5 Computer aided design in secondary schools (1988–91, 11–18 age group).

■ To install computers in selected high schools and develop the use of computers in aspects of design across the art/design curriculum.

Ⓣ LEA adviser, 1 seconded teacher

▼ Reports/evaluations

6 Teaching/learning strategies in applied science and technology (1988–91, 14–19 age group).

■ A collaborative project with 4 LEAs to enable experienced teachers to review teaching and learning strategies and to produce materials to support modified practice in schools and colleages

Ⓣ 16 teachers seconded 1 day a week

▼ Reports/evaluations; books; resource materials

89. Sandwell
PO Box 41, Shaftesbury Hse, 402 High St, West Bromwich B70 9LT

☎ 021 525 7366

Ⓟ Director of education

90. Sefton
Town Hall, Bootle L20 7AE

☎ 051 933 6003

Ⓟ Director of education

91. Sheffield
PO Box 67, Leopold St, Sheffield S1 1RJ

☎ 0742 26341

Ⓟ Chief education officer

92. Shropshire
Education Department, Shirehall, Abbey Foregate, Shrewsbury, Shropshire SY2 6ND

Ⓟ County education officer

Projects and curriculum initiatives

1 Whole school curriculum planning and review (ongoing, 5–18 age group).

■ The establishing of annual school development plans incorporating the national curriculum, TVEI and INSET plans. These are used as a basis of a collaborative review procedure between schools and the LEA, involving agreed indicators of good practice

▼ Reports/evaluations; policy documents

2 Shropshire design and technology team (ongoing, 5–16 age group).

▼ To develop design and technology across the curriculum and to establish and operate a GCSE course entitled 'Technology for all'

▼ Resource materials; policy documents; discussion documents; examination syllabus (approved by MEG)

Comment A major resource centre forms the focus of inservice training and curriculum research. This project is TVEI-related.

3 Shropshire school development group (ongoing, 5–16 age group).

■ To develop collaboration and cooperation in delivering the national curriculum.

▼ Reports/evaluations; policy documents

Comment The LEA is divided into 16 clusters of primary schools, approximately 15 to each cluster. These groupings are also used for INSET.

93. Solihull
Education Department, Council Hse, Solihull, West Midlands B91 3QU

☎ 021 704 6000

Ⓟ Director of education

Projects and curriculum initiatives

1 English (ongoing, 11–16 age group).

▼ Reports/evaluations; resource materials; discussion documents

2 Records of Achievement (ongoing, 5–16 age group).

▼ Reports/evaluations; resource materials; policy documents.

3 Cross-curricular activities (ongoing, 5–16 age group).

▼ Reports/evaluations

4 Technology (ongoing, 5–16 age group). Reports/evaluations; resource materials; policy documents.

94. Somerset
County Hall, Taunton TA14 6QS

☎ 0823 333451

Ⓟ Chief education officer

Projects and curriculum initiatives

1 Review and development – Somerset teacher appraisal scheme (ongoing, all phases).

▼ Books; resource materials; policy documents

2 Wessex project – modular A-level developments (ongoing, post-16 age group).

▼ Resource materials; general information

3 Somerset Thinking Skills course (ongoing, 11–16 age group, with potential for older students and adults).

■ To emphasise the acquisition and development of thinking skills

▼ Books; resource materials

4 Interpreting the national curriculum – a way forward for early education (ongoing, all phases).

■ To give general guidance on the national curriculum

▼ Reports/evaluations; books; resource materials; discussion documents.

95. South Tyneside
Town Hall and Civic Offices, Westoe Rd, South Shields NE33 2RL

☎ 091 455 4321   Ⓣ 538205

Ⓕ 091 4550208

Ⓟ Chief education officer

Projects and curriculum initiatives

1 National curriculum strategy in primary schools (in association with Newcastle Polytechnic) (1989–93, 4–11 age group).

■ A collaborative enquiry as a means of enabling teachers to respond to the long-term demands of the national curriculum. This will lead to a critical history of LEA strategy over a specified period. Action research groups have been established in various curriculum areas

▼ Reports/evaluations; policy documents; discussion documents

2 Economic awareness in the primary school (1989–90, 4–11 age group).

■ An investigation of the place of economic awareness in the primary curriculum

▼ Reports/evaluations

3 Records of Achievement and assessment policies in the secondary school (1988–92, 11–18 age group).

■ The development of a system for all comprehensive schools and the college

▼ Reports/evaluations; policy documents

4 Active learning in the secondary curriculum (1989–91, 11–16 age group).

■ The development of good practice in pilot schools

▼ Reports/evaluations; policy documents

96. Staffordshire
Tipping St, Stafford ST16 2DH
☎ 0785 223121
Ⓟ Chief education officer

97. Stockport
Stopford Hse, Stockport, Cheshire SK1 3XE
☎ 061 474 3876
Ⓟ Chief education officer
Projects and curriculum initiatives
1 Greater Manchester Mathematics
Challenge (ongoing, 11–13 age group).
■ To provide an open challenge consisting
of 2 question papers; to provide a stimulus for
promoting enjoyment in mathematics.
Ⓣ A committee of advisers, advisory
teachers, and HE lecturers
▼ Resource materials
2 Recording achievement – the
development of a formal assessment process
(1993–95, 3–19 age group).
■ To use the Stockport ROA as a focal
point for continuity and progression. The
Summary Record is based on a formative
assessment process integral to the delivery of
the whole curriculum. It includes regular
discussions between students and tutors to
enable students to set targets as a positive aid
to future learning
▼ Reports/evaluations; policy documents;
discussion documents
3 Education in a multi-ethnic society
(1988–91, 3–19 age group).
■ To develop the cross-curricular
dimension within the national curriculum and
beyond. To develop teaching and learning
styles and resource material which will
increase awareness of cultural diversity within
specific national curriculum subject attainment
targets. To address the implications for
management of the introduction of an equal
opportunities policy in institutions.
Ⓣ 1 adviser and 1 advisory teacher
▼ Reports/evaluations; resource materials
4 Stockport science project (ongoing,
11–16 age group).
■ To produce a limited Mode 2 GCSE
course available through LEAG and to support
with resources. To adapt the course to fit the
national curriculum Key Stage 4
▼ Books; resource materials

98. Suffolk
St Andrew Hse, County Hall, Ipswich IP4 1LJ
☎ 0473 230000
Ⓟ County education officer

99. Sunderland
Box 101 Civic Centre, Sunderland SR2 7DN
☎ 091 567 6161
Ⓟ Director of education

100. Surrey
County Hall, Penrhyn Rd, Kingston upon
Thames, Surrey KT1 2DJ
☎ 01 541 8800   Ⓣ 263312
Ⓕ 01 541 9005
Ⓟ Chief education officer

Projects and curriculum initiatives
1 Surrey flexible learning project (1989–90,
12–18 age group).
■ To identify situations in which flexible
learning is appropriate and to describe
examples of good practice
▼ Resource materials
2 Supply teachers project (ongoing,
primary and secondary phases).
▼ Discussion documents
3 Curriculum and assessment unit
(ongoing, secondary and FE age group).
■ To support the introduction of the
national curriculum, Records of
Achievement, and the national record of
vocational achievement in schools and
colleges
▼ Reports/evaluations; policy documents;
discussion documents
4 Multi-ethnic education project (1988–93,
primary and secondary phases).
▼ Discussion documents

101. Tameside
Council Offices, Wellington Rd, Ashton-under-
Lyne, Lancashire OL6 6DL
☎ 061 330 8355   Ⓣ 669991
Ⓕ 061 344 3070
Ⓟ Education officer, curriculum and inservice
Projects and curriculum initiatives
1 Mental mathematics for GCSE (1988–90,
14–16 age group).
▼ Books
2 Primary science guidelines (1987–89,
3–11 age group).
▼ Resource materials; policy documents
3 Thematic approach to the primary
curriculum including the national
curriculum (1988–90, 4–11 age group).
▼ Resource materials
4 Mathematics guidelines (1987–90, 3–19
age group).
▼ Books
5 Monitoring, recording and reporting
pupils' progress and achievement (ongoing,
4–12 age group).
▼ Resource materials; discussion
documents
6 Industrial change (1988–90, 11–16 age
group).
▼ Resource materials
7 Whole school development (1987–90,
4–11 age group).
▼ Resource materials; school-based
INSET materials
8 Health-related fitness (1988–90, 3–19
age group).
▼ Resource materials

102. Trafford
PO Box 19, Tatton Rd, Sale, Greater
Manchester M33 1YR
☎ 061 872 2101
Ⓟ Chief education officer

103. Wakefield
County Hall, Wood St, Wakefield WF1 2QL

☎ 0924 367111
Ⓟ Chief education officer

104. Walsall
Civic Centre, Darwall St, Walsall WS1 1DQ
☎ 0922 650000
Ⓟ Chief education officer
Projects and curriculum initiatives
1 Secondary to primary retraining
(ongoing, primary phase).
▼ Reports/evaluations; policy documents
2 Return to teach – updating (ongoing,
primary phase).
▼ Policy documents
3 Walsall Records of Achievement
(ongoing, secondary phase-extension to
primary phase later).
▼ Reports/evaluations; resource materials;
policy documents
4 PLANS (ongoing, pre-school).
■ To help pre-school handicapped children
and their parents
▼ Books
5 Schools–industry project (ongoing,
primary and secondary phases).
▼ Reports/evaluations; resource materials;
policy documents; video

105. Warwickshire
22 Northgate St, Warwick CV34 4SR
☎ 0926 410410
Ⓟ County education officer
Projects and curriculum initiatives
1 Language development – cross phase
(i.e. middle–secondary liaison) (1988–89,
middle and secondary phases).
Ⓣ 1 seconded teacher
▼ Reports/evaluations
2 Music guidelines publications (ongoing,
all age groups).
▼ Resource materials
3 Home–school link pilot initiative
(ongoing, 8–18 age group).
■ To facilitate discussions on topics chosen
by parents to encourage greater 2-way
understanding between home and school; to
provide opportunities for parents to talk and
teachers to listen
▼ Reports/evaluations; resource materials.
4 Home–school liaison review (ongoing,
5–18 age group).
■ To provide a structured framework to
help schools to review their policy and
practice in the field of home–school liaison;to
suggest a model for action to aid
developments; to provide the LEA with
feedback to allow INSET and resources to be
targeted
▼ Review document

106. West Sussex
County Hall, West St, Chichester, West
Sussex PO19 1RF
☎ 0243 777100   Ⓣ 86279
Ⓕ 0243 777952
Ⓟ Chief education officer
Projects and curriculum initiatives
1 Records of Achievement (1985–97, 5–19
age group).
▼ Resource materials; policy documents

2 Profiles and portfolios (1990–1, 4–5 age
group).
▼ Resource materials; discussion
documents
3 New horizons: science 5–16 (in
association with Cambridge University
Press) (1989–93, 5–16 age group).
▼ Books; resource materials; INSET
materials
4 The West Sussex pilot scheme
of teacher appraisal (1988–92, all phases).
■ To emphasise that appraisal is a positive
process; to raise the quality of education by
encouraging professional growth and
development
Ⓣ 21 teachers, 7 advisers and 3 officers,
with a seconded headteacher as project
coordinator
▼ Policy documents

107. Wigan
Gateway Hse, Standishgate, Wigan WN1 1XL
☎ 0942 827892
Ⓟ Director of education

108. Wiltshire
County Hall, Bythesea Rd, Trowbridge,
Wiltshire BA14 8JB
☎ 0221 43641
Ⓟ Chief education officer

109. Wirral
Municipal Offices, Cleveland St, Birkenhead
L41 6NH
☎ 051 647 7000
Ⓟ Director of education

110. Wolverhampton
Civic Centre, St Peter's Square,
Wolverhampton, West Midlands WV1 1RR
☎ 0902 27811   Ⓣ 335060
Ⓕ 0902 26644
Ⓟ Chief education officer
Projects and curriculum initiatives
1 Community involvement in nursery and
infant years (1989–90, nursery and infant
phases).
■ To support and encourage the
involvement of the community in the
educational process in the nursery and early
years of education; to develop a partnership
between school and parents which is
maintained throughout a child's time in school.
▼ Project book
Comment By increasing the involvement of
parents and the community, the project seeks
to ease the transition from home to school and
to build on early learning experiences.
Stronger links are intended to encourage a
continuity of development in the areas of
language, culture and cognition
2 Wolverhampton staff development
project (1989–90, all phases).
■ To establish and develop a systematic,
planned teacher/lecturer development needs
programme; to support schools and colleges
in the systematic identification of curriculum
and professional development needs
▼ Policy documents; project book
Comment This project is seen as central to

the effective implementation of the LEA's strategy for curriculum and professional development.

3   Newspapers and publishing (1989–90, all phases).

■   To provide a framework for the study of newspapers as an important section of the media and as a source of information in many subjects of the curriculum; to encourage the production of school publications which could include newspapers

▼   Policy documents; project book
Comment   The 'Enterprise Publishing Kit', developed by the Cleveland Gazette, is the basis of this project. The kit covers all practical aspects of production and provides guidelines for setting up a real project, with pupil notes on editorial work, finance, production and marketing, apart from general management.

4   Storytelling (1989–90, all phases).

■   To involve a diversity of schools, either individually or in consortia, in consideration of how they might foster the development of the arts curriculum by the use of an artist or arts company in one or more of these art forms: literature, music, dance and the visual arts including photography and media studies

▼   Policy documents; project book
Comment   Each school will have the opportunity of engaging artists for up to 30 hours for workshop or residency. Individual timetables will be negotiated through the LEA with the artists involved.

111. States of Guernsey
PO Box 32, Education Department, St Peter Port, Guernsey CI
☎   0481 710821
Ⓟ   Assistant Director
Projects and curriculum initiatives
1   Pre-vocational education (ongoing, 14–16 age group).
Ⓣ   St Peter Port secondary school and FE College staff
▼   Policy documents; course programme and introduction to parents
Comment   This is based on the C and G Foundation courses.
2   Curriculum design for MLD Special School (1987–90, 8–15 age group).
■   To prepare for the building of a new school
Ⓣ   Headteacher, Exeter University staff
▼   Policy documents; curriculum statement and submission to Exeter University for a group CPS
3   Review of Guernsey schools and quadrennial report to Education Council (1988–91, primary and secondary phases).
■   2 parallel workshops of secondary and primary headteachers to produce an instrument for the review of Guernsey schools and quadrennial report to Education Council
▼   Policy documents; review instrument
4   HEA guidelines (1988–9, primary and secondary phases).
■   To produce guidelines for health education in schools
Ⓣ   1 senior officer, 1 Teachers' Centre representative, 1 health promotion officer

▼   Policy documents

112. States of Jersey
PO Box 142, St Saviour, Jersey CI
☎   0534 71065
Ⓟ   Director of education

113. Isle of Man
Government Offices, Bucks Road, Douglas, Isle of Man
☎   0624 26262
Ⓟ   Chief education officer
Projects and curriculum initiatives
1   Primary school management (1989–91, 4–11 age group).
■   To service and train primary school headteachers, leading to an accredited Advanced Diploma and entry to MA courses
Ⓣ   2 LEA advisers, 4 HE lecturers
▼   Reports/evaluations; resource materials; initial remit course outlines.
2   Primary deputy heads professional development (1988–90 and ongoing, 4–11 age group).
■   To service and train primary deputy heads and to prepare for headship
Ⓣ   1 LEA adviser, 3 HE lecturers
▼   Reports/evaluations; resource materials; initial remit course outlines.
3   Training trainers (1988–90, 4–11 age group).
■   To prepare curriculum coordinators to assist in curriculum development and INSET initiatives
Ⓣ   1 LEA adviser, 4 HE lecturers
▼   Initial remit course outlines

114. Clwyd
Education Department, Shire Hall, Mold CH7 6ND
☎   0352 2121
Ⓟ   Director of education

115. Dyfed
Education Department, Pibwrlwyd, Carmarthen, Dyfed SA31 2NH
☎   0267 233333
Ⓟ   County education officer
Projects and curriculum initiatives
1   Theatre in education (1989–90, 5–11 age group).
■   To develop initiatives involving communication and relationships; to prepare for performances, usually bilingually
▼   Reports/evaluations; discussion documents
2   Bilingual supported self study (1989–90, 14–18 age group).
■   To produce bilingual supported self-study materials in cooperation with Gwynedd and Powys
▼   Resource materials
3   Prompt writer and concept keyboard (1989–90, primary).
■   To prepare files and overlays for Prompt Writer and Concept Keyboard in English and Welsh
▼   Resource materials
4   Flexible learning development programme

Curriculum Handbook

in English (1989–90, 16–18 age group).
■ A joint project with Powys to investigate collaborative writing and analysis for A level coursework. Textual and personal writing approaches are major concerns of the project
▼ Discussion documents
5 Police and education 1987–9, 5–11 age group).
■ To focus on cross-curricular developments relating to the police and their potential for assisting in curriculum delivery.
▼ Discussion documents
6 Satellites in education (1989–90, 7–18 age group).
■ To produce a wide range of materials, supported by British Telecom
▼ Reports/evaluations; books; resource materials; video
7 Wales Design Technology Research Project (1989–90, 5–13 age group).
■ To develop strategies and materials for delivering design and technology at Key Stages 1, 2 and 3 (up to Level 6). This project focuses on secondary schools and their contributory primary schools
▼ Reports/evaluations; resource materials; discussion documents
8 Teachers' needs in relation to science concepts in primary schools (1989–90, 5–11 age group).
■ To work with Aberystwyth University to identify and clarify teachers' needs in relation to science concepts in primary schools and to follow these up with resource support
▼ Reports/evaluations; resource materials.
9 Graded Assessments in Science Project (GASP) (1990–92, 11–16 age group).
■ To trial graded assessments in science in one school with the aim of eventual dissemination to all Dyfed secondary schools
▼ Reports/evaluations
10 Mobile fieldwork laboratory (1988–90, 5–11 age group).
■ To provide a mobile fieldwork laboratory and national curriculum support for primary schools
▼ Resource materials; discussion documents
11 Primary–secondary transition in English (1989–91, 9–12 age group).
■ To provide opportunities for primary and secondary schools to speak, listen, read and write for a variety of audiences, leading to shared schemes of work, shared anthologies or newspapers, poetry readings, group storytelling and other collaborations.
▼ Resource materials
12 Dance education in schools (1988–91, 5–13 age group).
■ To provide worthwhile dance experiences for primary and secondary pupils using secondary staff expertise to work with primary colleagues.
▼ Discussion documents

116. Gwent
County Hall, Cwmbran, Gwent NP44 2XG
☎ 0633 838838
Ⓟ Director of education

117. Gwynedd
Castle St, Caernarvon, Gwynedd LL55 1SH
☎ 0286 3507   Ⓕ 0286 3993
Ⓟ County education officer
Project and curriculum initiatives
1 Olympus project (1989–91, 14–18 age group).
■ To complement and coordinate the use of free time granted to educational parties on the Olympus Broadcasting satellite, and to explore the use of communication technology in support of distance learning in a European context
▼ Reports/evaluations; resource materials; discussion documents; video tapes
2 Technology in the national curriculum 1989–90, 5–18 age group).
■ To develop curriculum support materials for the introduction of technology as a foundation subject in the national curriculum
▼ Books; resource materials
3 Flexible learning within the sixth form core (1989–90, 16–18 age group).
■ To produce flexible learning materials to support the WJEC A(S) general studies syllabus
▼ Books; resource materials; policy documents
4 Joint support activities project involving Gwynedd, Dyfed and Powys (1988–91, 16–18 age group).
■ To develop bilingual, flexible learning materials and to test various delivery systems in support of these materials
▼ Reports/evaluations; books; resource materials; discussion documents

118. Mid Glamorgan
County Hall, Cathays Park, Cardiff CF1 3NF
☎ 0222 820820
Ⓟ Director of education

119. Powys
County Hall, Llandrindod Wells, Powys LD1 5LG
☎ 0597 826448   Ⓕ 0597 826230
Ⓟ Chief education officer
Projects and curriculum initiatives
1 ESG Rural Schools Project 1985–90, primary phase).
■ To develop cluster groups
▼ Reports/evaluations; policy documents
2 Resource-based learning (1989–92, all phases).
3 Religious education (1989, all phases).
4 English in the national curriculum (1990, all phases).
■ To develop work in drama for primary and secondary schools, and in reading for primary schools
5 TVEI extension (1989–94, secondary phase).
▼ Reports/evaluations; policy documents; discussion documents
6 PSE (health education) (1986–92, all phases).
▼ Reports/evaluations; policy documents; discussion documents

Curriculum Initiatives in Local Education Authorities

120. South Glamorgan
County Hall, Atlantic Wharf, Cardiff CF1 5UW
☎ 0222 872751　Ⓕ 0222 872777
Ⓟ Chief education officer
Projects and curriculum initiatives
1 Musicianship development through singing based on Welsh folk song (1985–90, 7–11 age group).
▼ Books
2 Performing Rights Society Award (1989–90, 14–15 age group).
■ To encourage pupils to develop their composing techniques, using elements from different musical genres and aided by 3 composers in residence – ethnic music, jazz and music–drama
▼ Reports/evaluations; resource materials

121. West Glamorgan
County Hall, Swansea SA1 3SN
☎ 0792 471111
Ⓟ Director of education

122. Borders Regional Council
Newtown St Boswells, Roxburghshire TD6 9DE
☎ 0835 23301　Ⓕ 0835 22145
Ⓟ Director of education
Projects and curriculum initiatives
1 Teacher Appraisal (1988–9, all phases).
■ To pilot staff development and career review in a variety of educational institutions on a volunteer basis; to develop training for appraisers and appraisees
Ⓣ 1 depute director and 2 senior advisers
▼ Resource materials; policy documents
2 Preparation for management for unpromoted teachers (1987–8, primary phase).
■ To encourage teachers to prepare for management via INSET of one year including residential experience, seminars, and personal projects.
Ⓣ 1 senior adviser and 2 primary advisers
▼ Reports/evaluations
3 Electronics in measurement (1988–90, secondary phase).
■ To provide a short course for teachers and pupils on the use of electronic devices in school and industry for measuring purposes
Ⓣ 1 adviser, 3 principal teachers, 1 national development officer
▼ Resource materials

123. Central
Central Regional Offices, Viewforth, Stirling FK8 2ET
☎ 0786 73111
Ⓟ Director of education

124. Dumfries and Galloway
30 Edinburgh Rd, Dumfries DG1 1JQ
☎ 0387 63822
Ⓟ Chief education officer
Projects and curriculum initiatives
1 Ahead in management (1988–9, primary phase).
■ An open learning package in management for primary headteachers

commissioned from SCOTTSU
▼ Resource documents
2 Technology across the curriculum (1988–90, 14–16 age group).
■ An attempt to identify technological components in subjects across the curriculum to provide schools with a tracking mechanism
▼ Reports/evaluations
3 Enterprise education (1989–92, 14–18 age group).
■ An INSET programme to develop methodology in such a way as to introduce a more enterprising approach to teaching and learning
▼ Reports/evaluations; resource materials; discussion documents
4 Economic awareness (1988–92, 12–18 age group).
■ To develop materials to introduce elements of economic awareness into subjects across the curriculum
▼ Reports/evaluations; resource materials; policy documents

125. Fife
Fife Hse, North St, Glenrothes, Fife KY7 5LT
☎ 0592 754411　Ⓣ 727461
Ⓕ 0592 758582
Ⓟ Director of education
Projects and curriculum initiatives
1 TVEI-funded curriculum enhancement package (1988–90, 12–18 age group).
Ⓣ 1 adviser (special needs) and 6 teachers
▼ Reports/evaluations; resource materials; policy documents
2 Orientation programme (1988–9, 12–18 age group).
Ⓣ 1 member of Moray House staff and 9 school staff (Lochgelly North)
▼ Reports/evaluations; resource materials
3 FACCT Project (ongoing, secondary phase).
▼ Reports/evaluations; resource materials
4 Intensive interaction school staff/college support (1989–90, 5–18 age group).
▼ Reports/evaluations
5 Craft, design and technology (primary) (1989–91, 5–12 age group).
▼ Resource materials
6 Health education (1989–91, 5–12 age group).
▼ Reports/evaluations; books; resource materials; policy documents
7 Writing school policies in environmental studies (1988, 5–12 age group).
▼ Reports/evaluations; policy documents
8 Regional provision of micro-computers in primary schools (1983–90, 5–12 age group).
▼ Reports/evaluations; resource materials; policy documents; discussion documents
9 Induction, support and assessment of probationary teachers in the primary school (1988–90, 5–12 age group).
▼ Reports/evaluations; policy documents; discussion documents

126. Grampian
Woodhill Hse, Westburn Rd, Aberdeen AB9 2LU

113

☎ 0224 682222   Ⓣ 739277
Ⓕ 0224 697445
Ⓟ Director of education
Projects and curriculum initiatives
1 Learning for a changing world (1989–93, 12–16 age group).
■ To encourage the development of courses which will give all pupils a better opportunity to develop economic awareness, technological capability, and pre-vocational skills
Ⓣ Coordinator, 9 teacher tutors, consultants
▼ Policy documents
Comment This project is sponsored by BP. External consultants are provided by CRAC.
2 Industry link scheme (ongoing, 5–11 age group).
■ To develop links between a community primary school and local industries and thereafter to extend those links into other areas of the community
Ⓣ Primary adviser, schools–industry liaison officer, headteacher, deputy headteacher, 2 teachers
▼ Curriculum awards submission outlining the scheme; extracts from DTI publication on teacher placement in industry giving background to the scheme
3 Enquiry skills progression (1988–9, 5–14 age group).
■ To prepare a progression of enquiry skills and to foster primary–secondary curricular liaison
Ⓣ 1 secondary headteacher, 1 primary headteacher, 1 secondary teacher, 1 primary teacher, 1 secondary librarian, 4 CDOs
▼ Book on enquiry skills

127. Highland
Regional Bldgs, Glenurquhart Rd, Inverness IV3 5NX
☎ 0463 234121
Ⓟ Director of education

128. Lothian
40 Torphichen St, Edinburgh EH3 8JJ
☎ 031 229 9166
Ⓟ Director of education
Projects and curriculum initiatives
1 National Certification (1984–94, 14–18 age group).
■ Development of local resource materials, teaching packs, student materials and associated staff development initiatives for new SCE and SCOTVEC courses, modules and syllabuses
Ⓣ 60 members of staff
▼ Publications list
2 5–14 programme (1989–94, 5–14 age group).
■ Development of local resources and associated staff development initiatives in areas such as thematic work with national attainment targets in mind
Ⓣ 30 members of staff
▼ Publications list
3 Cross-curricular developments (1987–93, 5–18 age group).
■ Development of local resources and

associated staff development initiatives in specific areas of need, including AIDS/HIV
Ⓣ 15 members of staff
▼ Publication list
4 Management training

129. Strathclyde
6 India St, Glasgow G2 4PF
☎ 041 204 2900   Ⓣ 77428
Ⓕ 041 204 2870
Ⓟ Director of education
Projects and curriculum initiatives
1 Health education (1989, 5–16 age group).
2 Primary languages (1989–92, 5–12 age group).
3 Educational computing (5–16 age group).
4 Standard grade development (14–16 age group).

130. Tayside
Tayside Hse, Dundee DD1 3RJ
☎ 0382 23281
Ⓟ Director of education

131. Orkney
Orkney Islands Council, Kirkwall, Orkney KW15 1NY
☎ 0856 3535
Ⓟ Director of education
Projects and curriculum initiatives
1 Record of Achievement in secondary schools (1988–9, 15–16 age group).
■ To develop pilot Records of Achievement profiles for use in years S3 and S4
Ⓣ 2 assistant headteachers, 3 principal teachers, 1 careers officer
▼ Reports/evaluations; policy documents; record and rationale
2 School exchange plus work placements for 2 weeks in Germany (1989, 15–16 age group).
▼ Reports/evaluations; policy documents; correspondence with German schools, employers, parents, and insurance
Comment This was funded by TVEI

132. Shetland
1 Harbour St, Lerwick, Shetland ZE1 0LS
☎ 0595 3535
Ⓟ Director of education

133. Western Isles
Stornoway, Isle of Lewis PA87 2BW
☎ 0851 3773
■ Curriculum development officer
Projects and curriculum initiatives
1 Curriculum development – standard grade (1989–91, 12–16 age group).
■ To produce materials to support teaching in the following curriculum areas: biology; chemistry; physics; science
Ⓣ 1 staff member
▼ Resource materials
2 S1/S2 geography/history (1990–1, 12–14 age group).
■ The development of courses in geography and history

T 1 staff member
3 TVEI Pilot (1987–92, 14–18 age group).
▼ Resource materials
4 Standard grade development (1987–90, 12–16 age group).
■ To produce teaching materials for the teaching of Gaelic
▼ Resource materials; policy documents; discussion documents
5 Gaelic medium teaching (secondary) (1989–91, 12–14 age group).
■ To produce teaching materials for teaching history and geography in Gaelic
▼ Books; resource materials; discussion documents
6 Gaelic materials (secondary) (1988–91, 12–17 age group).
■ To commission production and publication of books, tapes and photographic stimuli to encourage fluent speaking of Gaelic
▼ Books; resource materials
7 ABAIR E (1987–93, 12–16 age group).
■ To produce a Gaelic learners course
▼ Resource materials
8 Gaelic open learning course (1988–91, 16+ age group).
■ To produce an open learning course incorporating text and tape, related to SCOTVEC language: Gaelic modules
▼ Resource materials
9 Gaelic higher grade development (1990–91, 16–18 age group).
■ To give support to revised courses
10 Bilingual education (ongoing, 5–18 age group).
■ To research into bilingual education, to evaluate, make recommendations and review materials
▼ Reports/evaluations; policy documents; discussion documents
11 Gaelic arts (ongoing, 10–18 age group).
■ To develop initiatives in Gaelic arts which will be applicable to education, in cooperation with other agencies
▼ Reports/evaluations; discussion documents

134. Belfast
40 Academy St, Belfast BT1 2NQ
☎ 0232 239211
Ⓟ Chief officer

135. North-eastern Education and Library Board
County Hall, 182 Galgorm Rd, Ballymena, Antrim BT42 1HN
☎ 0266 653333   Ⓕ 0266 46071
Ⓟ Senior education officer
Projects and curriculum initiatives
1 Records of Achievement: a Board based pilot study (ongoing, 11–16 age group).
▼ Policy documents
2 Causeway school project (1988–9, primary phase).
▼ Resource materials
3 11–16 curriculum review and development (1984–9, 11–16 age group).
■ To enable all secondary schools to provide a broad, balanced, differentiated and relevant curriculum
▼ Resource materials; discussion documents; magazines; individual school reports
4 Writing in primary schools (1989–90, 7–11 age group).
■ To extend children's language experience by writing for other schools about the environment and local cultural events.
T 1 Board officer, 1 project teacher
▼ Reports/evaluations
5 DTP in secondary schools (1988–91, 12–18 age group).
■ To introduce DTP to all secondary schools in the Board's area as a cross-curricular activity supporting work in English, history, geography, home economics, science, etc.; to provide hardware, software and inservice training for each school, enabling DTP to be used by pupils across the curriculum
T 1 Board adviser, 2 staff at Area Resource Centre
▼ Resource materials; policy documents
6 Preparation and publishing of teaching materials on local seventeenth century history (1988–90, 11–15 age group).
■ To provide classroom teaching materials on seventeenth century history based on the geographical area of the Board and suitable for use by pupils preparing for the GCSE examination
T 2 Board advisers, 2 teachers, supported by staff of Area Resource Centre
▼ Books; resource materials
7 Video in careers/counselling in selected secondary schools (1989–91, 12–18 age group).
■ To promote the use of school-produced video in careers and enterprise education and in the economic understanding area of the curriculum; to provide sample videos produced on equipment available to schools and training required to produce similar videos
T 1 field officer with support from staff at Area Resource Centre
▼ Resource materials; discussion documents; videos.

136. South-eastern Area Education and Library Board
18 Windsor Ave, Belfast BT9 6EF
☎ 0232 381188
Ⓟ Chief officer

137. Southern Area Education and Library Board
3 Charlemont Pl, The Mall, Armagh BT61 9AX
☎ 0861 523811   Ⓕ 0861 526950
Ⓟ Education officer

138. Western Education and Library Board
1 Hospital Rd, Omagh, Co. Tyrone BT79 0AW
☎ 0662 44931 and 44431
Ⓕ 0662 41443
Ⓟ Education officer
Projects and curriculum initiatives

Curriculum Handbook

1 Small schools specialist support scheme (1987–90, primary phase).
■ For support teachers to work alongside class teachers and involve them in the process of review, development and implementation, encouraging them to start at their own baselines and move at their own pace, in response to what they see as their needs and the needs of their pupils
Ⓣ 25 seconded teachers under the guidance of an Education Officer support 120 primary schools
▼ Reports/evaluations; resource materials; policy documents
2 Development of science in larger primary schools (1988–90, primary phase).
■ To support the implementation of science in the whole school curriculum
Ⓣ 1 primary adviser and 8 seconded field officers
▼ Reports/evaluations; resource materials; policy documents
3 Technology and design support (1990–91, secondary phase).
■ To support the development of technology and design in the whole curriculum
Ⓣ 1 adviser and 12 seconded or short term contract teachers
▼ Reports/evaluations; resource materials; policy documents
4 11–16 Programme (1985–90, secondary phase).
■ To work towards the implementation of the Northern Ireland Curriculum in all post-primary schools in the Board's area. It is directed at all aspects of school life, and takes account of each school's distinctive features.
Ⓣ This joint Board/DENI/School initiative uses a regional coordinator, an adviser and an inspector from DENI and 7 seconded field officers
▼ Reports/evaluations; books; resource materials; policy documents; discussion documents

139. Service Children's Education Authority – SCEA
HQ Director of Army Education, Ministry of Defence, Court Rd, Eltham, London SE9 5NR
☎ 081 854 2242
Ⓟ M.P. O'Sullivan, SCEA 2a, Curriculum

Section 7

Curriculum Initiatives in Institutions of Higher Education

This section contains entries on curriculum initiatives which are located in institutions of higher education (HE). All of the HE institutions were circulated with requests for information. Some returns indicated that that institution was no longer active in the fields requested; others indicated that though they were actively involved there was little in the way of publicly available information. Hence, this section very fairly reflects both the spread of interests in curriculum initiatives which are represented in HE institutions and the extent of research and development initiatives in the curriculum field. There was a very positive and full return to this section.

Several of the larger institutions requested the opportunity to include more than the original six projects which the authors asked for; in all cases these requests were granted. However there are some institutions which are still engaged in much more research than can be included here; in this case judicious inclusion was subject to editorial control.

Very many institutions put their returns in a priority order: where this was the case it has been honoured here. Details on funding monies and the size of project team has been included where it was given, so that readers have an indication of the size of various projects. It is also noticeable that very many funded research projects are jointly mounted by HE institutions and LEAs; a clear example of this can be seen in the proliferation of TVEI evaluations.

One has to notice the very high representation of funded policy-driven research in this section, and the dearth of 'pure' research or methodological interests in the institutions which sent returns. This surely is indicative of a 'value for money' and 'service' mentality which HE institutions have had to take very seriously in the current political climate if they are to survive. Not surprisingly perhaps one can detect the very strong influence of the National Curriculum and government-sponsored initiatives driving research interests. The long term effect of this on HE institutions is difficult to foresee, but it could well signal the depletion of the wider view of education which HE institutions have traditionally been able to take.

1. Bangor Normal College

Bangor, Gwynedd LL57 2PX
☎ 0248 370171
Ⓟ W. Davies, Dean
Projects and curriculum initiatives
1 Investigating mathematics in the primary school (£15,000) (1988–9).
■ To promote investigational methods of teaching mathematics through the medium of Welsh
Ⓣ Dr G. Roberts + 3
▼ Books
2 Calculators in the primary school (£29,000) (1989–90).
■ To develop resources in Welsh to assist

teachers in the integration of the calculator within the mathematics curriculum
Ⓣ Dr G Roberts + 8
3 Welsh PRiME INSET (1989–90).
■ To promote a Welsh version of PRiME INSET packs
Ⓣ Dr G. Roberts + 3
4 Unedal HMS iaith ysgal Ganglog (School based inservice training language units (£17,000) (1988–90).
■ To offer guidance and suggest routes for school based inservice training sessions concentrating on good practice in language development across the primary curriculum
Ⓣ Mr L Williams + 2
▼ Discussion documents
5 Cwrs Newld Cyfrwng (Language conversion course) (£55,000 (1988).
■ To give Welsh speaking secondary school subject teachers (or proficient Welsh learners) the necessary confidence and ability to teach through the medium of Welsh; to provide a refresher teacher training course specialising in the use of language across the curriculum
Ⓟ Mr L. Williams
▼ Resource materials; discussion documents; videotape

2. Bath College of Higher Education

Newton Park, Bath BA2 9BN
☎ 0225 873701
Ⓟ Director

3. Bedford College of Higher Education

Cauldwell St, Bedford MK42 9AH
☎ 0234 45151
Ⓟ Director

4. Bishop Grosseteste College

Lincoln, Lincolnshire LN1 3DY
☎ 0522 527347   Ⓕ 0522 530243
Ⓟ Dr R. Withers, Deputy principal
Projects and curriculum initiatives
1 Primary science materials (1988–90)
■ To develop and trial science materials for primary schools
▼ Resource materials
2 Early writing project (1988–90)
■ To undertake activities in classrooms and to document emergent writing
▼ Report evaluations; books
Comment The work is being undertaken in primary schools in Cambridgeshire.

5. Bolton Institute of Higher Education

Deane Rd, Bolton, Lancs, BL3 5AB
☎ 0204 28851
Ⓟ R. Harris, Principal lecturer in education
Projects and curriculum initiatives
1 Inservice training for TVEI (1988–90)
■ To develop a training programme for FE staff becoming involved in TVEI
▼ Report evaluations; resource materials; a framework for validation

6. Bradford and Ilkley Community College
Room 230, Great Horton Rd, Bradford BD7 1AY
☎ 0274 753026
Ⓟ Principal

7. Bretton Hall College
West Bretton, Wakefield WF4 4LG
☎ 0924 85261   Ⓕ 0924 830521
Ⓟ Professor R. George, Academic director
Projects and curriculum initiatives
1 Early years reading (1987–91, 3–8 age group)
▼ Reports/evaluations
2 Bretton writing (1988–91, primary age group).
▼ Reports/evaluations
3 Interrelated arts in schools (1988–91, secondary age group)
▼ Reports/evaluations
4 National arts education archive (1985–, continuing education)
▼ Reports/evaluations; books; resource materials; discussion documents
5 Academy of performing arts (1989–, continuing education)
▼ Archive collection

8. Brighton Polytechnic
Eastbourne Campus, Trevin Towers, Gaudick Rd, Brighton BN20 7SP
☎ 0323 21400
Ⓟ S. Modgil, Reader
Projects and curriculum initiatives
1 Telsoft interactive video education centre (1986–91)
■ To provide a physical centre to which teachers may refer for training, information and assistance in the design, production and use of interactive video in education. To produce a series of IV packages for INSET in business education
▼ Reports/evaluations; discussion documents; resource materials; user guides
2 Countryside research unit (1979–, all age groups)
■ To be a focus for countryside related research. To develop a consultancy role in countryside projects
▼ Reports/evaluations; planning documents; resource materials; discussion documents
3 The Tidy Britain group schools research project (1973–, 4–18 age groups).
■ To increase public consciousness and appreciation of the environment, particularly through the prevention of litter and improve waste management. To integrate education for personal responsibility for the environment into the formal school curriculum
▼ Reports/evaluations; discussion documents; resource materials; books; policy documents; project packs; videos
4 The book trust research project (1989–92, pre-school age group).

9. Bristol Polytechnic
Redland Hill, Redland, Bristol BS6 6UZ

☎ 0272 741251
Ⓟ Len Barton, Head of department
Projects and curriculum initiatives
1 Interpreting, adapting and implementing the national curriculum (£1,750) (1989–90, secondary age range).
Ⓟ Dr David Halpin
■ To report on the ways in which four secondary comprehensive schools adapt the national curriculum to existing institutional needs and priorities; to characterise the changing nature of teachers' concerns about the national curriculum
▼ Working paper which includes details of research design
2 Evaluation of aspects of the implementation of the training grants scheme in one LEA (£55,000) (1988–90, primary and secondary age ranges).
Ⓟ Dr David Halpin
■ To evaluate specific models of INSET delivery and to assess their impact in teachers' classrooms and schools generally
▼ Various interim reports
3 Learning about AIDS (£200,000) (1986–90)
Ⓣ Dr P. Aggleton
■ To develop and disseminate materials for use in INSET in relation to HIV Aids education
▼ Training and resource packs; reports/evaluations; books
4 AIDS: working with young people (£120,000) (1988–90, 14–25 age group).
Ⓣ Dr P Aggleton + 3
■ To develop and disseminate materials for use with young people in informal settings
▼ Resource materials; books

10. Brunel University
Runnymede Campus, Englefield Green, Egham, Surrey TW20 OJZ
☎ 0784 431341
Ⓟ Professor N. Harris, Head of education
Projects and curriculum initiatives
1 Development of enterprise education materials (£30,000, Electricity Council) (1988–9, 14–16 age group).
Ⓣ 2 university teachers and 4 teachers
▼ Resource materials
2 Development of curriculum resource materials (£40,000, Electricity Council) (1988–9, 14–16 age group).
Ⓣ 2 university teachers and 8 teachers
▼ Resource materials
3 Development of graphics system for national database (funding from National Educational Resources Information Services (NERIS) (1988–90, 8–18 age group).
Ⓣ 3 university staff
▼ Reports/evaluations; NERIS database
4 TVEI evaluation: Hillingdon (1987–91, 4–18 age group).
▼ Reports/evaluations
5 TVEI evaluation: Hounslow (1988–91, 14–18 age group)
▼ Reports/evaluations
6 TVEI evaluation: Waltham Forest (1989–91, 14–18 age group).
▼ Reports/evaluations

11. Buckinghamshire College of Higher Education
Queen Alexandra Rd, High Wycombe HP11 2JZ
☎ 0494 22141
Ⓟ Principal

12. Bulmershe College of Higher Education
Woodlands Ave, Earley, Reading RG6 1HY
☎ 0734 663387
Ⓟ Principal

13. Cambridge Institute of Education
Shaftesbury Rd, Cambridge CB2 2BX
☎ 0223 69631 Ⓕ 0223 324421
Ⓟ Howard Bradley, Director
Projects and curriculum initiatives
1 Evaluation of the school teacher appraisal pilot study (DES funding) (1987–9, 3–18 age group).
Ⓣ Howard Bradley + 5
▼ Reports/evaluations; books
2 Shakespeare and schools – Leverhulme funding (1986–9, primary and secondary age groups)
■ To research and develop methods to improve the quality of pupils, encounters with Shakespeare in schools and colleges
Ⓟ Rex Gibson
▼ Reports/evaluations; books; resource materials; termly magazine *Shakespeare and Schools*
3 Primary school staff relationships, and whole school curriculum development project (ESRC funding) (1985–90, primary age group).
■ Through case studies to consider organisational culture, the culture of collaboration, collegiality, leadership, notions of whole school
Ⓟ Geoff Southworth
▼ Reports/evaluations; books; articles
4 Support for innovation project (MSC and LEAs funding) (1986–8, infant to sixth form age groups)
■ To support and coordinate curriculum and staff development activities
Ⓟ Howard Bradley
▼ Reports/evaluations; discussion documents; video pack
5 (a) Information skills in TVEI and the role of the librarian (British Library funding) (1985–8, 14–18 age groups). (b) Information skills in GCSE and the role of the librarian (British Library funding) (1989–90, 11–18 age group).
Ⓟ David Hopkins
▼ Reports/evaluations; video tape and discussion material
6 School development plans (jointly with University of Cambridge Department of Education) (DES funding) (1989–90, 3–18 age groups).
■ To produce advice for governors, heads, teachers on whole school planning
Ⓣ Professor D. Hargreaves and Dr D. Hopkin; Research associate, Marilyn Leask
▼ Books; consultation

14. Cambridgeshire College of Arts and Technology
East Rd, Cambridge CB1 1PT
☎ 0223 63271
Ⓟ Principal

15. Canterbury – Christ Church College
North Holmes Rd, Canterbury CT1 1QU
☎ 0227 762444 Ⓕ 0227 470442
Ⓟ D.R. Greenstreet, Schools tutor
Projects and curriculum initiatives
1 IT–INSET initiative: PGCE junior course. To have tutors, students and teachers working in collaboration in classrooms on programmes which match schools' INSET needs and students' training, in which the roles of the teacher alternate between teacher, observer, evaluator
Ⓣ Carl Parsons, Steve Varley + 3
▼ Reports/evaluations
2 TVEI school-based project: PGCE secondary (1989–, 11–18 year olds).
■ To support 12 PGCE students based in a school working across Canterbury TVEI consortium, with 0.5 LEA secondment
Ⓣ Mrs Jenny Hawkins + 4
▼ Reports/evaluations; resource materials; policy documents
3 Creative arts project: PGCE junior course (1988–, 1–11 age group).
■ To have students assessed by an audio-visual television presentation of a cross-arts programme which they have devised and carried out with children in schools
▼ Reports/evaluations

16. Central School of Speech and Drama
Embassy Theatre, Eton Ave, London NW3 3HY
☎ 071 722 8183/4/5/6
Ⓟ Audrey Laski, Director, teacher courses

17. Charlotte Mason College
Rydal Rd, Ambleside, Cumbria LA22 9BB
☎ 05394 33066 Ⓕ 05394 3326
Ⓟ Mr M Waters, Director of staff development and research
Projects and curriculum initiatives
1 Approaches to teaching – critical studies in art education (1985–90, key stages 2 and 3).
▼ Books
2 Infant school science – design and technology (1988–90, 3–7 age group).
3 Investigating and evaluating approaches to teaching critical and contextual studies in art and design education (key stages 2 and 3).
▼ Resource material
4 Mathematics in nursery school and classes (£290) (1988– ,3–4 year olds).
Ⓣ Tutor, headteacher, secretary
▼ Books (in preparation)

18. Chester College
Cheyney Rd, Chester CH1 4BJ
☎ 0244 375444 Ⓕ 0244 373379
Ⓟ Judith Roden, Senior lecturer in science education

Projects and curriculum initiatives
1 The effects of students practising the role of curriculum leader with fellow students within initial training (1989–90, 5–11 age group).

19. Christ's and Notre Dame College
Woolton Rd, Liverpool L16 8ND
☎ 051 722 7331
Ⓟ Principal

20. City of Birmingham Polytechnic
Faculty of Education, Perry Barr, Birmingham B42 2SU
☎ 021 331 5000
Ⓟ Dean, Faculty of education

21. College of Ripon and York St John
The College, Lord Mayor's Walk, York YO3 7EX
☎ 0904 656771
Ⓟ Principal

22. College of St Paul and St Mary
The Park, Cheltenham GL50 2RH
☎ 0242 513836
Ⓟ Principal
Projects and curriculum initiatives
1 Foundations project: a personal development project for schools (funding from the Marriage Research Centre and a consortium of schools) (1989–92, 13–19 age group).
Ⓟ Professor R. Whitfield, Honorary director or Mrs A. Parrack, Administrative secretary
▼ Topic webs; brochure

23. Craigie College of Education
Ayr KA8 OSR
☎ 0292 260321
Ⓟ Principal

24. Crewe and Alsager College of Higher Eduation
Hassall Rd, Alsager, Stoke on Trent ST7 2HL
☎ 0270 882500   Ⓕ 0270 583433
Ⓟ Dr T. Evans, Dean of postgraduate and inservice board
Projects and curriculum initiatives
1 Evaluation of the management of Records of Achievement (1988–90, 11–16 age group).
Ⓣ 3 staff
▼ Reports/evaluations
2 Introduction of teacher appraisal, awareness and skills training (1988–93, 5–18 age group).
Ⓣ 1 tutor and seconded teachers
▼ Resource materials
3 Training for seconded teachers acting as ROA coordinators (1987–92, 11–18 age group).
Ⓣ 3 staff
4 Training for governing bodies in managing schools (1989–90, 5–11 age group).
Ⓣ 4 staff
▼ Resource materials
5 Professional development of teachers in health education research

project (£50,000) (1987–91).
Ⓟ Dr Gaye Heathcote
▼ Reports/evaluations

25. Athrofa gogledd ddwyrain cymru North-east Wales Institute of Higher Education
Plas Coch, Moold Rd, Wrexham LL11 2AW
☎ 0978 290666
Ⓟ Executive principal

26. De la Salle College of Higher Education
Hopwood Hall, Middleton, Manchester M24 3XH
☎ 061 643 5331
Ⓟ Principal

27. Derbyshire College of Higher Education
Western Rd, Derby DE3 5GX
☎ Derby 47181   Ⓕ Derby 294861
Ⓟ G. Littler, Head, School of education
Projects and curriculum initiatives
1 Work in the primary school (1988–, 9–11 age group).
■ To investigate children's perceptions of 'work'; to inform curriculum development packages with collaborating teachers
Ⓣ John Dolan + team
▼ Policy documents; resource materials (in preparation) articles; papers
2 Evaluation of initial B.Ed degrees (1987–90, 18+ age group).
■ To evaluate experiences of a cohort of students and associated staff on an initial B.Ed course to provide data for course modification
Ⓣ Dr R. Roberts, research assistant + team
▼ Reports/evaluations
3 Action research in staff development (1988–).
■ To engage with LEA staff development coordinators in programmes of action research into monitoring and evaluation of staff development
Ⓣ Dr R. Roberts + team
▼ Interim report

28. Digby Stuart College of Higher Education - Roehampton Institute of Higher Education
Roehampton Lane, London SW15
☎ 081 946 2234 x 4221
Ⓟ Dr Barry Stierer, Lecturer in education
Projects and curriculum initiatives
1 Development of a profile for children at the point of school entry, i.e. the beginning of Key Stage 1 (1989–90, 5 year olds). (Joint research and development ream with Merton LEA).

29. Doncaster Metropolitan Institute of Higher Education
Waterdale, Doncaster DN1 3EX
☎ 0302 322122
Ⓟ Mr Paul Barratt, Principal lecturer

30. Dorset Institute of Higher Education
Wallisdown Rd, Poole, BH12 5BB
☎ 0202 524111
Ⓟ Principal

31. Ealing College of Higher Education
St Mary's Rd, Ealing, London W5 5RF
☎ 081 579 4111
Ⓟ Director

32. Edge Hill College of Higher Education
St Helens Rd, Ormskirk, Lancs. L39 1LP
☎ 0695 75171
Ⓟ Dr B. Sorsby, Senior lecturer
Projects and curriculum initiatives
1 Science processes and concept exploration (SPACE) project (with Liverpool University and Kings College London) (1987–92, 5–11 age group).
▼ Reports/evaluations; policy documents
2 'Landmarks' project (with the British Society for the History of Science) (1989–92, 11–16 age group).
■ To generate teacher resources for the history of science and technology
▼ Books; resource materials

33. Essex Institute of Higher Education
Victoria Rd South, Chelmsford CM1 1LL
☎ 0245 493131
Ⓟ Head of education

34. Froebel Institute
Grove Hse, Roehampton La, London SW15 5PJ
☎ 081 876 2242
Ⓟ Principal

35. Gloucestershire College of Arts and Technology
Oxstalls La, Gloucester GL2 9HW
☎ 0452 426700
Ⓟ Principal

36. Gwent College of Higher Education
College Cresc, Caerlon, Newport NP6 1XJ
☎ 0633 421292
Ⓟ Dean, Faculty of education and combined studies

37. Harrow College of Higher Education
Watford Rd, Northwick Park, Harrow, Middlesex HA1 3TP
☎ 081 864 5422
Ⓟ Nora Dean, Senior lecturer, Department of Interfaculty Studies
Projects and curriculum initiatives
1 Primary science and the national curriculum (1988, 5–11 age group).
■ To provide or consolidate a scientific background for teachers in the context of the national curriculum, by means of a 10 week course, collaborating with LEA.

38. Hatfield Polytechnic
School of Humanities and Education, Wall Hall Campus, Aldenham, Watford WD2 8AT
☎ 0923 852511   Ⓣ 262413
Ⓕ 0923 853216
Ⓟ Dr Robin Campbell, Head, Division of education and training
Projects and curriculum initiatives
1 Reading and the national curriculum (1989–93, 5–11 age group).
■ To evaluate the impact of the national curriculum on primary school practice related to reading development
Ⓣ Dr Robin Campbell + 1
Proposal papers
2 An evaluation of sustained silent reading (SSR) (1988–92, 5–11 age group).
Ⓟ Dr Robin Campbell and Mrs Gillian Scrivens
▼ Two papers

39. Homerton College
Cambridge CB2 2PH
☎ 0223 411141   Ⓕ 0223 411622
Ⓟ Sylvia Williams, Assistant deputy principal
Projects and curriculum initiatives
1 PLUM (Primary LOGO use in mathematics (1986–91, middle infant age range).
■ A study of longitudinal development of the mathematics curriculum for children who are using LOGO
Ⓣ Hilary Shuard and Katrina Blythe (with the Nuffield Foundation)
▼ Books
2 PLUM Phase 2 – NCET/MESU and LEA funding (£7,500 per annum) (1989–91, middle infant age range).
■ To extend the work of the PLUM project to 11 more LEAs
Ⓣ Hilary Shuard, Katrina Blythe, Janice Stane
▼ Books
3 CAN (Calculator Aware Number curriculum) (LEA funding) (1989–92, junior age range).
■ To continue development of Calculator Aware Number curriculum until oldest group pass 12 years).
▼ Resource materials
4 Science software project (1988–90, all age groups).
■ To produce software and support materials to assist the implementation of the national curriculum for science
▼ Resource materials (software)
5 Mathematics software (MESU/NCET funding) (1988–9, secondary age range).
■ To develop software with curriculum materials
Ⓟ Christine Mayle
▼ Books; resource materials
6 Curriculum development in IT: visual creativity and the computer (1988–90, all age groups).
■ Development of art software and

curriculum support materials
Ⓟ Michael Cooper
▼ Resource materials (software)

40. Huddersfield Polytechnic
Queensgate, Huddersfield HD1 3DH
☎ 0484 22288
Ⓟ Dean of education

41. Humberside College of Higher Education
Cottingham Rd, Hull HU6 7RT
☎ 0482 41451
Ⓟ Head, Teacher education

42. Jordanhill College of Education
Southbrae Dr, Glasgow GL13 1PP
☎ 041 959 1232
Ⓟ Principal

43. King Alfred's College
Sparkford Rd, Winchester, SO22 4NR
☎ 0962 841515   Ⓕ 0962 842280
Ⓟ Dr B. Tippett, Dean of academic affairs
Projects and curriculum initiatives
1 WARN project (Wessex Action Research Network Project) (1988–, 5–18 age group).
■ To offer members the following: support network; resource base; data bank; research forum; means of publishing classroom research; directory of members' research activities
Ⓣ Chris Hall + 6
▼ Bulletin; conference papers; directory
2 The GRASP Project (Getting Results and Solving Problems) (DTI and Comino Foundation funding) (1987–90, 5–18 age group).
Ⓣ Jose Chambers + 1
▼ Reports/evaluations; resource materials; discussion documents
3 TESCA environmmental science project (1986–90, 4–11 age group).
■ To support groups of students in years 3 and 4 of B.Ed courses working on commissions provided by schools in the area of curriculum development in science and/or general education
Ⓟ Charly Ryan and John Bentley
▼ Reports/evaluations; books; resource materials
4 The Ilford Project (1984–, 5–12 age group).
■ To use photographic materials to enhance and accelerate children's learning across the whole primary curriculum
Ⓟ Stephen Hewitt
▼ Reports/evaluations; books; resource materials
5 Religious education project (1988–, 4–7 age group).
■ To use story, symbol and ritual for promoting religious literacy and understanding by developing calm reflection, concentration and awareness
Ⓣ Clive Erricker and teachers from Northam First School
▼ Reports/evaluations; books; resource materials

44. Kingston Polytechnic
Faculty of Education, Kingston Hill Centre, Kingston Hill, Kingston upon Thames, KT2 7LB
☎ 081 549 1141
Ⓟ Dr M. Gibson, Acting head, Undergraduate initial teacher training
Projects and curriculum initiatives
1 Practical problem solving in the primary (PS) curriculum: a cross-curricular approach to teaching and learning (1984–90, 5–13 age group).
▼ Resource materials; policy documents; discussion documents
2 Special educational needs (5–13 age groups).
▼ Resource materials; policy documents; discussion documents
3 Gifted children (5–13 age group).
▼ Resource materials; policy documents; discussion documents
4 Conflict management in the classroom: a cross-curricular approach (1988 onwards, 5–18 age group).
▼ Resource materials; policy documents; discussion documents; 'ways and means' publication
5 Industrial experience (1989–, 5–13 age group).
■ To enhance economic awareness through taught and experiential components, work shadowing being a major feature
▼ Resource materials; policy documents
6 Teacher appraisal (1987–90, 21+ age group).
■ To develop classroom observations leading to enhanced teaching performance
▼ Reports/evaluations; resource materials; policy documents; discussion documents

45. La Sainte Union College of Higher Education
The Avenue, Southampton S09 5HB
☎ 0703 228761
Ⓟ Principal

46. Leeds Polytechnic
Beckett Park, Leeds L86 3QS
☎ 0532 759061
Ⓟ Head of education department

47. Leicester Polytechnic
Scraptoft Campus, Leicester LE7 9SU
☎ 0533 431011
Ⓟ Head, School of education

48. Liverpool Institute of Higher Education
Standpark Rd, Liverpool L16 9JD
☎ 051 722 2361
Ⓟ Rector

49. Liverpool Polytechnic
School of Education, I.M. Marsh campus, Barhill Rd, Aigburth, Liverpool L17 6BD
☎ 051 724 2321   Ⓕ 051 709 0172
Ⓟ Sue Thompson, TVEI Coordinator
Projects and curriculum initiatives
1 TVEI staff development programme

Curriculum Handbook

(£100,000, Training Agency) (1989–91, 4–18 age group).
■ Staff development for TVEI, enhancement of initial teacher training curriculum, production of materials and identification of good practice. The project will involve development work and partnership between education, industry, business and commerce
Ⓟ Sue Thompson, Coordinator
▼ Work of projects to be disseminated by TVEI agency

50. Loughborough University of Technology
Department of Education, Loughborough LE11 3TU
☎ 0509 222768 Ⓕ 0509 231948
Projects and curriculum initiatives
1 Evaluation of inservice training for secondary school teachers (£400 MESU) (1987–9, secondary age group).
■ Evaluation of the work of an advisory teacher for IT
Ⓟ Dr P. Wild, Lecturer
▼ Reports/evaluations
2 Sensitising PE teachers to the role of health-related exercise (£296,000 HEA) (1985–90, 11–16 age group).
■ To produce resource materials
Ⓣ L. Almond, Director of physical education + 4
▼ Books; resource materials; discussion documents newsletters
3 Group Task Management (GTM) (1986–, 11–18 age group).
■ To report an ongoing action research project in four LEAs describing a cross-curricular approach using group work within a simulated commercial environment, emphasis being placed on task and time management by pupils
Ⓟ H. Dentop, Lecturer
▼ 3 published articles

51. Luton College of Higher Education
Park Square, Luton LU1 3JU
☎ 0582 34111
Ⓟ Director

52. Manchester Polytechnic
School of Education, Wilmslow Rd, Manchester M20 8RR
☎ 061 445 7871
Ⓟ D. Hustler, Principal lecturer
Projects and curriculum initiatives
1 TVEI and initial teacher training: a staff development programme (£100,000) (1989–92, 14+ age group).
Ⓣ D. Hustler + 7 teacher trainers + LEA officers
▼ Resource materials; discussion documents; programme proposal
2 Educational uses of international electronic networks in teacher education (Europe and North America) – the PLUTO project (£100,000 IBM) – involving ten

European institutions (1988–90, all age groups).
Ⓟ R. Gwyn
▼ Reports/evaluations; policy documents; books; discussion documents
3 Evaluation of Cheshire LEA's Arts Education in a Multicultural Society project (£3,000) (1989–90, all age groups).
Ⓟ D. Hustler
▼ Reports/evaluations
4 Research on book art projects in primary schools in Greater Manchester (£2,000) (1989–90, 5–11 age group).
▼Reports/evaluations; books; resource materials
5 Design of investigational and practical activities in mathematics (1987–90, 5–16 age group).
Ⓣ G. Hatch + 4
▼ Resource materials
6 Local evaluation of TVEI and TVEE (£9,000) (1987–91, 14+ age group).
Ⓣ A. Goodwin + 7 with LEA officers
▼ Reports/evaluations

53. Middlesex Polytechnic
Trent Park, Cockfosters, Barnet EN4 OPT
☎ 081 368 1299
Ⓟ Dean of Education

54. Moray House College
Holyrood Rd, Edinburgh, Lothian EH8 8AQ
☎ 031 556 8455 Ⓕ 031 557 3456
Ⓟ Professor Donald Bligh, Director of research and enterprise
Projects and curriculum initiatives
1 Resources for environmental social studies teaching (REST) (ongoing, 5–12 age group).
■ To provide resource materials relating to environmental and social studies
Ⓟ Tom Masterton
▼ Over 60 REST booklets; resource materials
2 Multicultural resource and development unit (1985–, 5–18 age group).
■ The collation and production of resources in multicultural and anti-racist education
Ⓣ John Landon + 2
▼ Reports/evaluations; books; resource materials
3 Scottish development project in expressive arts (1990, 5–12 age group).
■ To coordinate the production of a number of school-focused inservice training packages in the various disciplines of the expressive arts
Ⓣ Archie McIntosh + 4
▼ Resource materials
4 Listening comprehension materials (1983–8, 13–16 age group).
■ To develop listening comprehension skills in mother tongue speakers of English in Scottish secondary schools
Ⓟ Mike Wallace
▼ Reports/evaluations
5 Resources for Scottish schools (1985, 5–18 age groups).

■ To collate and commission materials for the teaching of geography in secondary schools and environmental studies in primary schools
Ⓟ Norman Thomson
▼ Reports/evaluations; resource materials
6 Practical art appreciation and critical activity (1981–, 5–18 age groups).
■ To extend the response and appreciation of school children to blended experiences of practical art in the classroom and visits to galleries
Ⓟ Mike Hildred
▼ Reports/evaluations; resource materials

55. Nene College
Moulton Park, Northampton NN2 7AL
☎ 0604 715000 Ⓕ 0604 720636
Ⓟ Dr J. Campbell, Research committee chairperson
Projects and curriculum initiatives
1 Implementing the national curriculum (1989–91, 4–16 age group).
■ To describe a case study of cross-phase liaison and curriculum development in humanities
Ⓣ Supervisor and research student

56. Newcastle upon Tyne Polytechnic
Coach Lane Campus, Newcastle upon Tyne NE7 7XA
☎ 091 232 6002 Ⓣ 53519 Newpol G
Ⓕ 091 235 8017
Ⓟ Colin Biott, Principal lecturer
Projects and curriculum initiatives
1 TVEI Initial teacher education project (£100,000) (1989–91, secondary age group).
■ To create a model of ITT which is more formally and fully collaborative between LEAs, school agencies and other institutions of higher education
Ⓟ A. Fendley and B. Gillham
▼ Reports/evaluations; resource materials; discussion documents
2 National curriculum strategy in primary schools (£21,000) (1989–90, primary age group).
■ To record a critical history of an LEA strategy; to develop classroom practice through a set of action research projects
Ⓣ Colin Biott + 6
▼ Reports/evaluations
3 Local authority training grant scheme evaluation (£21,000); a collaborative research project with Newcastle University (1988–90, all age groups).
■ A series of related projects studying aspects of INSET provision and the roles of key participants
Ⓟ Colin Biott
▼ Reports/evaluations
4 Cross-curricular learning materials project (£1,200) (1989–90, secondary age group).
The production, trialling and evaluation of cross-curricular learning materials
Ⓟ Betty Wadsworth
▼ Reports/evaluations; resource materials
5 Curriculum development for school

leavers with learning difficulties (£2,000) (1988–91, secondary age group).
■ Enquiry and curriculum development in a school for young adults with severe learning difficulties; focusing on the national curriculum entitlement and post-school initiatives
Ⓟ Keith Humphreys
▼ Reports/evaluations; policy documents

57. New College Durham
Nevilles Cross Centre, Darlington Rd, Nevilles Cross, Durham DH1 4SY
☎ 091 384 7325
Ⓟ Mr Alan Lilley, Acting head of education
Projects and curriculum initiatives
1 The introduction of design and technology into the primary school: an action research project (1989–, 5–11 age group).
▼ Reports/evaluations; resource materials

58. Newman and Westhill College
Genners Lane, Bartley Green, Birmingham B32 3NT
☎ 021 476 1181
Ⓟ Director

59. North Cheshire College
Fearnhead, Warrington WA2 0DB
☎ 0925 814343
Ⓟ Director

60. North East London Polytechnic
Longbridge Rd, Dagenham, Essex RM8 2AS
☎ 081 590 7722 Ⓕ 081 590 7799
Ⓟ C. Broderick
Projects and curriculum initiatives
1 Educational implications of desktop publishing (NAB funding) (1988–90, primary and secondary age groups).
■ To look at the development of curricular materials across a range of ages and needs; to look at developments in curriculum organisation and management related to DTP.
Ⓣ Dr P. Williams + 2
▼ Reports/evaluations; discussion documents

61. Northern College of Education
Hilton Place, Aberdeen AB9 1FA
☎ 0224 482342 Ⓕ 487046
Ⓟ Dr John Taylor, Vice principal
Projects and curriculum initiatives
1 Investigation of differentiation in primary schools (£77,978) (1987–9, 5–12 age group).
■ How to identify and make effective provision for a range of abilities in the classroom such that the needs of the very able and of children with learning difficulties are met
Ⓟ Dr Mary Simpson
▼ Report
2 Business studies teacher development network (£97,000) (1989–91, 12–18 age group).
■ To identify needs of business studies teachers in each participating authority, prepare materials and resources to meet these needs and facilitate their access by all participants

Ⓟ Mr James Grant
▼ Reports/evaluations; resource materials
3 Industrial chemistry in the curriculum (£2,000) (1988–90, 14–18 age group).
■ To produce articles on selected areas of the chemical industry that relate to the teaching of school chemistry
Ⓟ Dr Joe MacDowall
▼ Booklet
4 Now learning through living (£30,000) (1986–8, 8–14 age group).
■ To produce a resource bank of materials; to stimulate work at all areas of the curriculum; to introduce children to the world of industry
Ⓣ Miss Hilda Doran + 6
▼ Research report on school trails of materials; six pupil books and teachers' guide published
5 Assessment of achievement programme – mathematics (£70,000) (1987–9, ages 9, 12, and 14, primary 4 and 7, secondary year 2).
■ Monitoring of mathematical attainment nationwide in Scottish primary and secondary schools
Ⓟ Dr Donald Macnab and Mr John Page
▼ Reports/evaluations
6 Micro computers in social subjects (£10,000) (1985–9, 12–18 age groups).
■ To identify software for balanced progressive coherent approach ; to identify school and classroom organisation that promotes the effective use of microcomputers in social subjects
Ⓟ Dr J. Jennings (Northern College of Education) and Mr R. Munro (Jordanhill College of Education)
▼ Reports/evaluations

62. North Riding College
Filey Rd, Scarborough YO11 3AZ
☎ 0723 362392   Ⓕ 0723 370815
Ⓟ Sue Billett, Principal lecturer Education and professional studies
Projects and curriculum initiatives
1 Monitoring the impact and uptake of TVEI (1985–9, upper secondary age group).
Ⓟ Dr R. Davis
▼ Four research studies
2 Implementing the national curriculum in schools (1988–90, primary age group).
▼ Reports/evaluations; discussion documents
3 Evaluation of an ESG small schools project in 20 schools (1986–91, 5–11 age group).
Ⓣ M. Bentley + 2
▼ Reports/evaluations
4 School governors and educational reform (1988–90, primary age group).
Ⓣ 3 staff
▼ Reports/evaluations; discussion documents
5 Four year olds in school (with Leeds University) (1989–90, 4 year olds).
Ⓣ LEA adviser and 2 education lecturers
▼ Reports/evaluations
6 New directions in the inservice training of teachers; a comparative international study (1986–9)
Ⓟ Dr R Davis

▼ Thesis

63. Norwich City College of Further and Higher Education
Ipswich Rd, Norwich NR2 2LJ
☎ 0603 660011
Ⓟ Jack Sanger, Head, Research and consultancy
Projects and curriculum initiatives
1 Parental perceptions of special needs students in FE (1988–90, 16–19 age group).
▼ Reports/evaluations
2 Teacher appraisal consultancies (5–18 age group).
▼ Consultancy papers
3 Notts./Staffs. development project (5–18 age group).
▼ Consultancy papers
4 Teaching Handling Information and Learning project (THIL) (1983–, 5–18 age group).
■ A grassroots action research, cross phase group of teachers working on major process issues in the classroom
▼ Resource materials
5 Tutor librarians as change agents in further and higher education (£20,050, British Library) (1988–9, 16+ age group).
▼ Reports/evaluations

64. The Open University
Walton Hall, Bletchley, Milton Keynes MK7 6AA
☎ 0908 653773 or 652654
Ⓟ Georgina Sykes, Administrative assistant
Projects and curriculum initiatives
1 Teaching moments (1988–, all age groups).
■ To promulgate and elaborate the observation that the only change that a teacher can make in their own practice is when they become aware of an opportunity to act differently
Ⓣ John Mason + 5
▼ Discussion documents
2 Primary maths coordinator project (1989–90, primary age group).
■ To develop materials for primary maths coordinators to become confident about national curriculum requirements in maths, and to assist their colleagues to do likewise
Ⓣ Joy Davis + 4
▼ Resource materials
3 INSET support for mathematics teachers (1986–, primary and secondary age groups).
■ To support the professional development of mathematics teachers through video tape, inservice packs and undergraduate level and diploma courses
Ⓣ John Mason + 7
▼ Over 20 inservice packs and videotapes; information documents
4 Case studies and analyses of the relationship between the design of CAL packages and the distribution of control over learning between designers, teachers and learners (1986–89, 5–18 age group).
Ⓟ Peter Scrimshaw
▼ Reports/evaluations; books; resource materials

Curriculum Initiatives in Institutions of Higher Education

5 Teachers into business and industry (1989–, 5–18 age groups).
■ To produce a support pack (5 units plus audio and video cassettes) for teachers going on secondment into business, industry and the public sector
Ⓟ Geoff Esland
▼ Resource materials
6 Advanced diploma in technology in schools (£600,000 MSC Training Agency) (1987–92, 12–18 age group).
■ To serve teachers of any subject who wish to introduce the teaching of technology into the curriculum
Ⓣ 5 staff
▼ Books; resource materials
7 Working with under-5s (1989–91, 3–5 age group).
■ To produce a pack of materials for INSET use in relation to 'rising fives' and younger children in educational settings
Ⓟ Professor Paul Light
▼ Reports/evaluations; resource materials; video
8 Oracy: an inservice pack for teachers – in collaboration with the national Oracy Project (P535) (1989–90, 5–16 age group).
■ To produce a pack of materials for teachers of all sectors, on understanding, developing and evaluating spoken language across the curriculum
Ⓟ 12 staff
▼ Resource materials
9 Physics for science teachers (£270,000 DES and BP) (1988–, 13–16 age group).
■ To produce a distance learning, inservice package for secondary science teachers that aims to provide the knowledge, skills and confidence to enable those without the necessary background to teach physics as part of a balanced science programme up to GCSE level
Ⓣ Katharine Pindar + 5
▼ Books; resource materials; discussion documents
10 Primary science: why and how (EHP 531) (£35,000) (1985–, 5–11 age group).
■ To produce a pack consisting of 40 hours of distance learning to help primary teachers who have no specialists knowledge of science
Ⓟ Ms E. Scanlon
▼ Books; resource materials; policy documents; discussion documents
Comment This project is extended from 1990 onwards to become a primary science and technology project (EHP532) which requires an additional 25 hours of study (£30,000 DES)
11 Every child's language: a short inservice pack course for teachers (P534) (1988–9, 5–12 age group).
To provide a short course for primary teachers (100 hours) developed from the existing OU pack of the same name
Books; resource materials
12 Computers and learning (EH232) (1989–91, 5–18 age group).
■ To provide a course for teachers of all sectors on using computers to assist teaching and learning

▼ Resource materials

65. Oxford Polytechnic
Wheatley, Oxford OX9 1HX
☎ 0865 741111
Ⓟ Dean, Faculty of educational studies

66. Plymouth Polytechnic/Polytechnic of the Southwest at Rolle
Faculty of Education, Douglas Ave, Exmouth, Devon EX8 2AT
☎ 0395 265334
Ⓟ Ros. Fisher, Senior lecturer in education
Projects and curriculum initiatives
1 Investigating the potential for English in the national curriculum (1989–90, 4–11 age group).
■ To carry out the investigation within a village project in a group of small rural schools with ESG funding
Ⓣ Ros. Fisher + 2

67. The Polytechnic
Castle View, Dudley DY1 3HR
☎ 0384 459741
Ⓟ Dean, Faculty of arts, design and education

68. Polytechnic of North London
Prince of Wales Rd, Kentish Town, London NW5 3LB
☎ 071 607 2789   Ⓕ 071 267 4223
Ⓟ Dr Greg Condry, Head, School of teaching studies
Projects and curriculum initiatives
1 Primary schools and industry centre (£10,000) (1986–, 3–11 age group).
■ To examine young children's understanding of the world of work
Ⓟ Alistair Ross + 3
▼ Curriculum guidance notes; case studies; seminar papers; resource guides
2 IMPACT project (Mathematics with parents and children and teachers) (40,000) (1987–, 5–11 age group).
■ A research and information project including parents in their children's learning, involving 3 LEAs and expanding to take in up to 15 LEAs
Ⓟ Ruth Matthews + 3
▼ Books; resource materials; journal articles

69. Queen's University of Belfast
School of Education, University St, Belfast BT7 1HL
☎ 0232 245133
Ⓟ Head of department

70. Roehampton Institute of Higher Education
Roehampton Lane, London SW15 5PU
☎ 081 878 8117
Ⓟ The Rector

71. St. Andrews College of Education
6 Duntocher Rd, Bearsden, Glasgow G61 4QA

☎ 041 943 1424
Ⓟ Mr Charles Stronach and Mr James O'Brian, Programme directors, inservice
Projects and curriculum initiatives
1 Primary Education Development Project (PEDP) (1985–9, primary age group).
■ Resource packaging on caring for the countryside (farms); weather; building and supermarket
Ⓟ Mr C. Stronach + 5
▼ Resource materials
2 Values Education (£10,000 per year, Gordon Cook Foundation) (1988–91, 10–14 age group).
■ To promote values education, including materials developed, within college courses and for schools
Ⓟ Mr Stephen Joyce and Dr A. Naylor
3 Computing and information technology (1988).
(a) Learning interword on the BBC – self-study material to learn the facilities of word processing package from Computer Concepts. Booklet divided into 8 units with disc containing exercises to assist learning (14–18 age group). (b) Problem solving in the primary school using control technology (7–12 age group) – using the Cambridge In-Control Kit to create problem solving environments from primary pupils, assuming no teacher knowledge of control technology; divided into 5 units. (c) Interaction of humans/computers (14–18 age group) – using self-study materials to examine ergonomics, screen design and dialogue design, supported by exercises on disc for Apple and BBC. (d) Information handling in environmental studies (9–12 age group) – classroom materials to develop information handling skills. (e)The use of hyper text as a learning medium within computing studies (14–18 age group) – examination of the graphics facilities afforded by hyper card on the Apple Mac to enhance self-learning for the pupils and recording facilities for the teacher
▼ Resource materials
4 Music: Scottish Development Programme in Expressive Arts (SDPEA) (1984–9, primary age group).
■ To produce 3 packages. Package 1: 2 instructional videos on use of omnichord and electronic keyboard, audio tape of songs with accompaniment, support booklet. Package 2: audio tape of songs with accompaniment on classroom instruments, support booklet for teachers and children. Package 3: creative music making: a development approach – a video tape, support booklet.
Ⓟ Mrs J. McGregor
▼ Resource materials
5 Learning resources (1989–91).
■ (a) Local evaluation of TVEI in Argyll and Bute (16+ age group). (b) Production of video material for inservice training – school boards management training (5–18 age group)
▼ (a) Reports/evaluations; (b) video
6 The Croftcroigh drama project (1986–, 5–18 age group).
■ To produce three booklets describing

drama for children with complex learning difficulties
▼ Reports/evaluations; resource materials; videos

72. St. Martins College
Bowerham, Lancaster LA1 3JD
☎ 0524 63446
Ⓟ Principal

73. St. Mary's College
19 Falls Rd, Belfast BT12 6FE
☎ 0232 327678
Ⓟ Principal

74. St. Mary 's College
Strawberry Hill, Waldeframe Rd, Twickenham TW1 4SX
☎ 081 892 0051
Ⓟ Mrs J. Northam, Dean, teaching studies

75. Sheffield City Polytechnic
36 Collegiate Crescent, Sheffield S10 2BP
☎ 0742 665274 Ⓕ 0742 670479
Ⓟ Professor Asher Cashdan, Head, Department of education
Projects and curriculum initiatives
1 Equal opportunities in science, maths and English (£14,000, European Commission) (£1989–90, primary and secondary age groups).
■ To develop a teacher education curriculum for students in primary and secondary areas
Ⓣ 6 staff and associated teachers
▼ Reports/evaluations; resource materials

76. Southbank Polytechnic
Borough Rd, London NW3 3HY
☎ 071 928 8989
Ⓟ Head, education department

77. South Glamorgan Institute of Higher Education
Cyncoed Site, Cyncoed Rd, Cardiff, CF2 6XD
☎ 0222 551111 Ⓕ 0222 747668
Ⓟ Delwyn Tattum, Reader in education
Projects and curriculum initiatives
1 EATE project to investigate the impact of information technology on the curriculum for B.Ed students in IT education (£20,000, DTI) (1989–91, primary age group).
Ⓣ 3 people
▼ Reports/evaluations
2 Castell Coch, Cardiff, as a location for environmental studies in the primary school (CADW (Wales) funding) (1989–90, primary age group).
Ⓣ 2 people
▼ Resource materials
3 Language and learning in the primary classroom (Mid-Glamorgan LEA funding) (1989–91, primary age group).
■ To run a part-time diploma for practising teachers in classroom investigations
Ⓣ Eric Hadley (for SGHIHE), Phil. Jackson (for Mid-Glamorgan)

▼ Validation document

78. Southampton Institute of Higher Education
East Park Terrace, Southampton S09 4WM
☎ 0703 229381
Ⓟ Principal

79. Southlands College
Wimbledon Parkside, London SW19 5NN
☎ 01946 2234
Ⓟ Principal

80. Stranmills College
Stranmills Rd, Belfast BT9 5DY
☎ 0232 381271
Projects and curriculum initiatives
1 Distance learning in primary science
(1989–90, primary age group).
■ To prepare materials for INSET in
primary science for teachers not within easy
travelling distance of an HE institution; to
enable them to meet the needs of the national
curriculum
Ⓣ Dr Barbara Erwin + 4 HE staff
▼ Books; resource materials (videos,
booklets); policy documents
2 BOB: a computer package for problem
solving (1987–91, primary and secondary age
groups).
■ To develop project work in 5 primary and
secondary schools
Ⓣ Leslie Caul + 7
▼ Reports/evaluations; resource materials;
policy documents; discussion documents
3 Children as poets: a study of processes
in the making of poetry (1888–91, primary age
group).
Ⓣ Dr G. Patterson + 17 teachers.
4 Writing into reading (£8,000, DENI)
1986–92, primary age group).
■ To provide a body of regional material
across the primary curriculum with a local
flavour written by parents, pupils, teachers
and local writers; to set up an exhibition in the
college
Ⓣ Neill Speers, Senior lecturer, + 10

81. Sunderland Polytechnic
Hammerton Hall, Gray Rd, Sunderland SR1
7EE
☎ 091 515 2000
Ⓟ Neil Hufton, director of INSET
Projects and curriculum initiatives
1 National business project (1985–90,
14–19 age group).
■ To support developments in TVEI related
to areas of business education, involving
teachers and industry; developing curriculum
materials and INSET provision
▼ Reports/evaluations; resource materials

82. Teesside Polytechnic
Borough Rd, Middlesbrough TS1 3BA
☎ 0642 218121
Ⓟ Brian Oldham, Head, Educational
development unit

83. Thames Polytechnic
Bexley Rd, Eltham, London SE9 2PQ
☎ 081 854 2030
Ⓟ Dean, Faculty of community studies

84. Thames Valley College of Further Education
Wellington St, Slough SL1 1YG
☎ 0753 34585
Ⓟ Director

85. Trent Polytechnic
School of Education, Burton St, Nottingham
NG1 4BU
☎ 0602 418248
Ⓟ Dean, School of education

86. Trinity and All Saints College
Brownberrie Lane, Horsforth, Leeds LS18
5HD
☎ 0532 584341
Ⓟ Principal

87. Trinity College, Carmarthen
Carmarthen, Dyfed SA31 3EP
☎ 0267 237971/2/3   Ⓕ 0267 230933
Ⓟ Malcolm Jones, Assistant principal,
educational studies
Projects and curriculum initiatives
1 Teaching non-Welsh speaking
teachers/learners to teach infant Welsh
classes (Welsh Office funding) (1989–90, 4–7
age group).
▼ Resource materials

88. University of Bath
School of Education, Claverton Down, Bath
BA2 7AY
☎ 0225 826826
Ⓟ Head, School of education

89. University of Birmingham
School of Education, PO Box 363,
Birmingham B15 2TT
☎ 021 414 4381
Ⓟ Ms Pamela Cotton, Executive secretary
Projects and curriculum initiatives
1 Development of microcomputer software
for educational and vocational applications
(for blind and partially sighted persons) (RNIB
funding) (1983–)
■ The research centre for the education of
the visually handicapped has a programme of
individual research and development projects
concerned with using and adapting
microcomputer technology to allow visually
handicapped children and adults to have
access to databases, educational materials,
and word processing systems. Software has
been developed so that output can be
produced in braille, large print, computer
graphics and synthetic speech
Ⓟ Dr M. Tobin and Mr M. Ross
▼ Regular newsletters; information sheets;
software documentation. The research centre
keeps copies of its published journal articles.
2 Braille and Moon (RNIB funding)
(1985–).

■ A series of experiments undertaken on various aspects of tactile reading by blind children and adults. Experimental comparisons are being made among alternative letter shapes with the aim of producing a more legible tactile code for older adults and for those with poor tactual ability
Ⓟ Dr M. Tobin
▼ Documents available. The research centre keeps copies of its published journal articles.
3 Speed of visual information processing (RNIB funding) (1985–).
■ To measure the speed of visual information processing on partially sighted pupils on tasks similar to those used with their fully sighted peers. Preliminary findings have indicated a large discrepancy between the average performances of the partially sighted and the published norms for the fully sighted
Ⓟ Dr M. Tobin
▼ The research centre keeps copies of its published journal articles
4 Longitudinal investigation of cognitive development and educational achievement in blind and partially sighted children (RNIB funding) (1973–).
■ To monitor aspects of psychological and educational development of blind and partially sighted children attending special schools for the visually handicapped in England and Wales
Ⓟ Dr M. Tobin
▼ The research centre keeps copies of published journal articles
5 Distance learning for teachers of children with language difficulties (£76,421 DES); a joint project with the School of Speech Therapy at Birmingham Polytechnic (1989–90).
■ To investigate the needs of teachers of children with speech and language problems; to develop a distance learning course for teachers, based on these needs
Ⓟ Carol Miller
6 Support for special needs (£100) (1984–7).
■ To study changing perceptions of the roles of advisory teachers and mainstream teachers in meeting the special educational needs of pupils with difficulties in learning in the ordinary school
Ⓟ Colin Smith (School of education) and Robin Richmond (Dudley LEA)
▼ Two journal articles

90. University of Bristol
School of Education, 35 Berkely Square, Bristol BS8 1JA
☎ 0272 303030
Ⓟ Director

91. University of Cambridge
Department of Education, 17 Trumpington St, Cambridge CB2 1QA
☎ 0223 332888/332891
Ⓟ R. Stranks, Secretary of the department
Projects and curriculum initiatives
1 Cambridge modular A levels project (£26,000 UCLES) (1989–90, 16–18 age

group).
Ⓟ Mr R. Walferd (Department of education), Mr J. Sadler (UCLES), Mr B. Heppel (SRA/Department of education). 0223 332878
▼ Reports/evaluations: resource materials; discussion documents
2 Cambridge modular A levels project (£28,000 UCLES) (1989–90, 16–18 age groups).
Ⓟ Mr J. Raftoan (Department of education), Mr J. Sadler (UCLES), Mr P. Mitchell (SRA/Department of education). (0223 332878)
▼ Reports/evaluations; resource materials; discussion documents

92. University College of Swansea
Department of Education, Hendrefoilan, Swansea SA2 7NB
☎ 0792 201231
Ⓟ Dr Garth Elwyn Jones, Director of research
Projects and curriculum initiatives
1 GCSE in Wales (£88,000 Welsh Office) (1989–90, 14–16 age group).
■ To investigate the response of maintained secondary schools in Wales to the curriculum and assessment demands of GCSE
Ⓣ Mr Richard Daugherty + 4
▼ Policy documents

93. University College of North Wales
School of Education, Deiniol Rd, Bangor, Gwynedd LL57 2UW
☎ 0248 351151 X 2930
Ⓕ 0248 370451
Ⓟ Professor Iolo Wyn Williams, Head, School of education
Projects and curriculum initiatives
1 Research and development work in RE, world education (5–18 age group).
■ To promote initial and inservice training of students, teachers of RE, and Sunday School teachers; to provide a Religious education resource centre
Ⓟ Rheinallt Thomas (0248 351151 x 2956)
▼ Many publications in Welsh and some in English
2 Prosiect Addysg Byd/World Education Project (1983–, primary and secondary age groups).
■ To promote development education to schools, colleges and community groups; to develop and disseminate teaching materials
Ⓟ Heather Morgan
▼ Teaching materials and newsletters
3 Joint project with Health Promotion Unit (Heartbeat Wales funded) (7–11 age group).
■ To increase regular participation in physical activity in and out of school
Ⓟ Christine Jenkins (Gwynedd Health Authority Health Promotion Unit) and Jogn Fazey, Della Fazey (UCNW Physical Education department)
▼ Pack of 60 workcards and guidelines
4 Teacher development in IT in science and technology (Training Agency funding)

(1989–91, 14–18 age group).

■ To investigate strategies for INSET and teacher development in above areas through case studies and strategic intervention

Ⓟ Martin Owen

▼ Discussion documents

5 Bilingual GCSE maths coursework project (1990–)

■ To provide resource materials for the GCSE in Welsh and English. Materials to be prepared relating to four topic areas, providing schools with flexible coursework packs for all levels of entry to GCSE. The packs will be based on ideas presented at the Royal Institution Mathematics Masterclass given at the University of Wales, Bangor, but will be structures for use with a wide ability range.

Ⓟ Heather McLeay

▼ Resource materials

6 Use of database of national curriculum for producing teaching schemes, management of resources, record keeping – joint project with LEA (1989–90, 5–16 age group).

Ⓟ J. Prys Jones

▼ Software

94. University of Durham

School of Education, Leazes Rd, Durham DH1 1TA

☎ 091 374 3000   Ⓕ 091 374 3740

Ⓟ Professor Frank Coffield, Chairman of research committee

Projects and curriculum initiatives

1 Science 5–16 (1988–91, key stages 1–4).

■ To provide a complete course for the national curriculum in science

Ⓣ Dr Richard Gott + 4

2 Science 14–16 (1989–91, key stage 4)

■ A continuation of 'Active Science' course already published.

Ⓣ Dr Richard Gott + seconded teacher

3 Language teaching and pupils' views of other cultures (£99,210 ESRC) (1985–88, 12–14 age groups).

Ⓣ Dr Michael Byram + 2

▼ Books; ESRC report

4 Microcomputer networking in primary schools (£9,750 funding) (1986–, primary age group).

Ⓣ Jack Gilliland, Charles Crook, John Steele, Geof Alred

▼ Reports/evaluations; software

5 Christian understanding in adolescence (£500) (1982–8, secondary age group).

Ⓣ David Day and Philip May

▼ Reports; articles

6 Evaluation and innovations in science teaching (part of £6,000 funding for innovation in science teaching project) (1987–9, secondary age group).

■ To carry out a long term mixed method evaluation of a science innovation which combines school based and school focused curriculum development.

Ⓟ Keith Morrison

▼ Reports; articles; seminar papers

7 The development of bibliographic data bases for use in initial teacher training (£1,000) (1988–).

Ⓣ Jack Gilliland, John Steele, Joyce Adams

▼ Discussion documents; the project uses the university mainframe computer

95. University of East Anglia

School of Education, Norwich, Norfolk NR4 7TJ

☎ 0603 56161   Ⓕ 0603 259388

Ⓟ John Shostak, Lecturer

Projects and curriculum initiatives

1 Evaluation of the National Problem Solving Project (£48,000) (1988–90, 5–13 age group).

Ⓣ Team of three

▼ Policy documents

2 Teaching, handling information and learning (£76,000) (1984–6, 5–18 age group).

Ⓟ Team of four

▼ Reports/evaluations; books

3 Talking and listening project (1988–9, 5–8 age group).

Ⓟ Team of two

▼ Reports/evaluations; resource materials; discussion documents

4 The culture of alcohol in relation to secondary school aged pupils (£25,000) (1989, 11–18 age group).

Ⓣ Three people

▼ Reports/evaluations

5 Children and the culture of arcade gambling (1990, 8–18 age group).

Ⓣ Two people

6 Language through projects (1983–8, 9–13 age group).

Ⓟ Dr Stephen Parker

▼ Resource materials (Hayhoe M., Parker S. (1983) 'Island: a theme pack of ideas for use in the middle years of education'; Parker S., Hayhoe M. (1989) 'Voyages: skills in everyday English')

7 The greenhouse effect – causes and consequences (1988–90, 11–14 age group).

Ⓟ David Wright, Lecturer

▼ Books; resource materials (teachers' book, pupils' book and photocopiable resources)

96. University of Exeter

School of Education, St Luke's, Exeter EX1 2LU

☎ 0392 57246   Ⓣ EXUNIV G 428944

Ⓕ 0392 411274

Ⓟ Dr P. Gurney, Administrator

Projects and curriculum initiatives

Three projects from the Schools Health Education Unit, Wolfson Laboratories, University of Exeter EX4 4QJ

☎ 0392 264722   Ⓕ 0392 263108

Ⓟ John Balding, Director, Schools Health Education Unit

1 Health Behaviour Survey Services (1981–, 13–19 age group).

▼ Reports/evaluations; books; resource materials

2 Attitudinal behaviour survey service (1978–, 8–19 age group).

▼ Reports/evaluations; books; resource materials

3 Journal: Education and Health (1983–,

5–19 age group).
▼ Books; journal
Comment The Unit's collection of Health
Related Behaviour data contains the
responses of more than 120,000 pupils in the
UK. It has developed the health related
Behaviour and Just a Tick questionnaires, and
publishes the journal *Education and Health*
from the Centre for Innovation in mathematics
teaching (0392 217113)
4 Enterprising mathematics (1986–91,
14–16 year olds).
℗ Professor David Burghes
▼ Reports/evaluations; resource materials
5 Maths focus (1989–, 11–18 age group).
℗ Professor David Burghes
▼ Resource materials
6 Wessex A-level maths (1990–, 16–18
age group)
℗ Professor David Burghes
▼ Policy documents
7 Aspects of Gymnastics and Independent
Learning Experiences (AGILE) (£22,000)
(1988–90, 8–14 year olds).
℗ Dr M. Underwood (0392 264852)
▼ Teachers' and pupils' books; resource
materials – 96 work cards; videotape
8 PEG – The application of knowledge
based and expert systems in the education of
children and students across the whole range
of national curriculum subjects and ages
(1982–92, 7–19 age group).
℗ Dr J. Nichol
▼ Reports/evaluations; books; resource
materials; discussion documents
9 ETHOS – enquiry into teaching history to
over sixteens; an improvement project aimed
at reforming the teaching of history via
syllabus development, resource improvement
and the changing of pedagogy.
℗ Dr J. Nichol
▼ Reports/evaluations; resource materials;
policy documents; discussion documents
10 Forms of assessment in RE (FARE)
(£200,000) (1989–91, 5–18 age group).
Ⓣ Two project officers and two directors
plus steering committee of RE advisers and
funding representatives and the project team.
℗ Dr J. Priestley (0392 264749)
▼ Policy documents; discussion documents
(in preparation); reports/evaluations, books,
resource materials
11 Early years IT–INSET (1989–, 5–7 age
group).
℗ Dr A. Peacock (0392 264833)
▼ Policy documents
12 Parental understanding of science in the
national curriculum (1990–3, 5–8 age group).
℗ Dr A. Peacock (0392 264833)
▼ Policy documents

97. University of Hull
School of Education, Cottingham Rd, Hull,
North Humberside HU6 7RX
☎ 0482 465031   Ⓕ 0482 466205
℗ Kathryn Carrick, Administrative assistant
Projects and curriculum initiatives
1 Aids, values and the curriculum (1987–9,
13–18 age group).
2 English as a subject: the perceptions of

students and teachers regarding its subject
matter, teaching methods and assessment
(£1,200) (1985–, 11–18 age group)
Ⓣ 2 people
▼ Books
3 The philosophy for children project
(1988–92, 7–11 age group).
■ To improve reasoning ability through the
discussion of philosophical topics
Articles
4 The Happy Heart Project (£12,000,
Sports Council; £28,000 Health Education
Authority) (1987–, 4–11 age group).
■ To promote physical activity amongst
primary children
Ⓣ 3 people
▼ Resource materials

98, University of Keele
Department of Education, Keele ST5 5BG
☎ 0782 621111
℗ Head of department

99. University of Leeds
School of Education, Leeds, West Yorkshire
LS2 9JT
☎ 0532 334653   Ⓣ 556473 UNILDS G
Ⓕ 0532 336017
℗ Dr Peter Medway, Lecturer in education
Projects and curriculum initiatives
1 Developing English for TVEI (£48,000,
Training Agency) (1989–90, 14–16 age group).
■ Documentation of good practice in
developing English for TVEI and work with
teachers in 10 schools
Ⓣ 3 people
▼ Newsletter; reports/evaluations
2 Economic change and society (IBM, BP,
Gatsby Foundation, Comino Foundation, DTI
funding) (1987–90/1, 16–18 age group).
■ Curriculum development project creating
a new, modular, broadening, advanced
supplementary AS level which seeks to
enable young people to understand the forces
transforming modern society and their place in
that society
Ⓣ 25 people
▼ Reports/evaluations; books; resource
materials; discussion documents
3 Health into mathematics (1987–90,
primary age group).
■ The first stage of the health across the
curriculum project funded by 'Child to Child'
and British Council
Ⓣ 8 people, based in Kenya
▼ Teachers' guide
4 Primary Needs Independent Evaluation
Project (PRINDEP) (£140,000) (1986–90,
5–11 age group).
■ A formative and summative evaluation of
Leeds City Council's 14 million pounds
programme to improve provision and practice
in its 230 primary schools.
Ⓣ Dr Robin Alexander + up to 9 + 14
seconded teachers
▼ Thirteen reports; two books
5 Pupils' design and technology capability
(1989–90, secondary age group).
6 Science and technology in action

(£80,000, Nuclear Electricity Information Group) (1989–90, 14–16 age group).

Ⓣ Professor R. Driver and Mr P. Scott, and associate teacher

▼ Reports/evaluations; resource materials; policy documents; discussion documents; inservice training materials

7 Physics of materials project (£24,500) (1985–, 16–18 age group).

■ To increase awareness of materials science and to introduce a technological element into A level physics courses

Ⓣ HE staff and 2 seconded teachers

Books

100. University of Leicester

School of Education, 21 University Rd, Leicester LE1 7RF

☎ 0533 522522

Ⓟ Maurice Galton, Director, School of education

Projects and curriculum initiatives

1 Science teaching action research (STAR) (£127,000) (1986–9, primary age group).

■ To define effective primary science by systematic observation of children's use of process skills and through collaborative action research, to develop inservice strategies to disseminate effective practice

Ⓣ M. Galton, S. Cavendish, L. Hargreaves, M. Shilling and W. Harlen (University of Liverpool)

▼ Books; articles

2 East Midlands Records of Achievement Project (EMRAP) (£7,000) (1989–90).

■ To evaluate applications of IT to RoA in Northamptonshire (ESG extension)

Ⓣ K. Fogelman, J. Edwards, D. Ball

▼ PRAISE report

3 Impairment of motor function of 5 years and cerebral pathology in the neonatal period (£45,765) (1989–90).

■ Follow up at 5 years of 150 very low birthweight babies (1500 grams) to assess motor impairment and intellectual progress

Ⓣ K. Fogelman, S. Dowling, M. Graham, M. Galton

4 Teaching and learning in the creative arts: arts assessment of creative development (DELTA) (£29,000) (1987–9, primary age group).

■ A study of assessment techniques used by teachers in the creative arts in the primary school

Ⓣ M. Galton, D. Hargreaves, S. Robinson

▼ Books; articles

5 Rural Schools Curriculum Enhancement National Evaluation Project (SCENE) (£117,463) funding (1989–91, primary age group).

■ Evaluation of ESG supported pilot projects in 14 LEAs, aimed at improving the quality of education for pupils in small rural primary schools

Ⓣ M. Galton, K. Fogelman, L. Hargreaves

6 Practical science with computers (£15,000) (1987–90).

■ To develop materials which enable and encourage science teachers to incorporate the use of microcomputers in practical science

lessons. The work is built on examples of good practice

Ⓣ L. Rogers, R. Barton and J. Bertram (of Warwick University)

▼ Trial materials (10 units); articles

7 Research programme for the speaker's commission on citizenship (£30,000) (1989–90).

■ A review of research evidence on citizenship, a qualitative study of active citizenship in schools in two counties and the planning and writing up of a national survey of active citizenship and volunteering

Ⓣ K. Fogelman, J. Edwards, M. Vlaeminke

8 TVEI evaluation in Northamptonshire (£70,000) (1990–93)

Ⓣ M. Whiteside

101. University of Liverpool

Department of Education, 19 Abercromby Square, Liverpool L69 3BX

☎ 051 794 2476   Ⓣ 627095 UNILPL G

Ⓕ 051 794 2512

Ⓟ Professor Wynne Harlen, Head, Department of education

Projects and curriculum initiatives

1 Barnardo's/Edge Hill College research project (£17,000) (1988–90)

■ An investigation into the use of a computer to help with the cognitive and sensory development of children with profound learning difficulties.

Ⓟ M. Hind

▼ Reports/evaluations

2 Spastics Society Research Project (£6,000, Spastic Society) (1986–9).

■ The production and evaluation of a suite of computer programs to help teach speech-impaired children to correct sequencing of Bliss symbols in short sentences and phrases with input via one or two switches.

Ⓟ M. Hind

▼ Reports/evaluations; resource materials

3 Use of IT in developing partnership between leader tutors in training PGCE (infant) students in a school context (1989–90, 5–7 age group).

■ Improved classroom practice and feedback

Ⓟ Diane Allanson

▼ Research submission

4 Liverpool Evaluation and Assessment Unit (1989–, 5–18 age group).

▼ Reports/evaluations: resource materials

5 Science Processes and Concepts Exploration (SPACE) – joint project with Kings College, London (£360,000) (1987–91, 5–12 age group).

■ Development of full range of classroom materials for science 5–12

Ⓟ Professor Wynne Harlen

▼ Reports/evaluations; books; resource materials

6 Science in Primary Teacher Education (SPRITE) (£57,000) – joint project with Reading University (1988–90, 5–12 age group).

■ Courses and materials for teacher education at pre-service and inservice levels

Ⓟ Professor Wynne Harlen

▼ Resource materials
7 Science component of STAIR consortium (Manchester) preparing national assessment materials for end of key stage 1 (£92,000) funding (1989–91, 5–7 age group).
Ⓟ Professor Wynne Harlen
▼ Reports/evaluations; resource materials
8 Science teaching action research (STAR) – joint project with Leicester University (£67,000) (1986–9).
■ Development of practice in primary science teaching through action research
Ⓟ Dr M. Schilling
▼ Reports/evaluations; books
9 Evaluation of museum displays in national museums and galleries on Merseyside (£35,000) (1988–90, all age groups).
Ⓟ Mr David Thomas
▼ Reports/evaluations
10 Developing navigational skills with young children (£10,000) (1989–90, 10+ age group).
Ⓟ Mr James Martland
▼ Reports/evaluations

102. University of London
Centre for Educational Studies, Kings College London, 552 King's Rd, London SW10 OUA
☎ 071 351 7312
Ⓟ Head of department

103. University of London
Goldsmiths' College, Faculty of Education, Lewisham Way, London SE14 6NW
☎ 081 856 2516   Ⓕ 081 469 0516
Ⓟ Jill Thorn, Faculty officer, Education
Projects and curriculum initiatives
1 Early years curriculum lobby (1988–, 3–8 age group).
■ To spread understanding of the early years curriculum and its role in relation to the national curriculum and assessment.
Ⓣ Vicky Hurst, Lecturer in early childhood education + 25
☎ 081 692 7171 x 2290
▼ Discussion documents
2 Reflecting on non-narrative texts (1986–, 7–11 age groups).
Ⓟ Margaret Mallett
3 The teaching of poetry in school (1983–91, 5–11 age group).
■ To develop an adequate theory of poetry and disseminate its strategies
Ⓟ Colin Walter
▼ Reports/evaluations; books

104. University of London
Institute of Education, 20 Bedford Way, London WC1H OAL
☎ 071 636 1500 x 287
Ⓕ 071 436 2186
Ⓟ Ms Jane Perry, Research administration officer
Projects and curriculum initiatives
1 GCSE oral commission assessment and inter-ethnic variation (£82,500 ESRC) (1988–90, 15+ age group).
■ To look at differences in discursive style between white majority and British born ethnic groups and relate these to English oral

assessment criteria for GCSE
Ⓟ Dr R. Hewitt
2 Curriculum research for pupils with moderate learning difficulties (£258,000, DES) (1985–9, primary and secondary age groups).
■ The implementation of an appropriately structured curriculum for children with moderate learning difficulties in special and ordinary schools
Ⓟ Dr P. Evans
3 National curriculum assessments for seven year old pupils (£1,680,000 SEAC) (1989–91, 7 year olds).
■ To develop national curriculum assessment tests for maths, science and language for use at the end of the first key stage.
Ⓟ Professor D. Lawton and Dr. M. Kingdon
4 National curriculum assessments for fourteen year olds (£1,600,000, SEAC) (1989–92, 14 year olds).
■ To develop national curriculum assessment tests for English for the third key stage
Ⓟ Professor D. Lawton
5 Group work with computers (£125,000 ESRC) (1988–91, primary/middle school age groups).
■ To develop a programme of computer-based group work for maths; to look at the relationship between the context, group processes, pupil attitudes and learning
Ⓟ Professor C. Hoyles
6 Educational achievement in the infant school: the contribution of teachers and parents (£512,000, ESRC) (1982–9, 5–8 year olds).
■ To look at the influence of parent contribution and teacher expectation of academic skill and achievement, and to explore relationships with gender, class and ethnicity; to explore school and teacher differences
Ⓟ Professor B. Tizard
7 Soviet British curriculum project (£44,000 from a consortium of charities) (1989–91, 15+ age groups).
■ To examine ways in which teachers handle ethnocentrism in teaching, focusing on history
Ⓟ Dr. H. Simons and Miss J. Maw
8 Television literacy in middle childhood and adolescence (£103,000, ESRC) (1989–91, 7–12 age group).
■ To look at the nature and extent of television literacy at different ages, the understanding and competencies used by children, to guide programme production and curriculum development
Ⓟ Mr D. Buckingham
9 The evaluation of the Hertfordshire 2000 project (£189,500, DES) (1987–90, secondary age group).
■ To develop a curriculum for 21st century involving parents and wider community and new technology
Ⓟ Dr J. Outson
10 The integration of TVEI technology options and mathematics (£157,000, Training Agency) (1988–90, 14–16 age group).

■ To develop modular assignments which integrate TVEI courses with the maths curriculum. Subject areas involved are design and technology, food technology and information technology/business studies
℗ Mrs A. Wolf
11 Computer based modellling across the curriculum (£112,300, Training Agency) (1989–91, secondary age group).
■ To develop materials to support the use of the computer as a tool for modelling in maths, business studies, science and geography
℗ Professor C. Hoyles
12 Global futures project (£100,500, Worldwide Fund for Nature) (1989–91, primary and secondary age group).
■ Focus on entitlement of pupils to preparation for responsible and active citizenship of global community and look at alternative futures and responsible exercise of rights
℗ Dr D. Hicks

105. University of Manchester
School of Education, Oxford Rd, Manchester M13 9PL
☎ 061 275 3456 ⓕ 061 275 3519
℗ Mr G. Wedlock, Senior administrative assistant
Projects and curriculum initiatives
1 Economic and industrial awareness programme (MVEIAP) (1986–, all age groups).
■ To provide INSET and consultancy support to LEAs, schools and teachers to develop economic and industrial awareness across the curriculum as an entitlement for all pupils
Ⓣ Mr R. Ryba and 3 development/field officers
▼ Reports/evaluations; resource materials; policy documents; discussion documents
2 Economic awareness teacher training programme (ECATT) (£340,000) (1986–92, 5–19 age group).
■ A partnership between the universities of London and Manchester, government, LEAs and industry/commerce to meet the economic awareness needs of schools/colleges
℗ Mr S. Hodkinson + 15
▼ Reports/evaluations; books; resource materials; policy documents; discussion documents
3 Mechanics in action project – joint project with Leeds University (£226,000) (1985–, 11–18 age group).
■ Secondary school curriculum development in practical problem solving in mathematics and in cross-curricular links between mathematics, science and technology
℗ Mr J. Williams + 8
▼ Reports/evaluations; books; resource materials; policy documents; discussion documents
4 Staged Assessments in Literary (SAIL) (£248,000, Joint Matriculation Board) (1986–9, secondary age group).
℗ 6 people
▼ Reports/evaluations; resource materials;

policy documents; discussion documents; teachers' handbook
5 Christianity in Britain – a multi-racial faith (£25,000, All Saints Education Trust) (1989–90, primary and lower secondary age group).
℗ Professor G. Verma + 3
▼ Introductory leaflet; reports/evaluations; resource materials
6 The development of course materials using existing software to support bilingual learners in the mainstream classroom (1989–, secondary age group).
℗ Mr G. Motteram

106. University of Newcastle upon Tyne
School of Education, St. Thomas St, Newcastle upon Tyne NE1 7RU
☎ 091 222 6000 ⓕ 091 222 8170
℗ Professor Tony Edwards, Dean, Faculty of education
Projects and curriculum initiatives
1 Interactive learning (£590,000) (1986–90, secondary age group).
■ To develop videodiscs and examine the impact of this new technology and pupils' learning
℗ Dr Madeline Atkins + 4
▼ Videodiscs; reports; articles
2 Supporting teaching in urban school
■ To investigate peer tutoring in science in a multiracial comprehensive school (£50,000) (1989–91, secondary age group).
℗ Dr Carol Fitzgibbon, Mr Bruce Carrington and researcher
3 Verbal interaction in foreign language classrooms (1986–, secondary age range)
■ Collaborative action research to identify strategies of teaching and learning
Ⓣ Mr David Westgate and FL department of a comprehensive school
▼ Conference papers; articles
4 Children's explanations of calculations (1988–, 5–8 age group).
■ Investigation of how young children verbalise calculations
℗ Mr Ian Thompson
▼ Articles
5 Uses of LOGO in mathematics teaching and learning (1988–, 5–9 age group).
▼ Articles

107. University of Nottingham
School of Education, University Park, Nottingham NG7 2RD
☎ 0602 484 848 Ⓣ 37346 UNINOT G
ⓕ 0602 420825
℗ Dr Keith Selkirk, Senior lecturer in education
Projects and curriculum initiatives
1 TVEI in initial teacher training (£100,000, Training Agency) (1989–91, 14–18 age group).
■ To familiarise ITT staff with TVEI promoted developments in schools and colleges
Ⓣ 3 people
▼ Reports/evaluations; books; resource materials

2 Religious experience and education project (£100,000) (1985–, 5–18 age group).
Ⓣ Two people
▼ Reports/evaluations; books; resource materials
3 Nottingham University language assessment consultancy (£25,000) (1989–91, 14 year olds).
■ To advise ELMAG group on key stage 3 SATs in English
Ⓣ 3 people
4 HELP (1988–90, 6–16 age group).
■ To compile an annotated catalogue of resource materials for use with children with SEN covering maths, reading, writing, spelling, language and cognitive development
Ⓣ 2 people
▼ Resource catalogue
5 An evaluation of schools–industry links in the East Midlands area (1989–91, 11–18 age group).
6 An evaluation of schools' and FE use of devolved INSET finance (£24,000, LEA) (1988–90, 5–18 age group).
Ⓣ 3 people
▼ Reports/evaluations

108. University of Oxford
Department of Educational Studies, 15 Norham Garden, Oxford OX2 6PY
☎ 0865 274024 Ⓕ 0865 270708
Ⓟ Brian Woolnough, Lecturer in education
Projects and curriculum initiatives
1 Geography, Schools and Industry Project (GSIP) (£210,000) (1984–91, 11–18 age group).
■ To promote and monitor the contribution of geography teachers to economic understanding in the curriculum, through school based curriculum development. GSIP currently involves teacher groups in 32 LEAs
Ⓣ Graham Corney + 2
▼ Project papers (two series); articles; newsletter; guidelines handbooks for teachers
2 Curriculum development through internship PGCE partnership (1987–,11–18 age group).
■ To improve the critical awareness and teaching practice of teachers in the curriculum subjects of mathematics, English, the sciences, modern languages, techhology, history and geography through involvement with the PGCE course as mentors
Ⓣ Hazel Hagger + 12 tutors and 80 mentors
▼ Booklets outlining the structure of the course and investigational activities for analysing classroom practice
3 The Oxford Project on Diversification of First Foreign Language Teaching (OXPROD) (£84,000, largely from the Leverhulme Trust) (1987–90, 11–16 age group).
■ To investigate pupils' experience of learning languages other than French as first foreign language; to examine organisational problems arising from a policy of diversification
Ⓟ David Phillips and Caroline Filmer-

Sankey
▼ Occasional papers; newsletters and articles
4 Primary School Teachers and Science (PSTS) (£60,000) (1989–90, 5–11 age group).
■ To investigate primary school teachers' understanding of science concepts; to establish the prevalence of selected misconceptions in a large sample of primary teachers; to produce INSET materials designed to help primary teachers improve their understanding of science concepts.
Ⓟ Mike Summers + 2
▼ Working papers describing the results of the research work of the project
5 Discussion of issues in school science (£64,000 ESRC) (1988–91, 16–18 age group).
■ To examine how students use knowledge from school, and from video excerpts, in small group discussions of science based social issues. The project is in the linked research programme on the Public Understanding of Science run by the Science Policy Support Group.
Ⓣ Joan Solomon and 1 research officer
▼ Papers on the discussion of kidney transplants, nuclear power and on the general uses of discussion in the science classrooms.
6 Reviewing practice in the 11–13 science curriculum (1985–7, 11–13 age group).
■ To help science teachers and head of science departments to reshape the science curriculum in the early years of secondary schooling. The project is part of the Secondary Science Curriculum Review
Ⓟ Terry Allsop
▼ Four booklets covering aims, reviewing language policy, assessment, problem solving and technology

109. University of Reading
Faculty of Education and Community Studies, Bulmershe Court, Earley, Reading RG6 1HY
☎ 0734 663387 Ⓕ 0734 352080
Ⓟ Dr A. Kemp, Head, Department of arts and humanities in education
Projects and curriculum initiatives
1 Microtechnology for creative music activities (£40,000, NCET (MESU)) (1987–9, primary and secondary age groups).
Ⓣ 4 people
▼ Books; resource materials; video
2 The use of computers for music education (£40,000, NCET (MESU)) (1987–9, secondary age group).
Ⓣ 4 people
▼ Books; resource materials; music computer cookbook
3 Multicultural music and microtechnology (£40,000, NCET (MESU)) (1988–9, primary and secondary age groups).
Ⓣ 4 people
▼ Books; resource materials
4 Electronic keyboards in music education (£40,000, NCET (MESU)) (1988–9, primary and secondary age groups).
Ⓣ 4 people
▼ Books; resource materials
5 Music education, special needs and

microtechnology (£40,000, NCET (MESU)) (1989–90, primary and secondary age groups).

Ⓣ 4 people

▼ Draft specification

6 Non keyboard microtechnology devices for music education (£40,000 NCET (MESU)) (1989–90, primary and secondary age groups).

Ⓣ 4 people

▼ Draft specification

7 Environmental education inservice training for teachers of children from 5–16 (1987–9, primary and secondary age groups).

Ⓟ Dr C. Gayford, Head, Department of science and technology education)

▼ Resource materials

Comment This project is run by the Council for Environmental Education and the University of Reading.

☎ 0734 875123   Ⓕ 07 044 734314

110. University of Sheffield

Division of Education, Floor 9, The Arts Tower, University of Sheffield, Sheffield, South Yorkshire S10 2TN

☎ 0742 768555   Ⓣ 547216 UGSHEF G

Ⓕ 0742 739826

Projects and curriculum initiatives

1 TVEI/PGCE staff development and course development project (1988–9, secondary age group).

Ⓟ Peter Lucas and Professor Jean Rudduck, Joint directors

▼ Reports/evaluations

2 Centre for the development of new teaching strategies in biotechnology (£170,000, Training Agency) (1988–91, 11–16 age group).

Ⓣ Jenny Henderson + 4

▼ Books; videotapes; pupils and teacher resource material

3 Light works – Interactive science for schools (£30,000, Nuffield Foundation) (1989–90, 4–12 age group).

■ To take 'hands on science' into schools. 15 exhibits on light colour and optics with full teachers' support material for activity based follow-up work; matched to national curriculum and cross cultural in character.

Ⓟ Chris Morris

▼ Resource materials; exhibition guides and notes

4 Mechanics in action project (£50,000) (1988–, 11–18 age group).

■ To develop and trial new teaching approaches and materials in mechanics, with particular emphasis on practical and project work

Ⓣ Chris True, John Scaife + 6

▼ Reports/evaluations; resource materials

111. University of Southampton

School of Education, Highfield, Southampton SO9 5NH

☎ 0703 595000   Ⓣ 47661

Ⓕ 0703 593556

Ⓟ Professor C. Brumfit, Head of school

Projects and curriculum initiatives

1 Hampshire modern language skills development programme (1986–1990/91, 11–14 age group).

■ The production of communicative activities/materials with continuous assessments – certification levels 1 and 2

Ⓟ Francine Chambers, adviser, lecturer and two full time seconded teachers per year

112. University of Sussex

Institute of Continuing and Professional Education (CAPE), Brighton, Sussex BN1 9G

☎ 0293 606755

Ⓟ Heather Nicholas, Information officer, CAPE

Projects and curriculum initiatives

1 Whole school development in information technology (1988–91, 11–18 age group).

■ To develop and disseminate INSET strategies and materials of proven effectiveness in the following areas: whole school policies for IT; school management of IT; school-focused staff development in IT.

Ⓣ Michael Eraut, Stephen Steadman, John Pearce

2 Groupwork with computers (1988–91, 9–12 age group).

■ To provide guidance to teachers seeking to gain the maximum benefit from collaborative learning approaches using computers

Ⓣ Michael Eraut and Professor Celia Hoyles (ULIE) + 5

▼ ESRC OU Paper INTER/3/88; 'Groupwork with Computers' available from Department of Psychology, University of Lancaster.

3 National Business Studies Teacher Development Network (1988–9, 14–16 age group).

■ To provide education and consultancy support to the activities of the network, focusing on networks, change strategies, needs assessment, local evaluation, materials evaluation

Ⓣ Michael Eraut and Gerald Cole

4 Effective management of flexible learning in schools (1989–90, 14–18 age group).

■ To support the management of the introduction and development of flexible learning systems for the 14–18 age group within TVEI aims and criteria, in the context of current educational reforms

Ⓣ Michael Eraut and Colin Nash

5 The Education Network Project (ENP) (1987–, 5–18 age group).

■ To build a network for collating information and analysing global change in the context of environmental and developmental systems and processes; to change the provision of education so that it takes account of the importance of environment and development issues, and implements through curricular programmes appropriate knowledge, skills and values

Ⓣ Colin Lacey and Roy Williams

▼ ENP newsletter; ENP occasional papers; books

113. University of Ulster at Coleraine

Faculty of Education, Coleraine, Co.
Londonderry BT52 1SA
☎ 0265 44141   Ⓣ 747597
Ⓕ 0265 55513

Projects and curriculum initiatives
1 European studies project (1986–92, 11–18 age group)
Ⓣ Dr Roger Austin, 6 full-time field officers and 36 schools
▼ Reports/evaluations; resource materials; video

114. University of Wales at Aberystwyth

Department of Education, King St, Aberystwyth SY23 2AX
☎ 0970 3177
Ⓟ Head, Department of education

115. University of Wales

College of Cardiff, School of Education, Cathays Park, Cardiff CF1 3NS
☎ 0222 874000
Ⓟ Head, School of education

116. University of Warwick

Institute of Education, Westwood, Coventry CV4 7AL
☎ 0203 523821   Ⓣ 317472
Ⓕ 0203 461606
Ⓟ Professor J. Tomlinson, director

Projects and curriculum initiatives
1 Mini-enterprises in schools project (£1,971,000) (1985–91, 9–18 age group).
■ To conduct research, provide inservice training and publications on enterprise. This is based at the Institute of Education
Ⓣ Professor J. Tomlinson, Mr. K. Crompton + 9
▼ Reports/evaluations; resource materials; books; booklets
2 Records of achievement in four schools (based at the Centre for Educational Development, Appraisal and Research) (£55,000 for 2 years) (1989–90, 12–18 age group).
■ To produce four case studies and a thematic report
Ⓣ Professor R. Burgess, research fellow, 2 teacher fellows
▼ Reports/evaluations; discussion documents
3 Solihull English project (£45,000) (1986–9, 11–14 age group), based in the Department of Arts Education). To improve the teaching of English in the secondary schools controlled by Solihull LEA.
Ⓣ David Hooley + 4
▼ Reports/evaluations; discussion documents; handbook; twice termly bulletin
4 The use of the school and environment as a resource for children's learning (£20,000 funding) (1988–90, primary age group), based in the Department of Education.
■ To help teachers use first hand experience as a means of producing work of depth and quality with children's learning
Ⓣ 10 people

▼ Reports/evaluations; interim and final reports
5 An assessment of the conceptual and perceived physical needs of parents, pupils and teachers in secondary schools in England (£900) (1986–7, 12–18 age group), based in the Department of Physical Education.
Ⓟ M. Ralph and O. Pritchard
▼ Booklet
6 Discussion in the classroom (£66,000, Leverhulme Trust) (1986–91, 12–18 age group), based in the Department of Science Education.
■ To study the use of discussion methods for teaching mathematics and to produce case studies of pupil-pupil discussions
Ⓟ Dr S. Pirie and Professor R. Schwarzenberger
▼ Reports/evaluations

117. University of York

Department of Education, Langwith College, Heslington, York YO1 5DD
☎ 0904 430000
Ⓟ Head of department

118. West Glamorgan Institute of Higher Education

Townhill Rd, Swansea, SA2 OUT
☎ 0792 203482
Ⓟ Principal

119. West London Institute of Higher Education

Lancaster Hse, Borough Rd, Isleworth, Middlesex TW7 5DU
☎ 081 891 0121
Ⓟ Principal

120. Westminster College

North Hinksey, Oxford OX2 9AT
☎ 0865 247644
Ⓟ Principal

121. West Sussex Institute of Higher Education

The Dome, Upper Bognor Rd, Bognor Regis PO21 1HR
☎ 0243 865581   X 241
Ⓕ 0243 828351

Projects and curriculum initiatives
Projects 1 to 3 are based in the Mathematics Centre.
Ⓟ Mr Phillip Bufton, Head of mathematics
1 Raising achievement in mathematics (£750,000) (1986–9, 11–16 age group).
■ To promote good practice in mathematics teaching across the age and ability range, by encouraging teachers to become actively involved in their own professional development and by creating opportunities for personal contact between teachers. The project covers 34 LEAs
Ⓟ Afzal Ahmed
▼ Reports/evaluations; resource materials; policy documents; discussion documents
2 Flexible learning approaches; sixth form mathematics (£72,000) (1989–90, 16+ age

group).

■ The mathematics A level with total in-course assessment, developed by the Mathematics Centre in conjunction with four institutions, will provide a focus for the project; it is intended that the work should be relevant to all sixth form mathematics teachers, including those teaching on courses such as BTEC, City and Guilds, CPVE and GCSE as well as A level and AS level. The aim of the project is to enable students and teachers to develop research skills and encourage them to make use of the human and material resources around them

▼ Reports/evaluations; books; resource materials; discussion documents

3 Teachers evaluating and assessing mathematics (1988–91, 14–18 age group).

■ To promote good practice in teacher based assessment of course work both at GCSE and A level, initiating, developing and assessing coursework in mathematics

▼ Reports/evaluations; resource materials
Project 4–6 are based in Bishop Otter College, College Lane, Chichester, West Sussex PO19 4PE (0243 787911)

Ⓟ Dr J. Brighton, Deputy director

4 Enquiry into the teaching of history to those over 16 – a joint project with Dr Jon Nichol of Exeter University (£50,000, Nuffield Foundation) (1988–91, 16–19 age group).

▼ Resource materials: discussion documents

5 Young Historians Scheme (£75,000, Leverhulme Trust) (1986–90, all age groups).

▼ Resource materials; discussion

documents; newsletter

122. Whitelands College
West Hill, London SW15 3SN
☎ 081 788 8268
Ⓟ Principal

123. Worcester College of Higher Education
Henwick Grove, Worcester WR2 6AJ
☎ 0905 748080
Ⓟ Principal

124. Wolverhampton Polytechnic
Faculty of Education, Gorway, West Midlands WS1 3BD
☎ 0922 720141   Ⓕ 0922 722099
Ⓟ Miss Jean McKay, Head, Initial teacher education

Projects and curriculum initiatives

1 Enterprise in teacher education (1989–91, nursery to secondary age group).

■ The project is one of a number of pilots developed at Wolverhampton Polytechnic under the Enterprise in Higher Education Initiative funded by the Training Agency. Via education–industry links and staff and curriculum development programmes the project aims to promote and develop enterprising characteristics in all the participants in the initial teacher training portfolio of courses

Ⓟ Mike Chatburn

▼ Reports/evaluations; resource materials; policy documents; discussion documents

Index

Curriculum Handbook

To use this index the reader first has to go to the subject heading sought, then the age phase within that subject heading. Against this there will be an entry which begins with a Roman numeral, this tells the reader the section of the book in which the subject appears. The next set of figures which follows tells the reader the number of the entry in that section – every institution, organisation, agency etc. is numbered in each section. Finally where an entry is followed by figures in brackets; this indicates the number of the project referred to in the institution's, organisation's or agency's listing.

A reader wishing to access, for example, primary science would look up Science, then the 'primary' subheading under 'Science'. One of the entries under this subheading is vii–4(1) which means section seven, entry four, project one of that entry – in this example it would be Bishop Grosseteste College, whose first project is 'Primary science materials'.

If there are no figures in brackets then this means that the organisation has not had a separate project listing.

Advertisers' Index